PRAISE FOR

ALONE: A LOVE STORY

This is a lyrical tribute to the intoxicating, dramatic, destructive, and ultimately empowering nature of love. I could not stop reading Michelle's story, and now I cannot stop thinking about it.

> — **ANNA MARIA TREMONTI**,
> acclaimed journalist and broadcaster

Page by page, Michelle Parise's story of love, betrayal, loss, and ultimately redemption is filled with moments of grace, humour, pain, hope, and wisdom. Beautifully and powerfully written, *Alone: A Love Story* left me heartbroken and inspired at the same time.

> — **TERRY FALLIS**, bestselling author of *Albatross*

Michelle Parise is the best company. Her passion and humour leap off the page.

> — **CAMILLA GIBB**, internationally acclaimed author

When someone hurts you deeply (like, REALLY deeply), it can turn you into a special correspondent from the wreckage that is your own heartbreak. It may take all your self-control not to grab strangers by the shirt collar and shout, "He hurt me!" When Michelle Parise's life blew up, she did the more socially acceptable and thoughtful version of this: she wrote her own love story. It's brave, resonant, and oh so raw. In *Alone: A Love Story*, Michelle turns her greatest shock into a story that lets you get close enough to feel its sting and understand its nuance. Her book doubles as a survival guide for when it's your turn to rethink your relationship with love itself. Plus, Michelle Parise channels some seriously steamy Canadian Bridget Jones divorcee realness, and I'm here for it.

— **ANDREA SILENZI**, host of the podcast *Why Oh Why*

For anyone who has had a marriage fall apart, *Alone: A Love Story* is a book to keep close. Parise is unflinching as she reports back from her broken heart and, as strange as this might seem, comforts by showing us the way from loneliness to standing tall . . . and alone.

— **LAURIE BROWN**, music journalist and host of *Pondercast*

Michelle Parise's writing makes me feel like I can be more myself. She is remarkable at rendering the (nearly) universal human experience of deceit into a tightly woven tapestry of vulnerability, rawness, and humour, and while she's doing it, makes you contemplate your inner life with more acceptance and compassion.

— **BRITT WRAY**, Ph.D., broadcaster,
and author of *Rise of the Necrofauna*

Alone: A Love Story is an emotional memoir of a life exploded — the end of a marriage, referred to as The Bomb — and the chaos that follows. But it's also about what blooms in the wreckage. Beautifully written, intimate, alive, and accessible, the story flows like a conversation with your most interesting, wise, and exciting friend.

— **EMILY URQUHART**, author of *Beyond the Pale*

You know that feeling, when a close friend shares a secret with you? The rush of surprise and empathy you get, as you hear the most intimate and heartbreaking details of someone's life? Michelle Parise has turned us into confidantes, revealing her experiences of love, dating, and divorce. *Alone: A Love Story* is equal parts pain and hope, served with a side of laughs — and we're all wiser for it.

— **DUNCAN McCUE**, CBC Radio host and author of *The Shoe Boy*

How do you know when an ending is actually a beginning? What's it like to love the ones we can't be with? Ardent, urgent, and honest, Parise's wildly intimate voice reminds us that as long as we are feeling — feeling longing or loss, collapse or curiosity, the things that make us human — we are never really alone.

— **ADRIAN McKERRACHER**, author of *What It Means to Write*

Alone: A Love Story is a courageous and full-throttled confessional. Michelle Parise has written a fierce and compassionate book about losing yourself to grief and then finding yourself again with humour and grace.

— **DAEMON FAIRLESS**, journalist and author of *Mad Blood Stirring*

Alone: A Love Story is a universal, human, female experience; it's a homecoming and a reckoning. Parise took her story, one of pain, rage, and ultimately hope, and decided to own it, to reframe it, to tell it to the world on her terms. *Alone: A Love Story* tells a unique, nuanced story of healing. We've seen enough stories about self-destructive "lost" women. Parise explores the more real female narrative: we bleed but we're masters at covering it up. Parise's writing is addictively, heartbreakingly great. She will inspire you and she will devastate you, and you will be better for it.

— KATIE BOLAND, actor, writer, and filmmaker

Dating, love, marriage, parenthood, and scrape-yourself-off-the-floor heartbreak is illuminated in *Alone: A Love Story*. Michelle takes us into the heart's dark corners with dark humour and deep honesty, pouring out her story like a funny, fierce friend who trusts you with everything. I don't know anyone who won't see themselves somewhere in this story (but be glad Michelle's the one doing the telling). Ultimately, *Alone: A Love Story* gives us something we all want: to feel less alone.

— CHRISTA COUTURE, author of *How to Lose Everything*

PRAISE FOR THE PODCAST
ALONE: A LOVE STORY

Michelle Parise knows how to shape and deliver a story that will keep you coming back for more.

— *THE ATLANTIC*

The storytelling is exemplary. The way the narrative unfolds, moving back and forth in time, conjures up the full scope of emotion — horror and anxiety and wonder and happiness. Parise's is a very particular story but in many ways it's universal and familiar. The thing I'm most struck by is the neat way she walks the tightrope between hope and despair, darkness and light.

— SHARON BALA, author of *The Boat People*

ALONE

A LOVE STORY

MICHELLE PARISE

ALONE

A LOVE STORY

DUNDURN
TORONTO

Publisher: Scott Fraser | Acquiring editor: Kathryn Lane | Editor: Jess Shulman
Cover designer: Laura Boyle
Printer: Marquis Book Printing Inc.

Library and Archives Canada Cataloguing in Publication

Title: Alone : a love story / Michelle Parise.
Names: Parise, Michelle, 1974- author.
Identifiers: Canadiana (print) 20200178423 | Canadiana (ebook) 20200178466 | ISBN
    9781459746909 (softcover) | ISBN 9781459746916 (PDF) | ISBN 9781459746923 (EPUB)
Subjects: LCSH: Parise, Michelle, 1974- | LCSH: Parise, Michelle, 1974-—Relations with men. |
    LCSH: Dating (Social customs) | LCSH: Man-woman relationships. | LCSH: Single mothers. |
    LCSH: Parenthood.
Classification: LCC HQ801 .P37 2020 | DDC 306.73092—dc23

We acknowledge the support of the Canada Council for the Arts and the Ontario Arts Council for our publishing program. We also acknowledge the financial support of the Government of Ontario, through the Ontario Book Publishing Tax Credit and Ontario Creates, and the Government of Canada.

Care has been taken to trace the ownership of copyright material used in this book. The author and the publisher welcome any information enabling them to rectify any references or credits in subsequent editions.

The publisher is not responsible for websites or their content unless they are owned by the publisher.

Printed and bound in Canada.

VISIT US AT

 dundurn.com | @dundurnpress | dundurnpress |  dundurnpress

Dundurn
3 Church Street, Suite 500
Toronto, Ontario, Canada
M5E 1M2

For my Birdie. May you always know
that love was the driving force.

PART

ONE

*Love is only real if it can rage like a bonfire
and also comfort like a fireplace.
It's both, at once, the pain and the warmth.
It's why my heart is always cranked to maximum.*

CHAPTER ONE

FALLING

LOSS

So, here I am on the edge of thirty-nine. Petulant, drunk, and obsessed with a charming but frustrating man in a white shirt and perfect jeans. I'm taking my one-millionth fancy cocktail and stumbling down a hallway to go see a tarot card reader. My friends all rolled their eyes, but I like the idea of someone telling me who I am and what my path is based on randomly turned up cards. Because seriously? Fucked if I know these days.

The Man with the White Shirt is mingling so excellently and effortlessly with my friends. His smile and those dark eyes and that body in those jeans — God, it hurts to look at him too long. He's so handsome I can hardly stand it sometimes, and whenever he's around everything softens in me. Usually. Tonight I'm all edges. I'm being a bit rude to him even. I'll tell you why later, stick with me.

Right now, I'm stumbling down the hallway to see the tarot card reader. She's, like, twenty-five, max, and drinking a gigantic glass of red wine. She locks the door and it's quiet and all fortune teller-y in this closet we're in. I'm drinking my strong fancy French cocktail as she shuffles the cards and thinking about how this is going to be such bullshit, but it's my birthday so fun! fun! And then she turns over the first card.

LOSS. It says loss.

More cards come and it's like they are shouting at me. FEAR. FUTILITY. *What. The. Fuck.*

They may as well say *Your husband cheated on you* and *Now you think no one can love you.*

"You used to know exactly who you were," she says. "You were stable, confident. But now you have a veil of uncertainty over you. That's because you're being tested. To help you figure out how you say yes to things and how you say no."

Whoa. *How* I say yes to things, *how* I say no. Not *if. How.* It's as if she's telling me I have choices. Some control over my life. I know that probably seems obvious to you, but right now? In this year? In this bar? This is *news.* This bullshit card reading has suddenly become really fucking real.

I return to my friends and try to be cheerful. White Shirt is there to greet me, all gorgeous and sweet. He's searching my eyes for a sign, but I just say, "It was fun! She said freaky things!" Inside I think, *Fuck, why can't this real thing he says he feels for me be real enough?*

I wake up the next morning in his bed, my head bashed in by booze I don't even know the name of. My veins filled with lead instead of blood. Hungover. Massively. It's my thirty-ninth birthday. I look at White Shirt as he lies sleeping, and I already feel far away. *How did I get here? I used to be married, for God's sake! What happened to my life, to love?*

I wonder this all the time now.

Y2K

It's 1999. I'm twenty-four years old and living an artsy city-girl's life. I work all day in public radio and spend my free time in used bookstores and going to see bands. Every Wednesday night you'll find me and my friends here in this bar, before we head out to a well-known dive for dancing. They all drink and party and stay in school forever, but not me. I rarely drink, and certainly don't drink to get drunk. I'm not being pious, I just love to experience life, and I feel like I'd be missing out if I put a filter on it.

I also, with every part of me, *love* love. I mean, I *love* it! Being in love and falling in love and writing about love and singing about it and *living* it. I've had one boyfriend after another since I was fifteen years old. All long, committed relationships. I haven't slept in a bed alone in years. Relationships are everything to me; I know no other way. I just love to get lost in another person, to learn everything about what interests them, to see what they see and feel what they feel.

And that's how it is with my boyfriend right now. We've been together since I was nineteen. He's a musician, and four years older than me, and so intelligent and mystical that, probably out of youth or just abject insecurity, I defer to him on just about everything. I think he's so much better than me — he's read every book, he knows every song, he's knowledgeable on all subjects, every topic imaginable. He's an atheist, and a passionate altruist. He's a vegetarian, so of course now I am, too. He's a devoted boyfriend, a real *partner*; we are honest and expressive and artistically inspired by one another. We have matching tattoos, because it's the nineties. It's been a perfect, symbiotic relationship. We say we'll be together forever.

But lately, things are different. The Musician has been talking about us having an open relationship. Like, *open* open. He thinks we're mature enough and secure enough to handle sleeping with other people while still maintaining our committed bond. I'm less sure — a big part of me feels like true love doesn't want to be shared. But that seems old fashioned, so I start to entertain the thought. *Could I really do something like that?*

The only guy I find even remotely interesting is this weird, brooding graduate student. A friend of a friend, who always seems to be around but doesn't exactly fit in. He's completely different than all the downtown artsy guys I know. A small-town boy, a scientist, here in the big city doing his master's degree. We've never really talked, but I find him kind of cute. He's tall, with awful glasses and the worst long hair. But there's something about him. I kinda like that he gives zero fucks about what anyone thinks of him.

The Scientist drinks three pints of beer to every regular guy's one. He whistles to get the waitress's attention, which we all find mortifying. He sits with us, but doesn't really talk to anybody. He hasn't seen the latest Thomas Vinterberg film. I don't even think he reads books! You can tell he thinks we're all a bunch of big-city snobs, which of course we totally are. But he likes Top-40 music. And watches *football*. The Musician can't stand him, but I have been completely awakened from my elitist stupor by his very presence.

On this Wednesday in the bar, The Musician is holding court as he always does, orating on some political issue or another with everyone's rapt attention. Bored, I look across the table and find The Scientist just staring at me, his arched eyebrow indicating he thinks my boyfriend is a blowhard and also that he knows that deep down I agree. And so I smirk at him, and he smirks back, and this is all it takes for us to fall in love.

It's that knowing smirk we will share for the next thirteen years — on our wedding day, at crowded parties when other blowhards speak, in the middle of huge arguments, during sex, when any of our parents speak at any time about anything, and several times in the delivery room when he stays awake with me for forty hours straight until our daughter is born. It's the same knowing smirk we still share today, long after the divorce. All I can call it is true love. There's no more truth than that look between us.

But back to 1999. Things are escalating between us. We find ways to sit beside each other or walk together or run into each other. He stares at me across the bar and I feel it before I even turn around. There's an electrical current that's been switched on. He's wild and wounded, and it's this sad complexity that draws me to him, a thing that I think I can somehow fix.

On this night in the bar, after the smirks, I leave the table and go down into the basement. Just as I'm about to go into one of the washrooms, a hand grabs mine. The Scientist is behind me. He doesn't say a word. He kisses me so hard and his body is so physically strong, the breath gets literally knocked out of me. It is the best kiss I've ever had. In fact, the kiss is better than any sex I'd ever had. Then he turns and leaves without a word. It was so aggressive and unexpected. The Musician is sooooooo Mr. I'm-A-Sensitive-Feminist guy, and this is just the complete opposite. From this moment on, we begin an intense relationship.

The Musician can't understand *why* I would pick The Scientist of *all people*. I mean, it was his idea to be open, and now he doesn't like that I've chosen this football-watching, beer-drinking guy in cargo pants. But it's too late. I'm done. Hooked. I'm less and less interested in The Musician and the life we've built together. I'm tired of our shabby apartment, our vegetarianism, our bohemian lifestyle. The Scientist has plans, and goals, and eats meat for Chrissake. He's driven and focused, and I'm enthralled by the contrast.

We fall in love with each other hard and fast, writing long emails back and forth all day, every day. Me from my ninth-floor office downtown, and him in his lab at the university uptown.

We are obsessed with each other. By the end of December, I'm packing up my things and preparing to move out of the apartment I share with The Musician. The Scientist and I meet on the day before Christmas Eve and he gives me a gift — our emails printed out and bound in a book. He's made two copies, one for each of us. He calls it *Our Book*. He says he loves me. He says he'll wait for me. His dark eyes are so shiny as he holds my hand across the table and says, "I don't want to share you with anyone."

When I get back to the apartment, I look around at all the boxes and think, *Only a few more days.* The Musician isn't there. I sit on the floor with *Our Book*. On the cover is a drawing The Scientist has done in pencil, a face with a tree for a body.

When I close my eyes, he is all I see.

THIRTEEN YEARS LATER

We're in a restaurant with our daughter, Birdie, having our weekly "family dinner." We've been separated for eleven months.

Out of the blue he says, "I was just reading *Our Book*. All the emails back and forth." It's like he's just put a fist through my chest. There's no way I'd be able to read it yet; there's no way I'd expect *him* to re-read it, not now or ever.

"Did it make you sad to read it?" I ask.

"Yeah," he says, "but a little happy too."

We smile at one another, but I want to jump across the table and shake him. I also want to crawl into his arms and feel his skin against mine. I want to kiss the nape of his neck and also punch him in his stupid face. It's complicated to love someone who's betrayed you, okay?

Afterward, as he walks me and Birdie to my apartment, he puts his arm around me. For the first time in almost a year, we walk like that, his giant parka and mine all bunched together. We stop outside my building. He kisses my forehead and says, "I love you." He waves at us as we go in.

This is how we are now. This is who we are. Together, alone.

HURRICANE

In the year 2000, after I've broken up with The Musician and moved out on my own, I figure my relationship with The Scientist is no big deal. I'm pretty sure that the sex is all we have between us. That we'll grow tired of each other, eventually, and move on to find people who we actually have something in common with.

I miss the kind of conversations I had with The Musician — long, intelligent talks about films, novels, philosophy, music. The Scientist never knows what I'm talking about. If I play a song by The Beatles, he can't tell who's singing! My vocabulary is too big for him, and I'm constantly dumbing myself down.

Sometimes I think wistfully of The Musician and the easy symmetry of our life before The Scientist upset the balance. But I'm electrically charged. I'm hooked on this man who burns incandescent. It feels different to love like this. It feels like a hurricane.

Other than great sex, all we mostly do is fight in these early days. We fight and fight and fight. Once, I throw a bowl of cherries at the wall, and it smashes into pieces, a fireworks display of red and white. Another time I put all his stuff in a bag and throw it off the rooftop of my apartment into the alleyway. He doesn't seem to care and doesn't call me for days, which makes me crazy. I imagine him doing horrible things I don't want to imagine him doing with cute university girls. But apparently he's just playing video games and waiting for me to cool down. We cannot understand each other, ever. It's all one giant miscommunication. We fight and fuck and fight and fuck.

So yeah, there is a *lot* of passion and drama in that first year together. But there is also a lot of growth. I become a much less judgemental person because of him. I stop writing people off because of things like political affiliation or the fact that they don't read books. He asks me to teach him about music, so one night we listen to Led Zeppelin, and I teach him to count time signatures out by slapping his thighs with his hands. I also attempt to teach him to distinguish between Beatles (it doesn't work; he still can't tell who's singing). I introduce him to foreign films, and he takes me to blockbuster action movies. We learn to love the things the other person loves. Or at least, we try.

To get to my three-hundred-square-foot apartment you have to take a fire escape in the alleyway of Honest Ed's — an old department store famous for its quirky signs and the way you'd get lost in its maze of cheap stuff. Light bulbs hang in strings in the alleyway, and young cooks and dishwashers of neighbouring restaurants are out by open doorways having smokes at all hours of the night. The rats as big as cats in the dumpster, you can hear them fighting as you fall asleep. I paint the entire apartment mustard; I can't imagine why now, but I do, and The Scientist helps me. We do the bathroom bright purple.

I am twenty-five and living alone for the first time ever. Sort of. Once I'm in and settled, The Scientist settles in mostly, too. He's writing his master's thesis and that's hard to do while living with roommates. So during the day while I'm at work producing radio shows, he's at my place writing his thesis on an old laptop at my vintage Formica table. He sleeps at my new place most nights, too, but not always. I hate when he isn't there because I don't know where he is. It makes me anxious, panicked, possessive.

His thesis work is in atomic physics, and some days I get home from work and the entire floor of my little apartment is covered in paper — all with the mad scratchings of a mathematician. It looks like that scene in the movie *A Beautiful Mind*, just equations everywhere, and then his shiny dark eyes, his tense jaw. It makes me love him just to think of it now.

Each day is the same. I come home from a full day's work, he's sitting at the table, head deep into the workings of the cesium atom. I walk in, say hello, and without a word he comes to me and kisses me, removing my purse with one hand, shutting the door with the other, and we have sex immediately, right there or wherever — it's only three-hundred square feet. And then we might eat some dinner, or he'll go right back to writing and I'll play guitar and sing, but quietly, so I won't bother him.

We're in a mustard-coloured cocoon at the turn of the century, and everything feels full of promise. Every moment feels electric, even the ordinary ones.

Eventually I begin to edit his thesis for him, for grammar only, obviously. I know absolutely nothing about physics, let alone this very specific thing he has done to an atom, or the giant machine he's built himself in order to do it. Sometimes it takes me an hour to edit two pages, not because of the physics, but because he has no idea how to write a sentence. He has no idea how to write at all, his brain full of math and machines and experiments, not syntax. About a month into the editing, he comes up to me, there at the table hunched over his thesis, and he says to me with all sincerity, "So are you starting to get some of this?"

I laugh and tell him no, I am in no way starting to "get" any of it. He asks how I can edit something I don't understand, so I try to explain that it's just grammar, it's just sentence structure, the content is irrelevant. He finds this fascinating. I find him fascinating. We're in awe of each other, since we're from totally different planets, since the other person seems capable of powers we can't possess. We are total opposites. We are madly in love.

And then for reasons I'll never understand, because we've never talked about it, he asks me to marry him. On September 13, 2001. Yeah, that's right, two days after 9/11. He phones to say I should meet him at our favourite Italian restaurant for dinner. Like every journalist in the world following the attacks, I've just worked about thirty hours straight. I haven't been home at all. I'm tired. And I want to get out of the newsroom to forget for a little bit the terrible things we've all watched, over and over again.

I don't know what he's thinking, at all, especially at a time like this. But here he is, asking me to marry him. He has a ring, even — a big diamond ring, just sparkling at me, and I laugh and laugh and laugh. I can't stop laughing. I seriously don't know what the fuck is going on. I don't even ever *want* to get married, to anyone! Let alone this complicated, adorable man I have nothing in common with. But I love him. He makes my life an incredibly charged and technicolour thing. Everything about him makes me feel alive.

I love him so much the thought of not loving him pains me. But I'm also slightly conflicted; do I really want something as important as marriage to begin right when a huge tragedy has just happened? I worry it's a bad sign, this proposal in the aftermath of terrorism so close to home, while airspace is still closed, while loved ones are still missing, while images of people jumping out of falling buildings are still playing on a loop in my mind.

I'm looking at this ring, and after a while he says, "So?" and I say, "Why not?" Because really, why not? I say, "I love you and you love me. Let's take a chance!"

And we do.

TEN YEARS LATER

I'm reading in bed. Downstairs I hear the now familiar sounds: the pop of a beer cap, the hum of the television, the punctuated laughter that seems forced, as if he is trying desperately to find joy in something. Earlier, I stood in the doorway of the TV room, lingering unnoticed.

"Why don't you come up to bed with me?"

He didn't. He never does anymore.

We just celebrated our ninth wedding anniversary. By celebrate I mean we had strained conversation over dinner, where he said he was tired about fifty times. I tried to make him laugh, but his face has turned into a hard piece of stone, his eyes expressionless. Our marriage is stuck. It's just ... *there*. And festering. He's motionless, unresponsive. I don't know what's happened to him, and it's making me bitter. Angry. I feel trapped and resigned.

Of course what has happened to him is *her*. I just don't know it yet.

COMPROMISE

We are engaged for a year, and during that year we learn that planning a wedding is the least romantic thing you can do. We spend that year rolling our eyes at each other in utter exasperation, or giving each other long resigned looks. Despite how independent and kooky we both are, we also want to please everyone and do what we think we "should" do.

And so we give in to every expectation and trope, and end up planning the most traditional of weddings. 160 guests. Open bar. Seven-course meal. A DJ named Pino. A photographer named Greg. We get no fewer than fifty phone calls a week from either my mother or his mother, each one more maddening than the next: *so and so can't sit beside Aunt whoever, make sure you invite this distant cousin who you've never met plus his entire family, what kind of ribbon are you going to get for the centrepieces — eighth of an inch or tenth of an inch?*

I have never cared less about anything in my entire life. Ribbon sizes and flowers and seating arrangements and shoes dyed to match my dress ... honestly, I hate it all. He hates it, too, but, like the world's best almost-husband, he does every little boring task with me. At one point he declares that making the seating arrangement for our reception is the single most difficult puzzle he's ever done, which is saying a lot for a physicist. He's there with me to choose the flowers, the reception hall, even the who-on-earth-cares ribbon for the honest-to-God-who-cares centrepieces. We are compromising, both of us, to make this wedding a thing that a wedding is supposed to be.

But the biggest compromise is this: he wants us to get married in a church. I do *not* want to get married in a church. I was raised Catholic, but I'm not exactly religious. I go to church for baptisms and confirmations and special days that are important to my father. I'm respectful of people's faith, but truthfully? I'm not too sure I believe in God. Sometimes I wish I did believe more, but I just don't. So getting married in a church seems wrong to me — starting our marriage by telling lies in front of all our friends and family, in front of a God that may or may not exist.

It is very important to The Scientist for some reason. Surprisingly important. He really wants us to get married in a church; he just thinks it's "right." He says it will make everyone happy, especially our parents. He asks me to consider the United Church. He thinks it will be less "church-y" for me. And so, for him, I say fine. I say fine to make my almost-husband happy, to make his parents happy. And to spare my own parents the embarrassment of their artsy, feminist daughter getting married in a forest, or on a hilltop, or worse — in a *restaurant*. So I say, *Fine. Fine! I will get married in a church.*

And we do.

On the Saturday of the Thanksgiving weekend in 2002, I wear a vintage 1960s wedding dress and hold a bouquet of bright red and orange flowers. He wears a tux with a tartan vest and stands nervously at the front of the church. I'm wearing the long two-tiered veil my mother and I made together, and everyone we know and love is all in one room, smiling and laughing and getting teary-eyed.

And there in front of everyone, at the moment that counts most, I forget my vows. I just totally, completely forget. I'm standing there, The Bride On Her Special Day, and for the life of me there are no words. I can't remember a single thing about the beautiful vows I've written. So on the spot I conjure every TV and movie wedding I've ever seen, and I make something up: *Sickness and health, good times and bad, all the days of our lives, blah blah blah.*

When I finish, he smirks, leans in, and whispers knowingly to me, "Those aren't your vows, Parise!" I throw my head back and howl with laughter. A fiddler plays as we walk down the aisle, my hand in his.

After photos, we take our brand new little black car and drive ourselves to the reception at the very north end of the city. The windows are down on this warm October day as we drive up the winding highway to get there. The wind picks up my long veil and takes it out the window, so that it's flapping along the side of the car, still attached to my head. People in other cars honk and honk at us. They wave and hoot out of their rolled-down windows. We laugh and wave back — this wonderful tradition between strangers.

He has his hand on mine and he gives it a squeeze. "How about that, Parise?" he shouts. "*You* just got married!" And I laugh because really, how about that! I'm so happy in this moment, so happy to have done this thing I didn't want to do and in a place I didn't want to do it in. Here he is, squeezing my hand with one hand and driving with the other.

Here he is, my *husband*, The Husband. My teammate, my partner, my best friend. In good times and in bad, sickness and health, all the days of our lives, blah blah blah.

This is why, nine years later, when I find out about the affair, I focus unreasonably on our little car. This same car from our happy wedding scene.

I wonder about the things I can never know for sure. *Did he drive it to her place? How many times did she sit in the passenger seat where I once sat with my wedding veil hanging out the window? Did she even notice Birdie's baby seat in the back? All the little baby toys and books, the smushed-up Cheerios on the seat? And if she did notice those things, didn't that matter?*

Oh, I know. It's just a car. It's just metal. But it was ours, together, and so it's more than just metal, more than the way we got to our wedding reception or to summer campsites. More than the thing that we used for cross-country road trips or for bringing our newborn baby home from the hospital.

Yeah, it's just a car. But it's all the life that was lived in that car, too. And that strangely hurts almost as much as thinking about his wedding band all over her skin.

CHAPTER TWO

WAITING

Married life is good. We spend a year in a basement apartment to save money to buy our own place. It's small and crammed with all of our stuff. Well, all of my stuff. He has nothing. I remember the first time I was ever in his room, in the house he shared with a bunch of guys. I asked, "Where's all your stuff?" And he shrugged and said he just left it all when he moved to this city. "I like to travel light," he said, but I didn't understand. I mean, he wasn't travelling at all, he was *living*, wasn't he?

I love my stuff. I'm nostalgic for an old bowl that belonged to my friend's late mother, and my grandmother's kitchen utensils, and the first piece of art I ever bought on my own. I would never leave any of my things behind. But he could. He did. I wondered what that said about him, what it meant that he was the kind of person that had no sentimental attachment to things, the kind of person that could just up and go whenever he wanted to. *Could it mean he was unsentimental about people, too?*

It was a distant early warning sign I chose to ignore. Obviously, because here we are, married and living in a tiny basement apartment with all of these things of mine I would never leave. He's brought into our marriage only his clothes, a box of university textbooks, a fishing tackle box filled with odds and ends, and thirty-five thousand dollars' worth of student loans. We also have all the things you get when you have a big wedding like we did. My side, the Italian side, fulfilled all the traditional gift requirements. Twelve place-settings of china, cutlery, and crystal stemware. Coffee makers, blenders, tablecloths, bedsheets, towels, and luggage sets. There are so many trays and platters, I don't even know what I would ever use them all for. But for now they're in boxes while we save money to buy a real home.

We're in the basement of an old house, so everything slopes. The ceilings are only six feet, three inches high, and The Husband is six foot two. He bends his head down to walk around. It's freezing cold in there all winter long, and sometimes it gets so bad that we turn the oven on and open the door so I can sit directly in front of it. At night he fills plastic bottles with hot water and puts them in our bed so that by the time I'm ready to sleep it is toasty between the sheets. He's gold in this way, The Husband. These little things.

There are all kinds of crazy little insects and spiders in all kinds of nooks and crannies, and when the people who live upstairs walk around it sounds like thunder. We are so happy. We hang out all the time. He watches TV and I read, both of us on the couch with our legs wound together. We play cards and talk and talk and talk. During hockey season, we walk down the street to our local bar to watch the game and eat plates of macaroni and cheese. They know our drinks, so we never have to order. We go to movies, we go dancing, we eat in restaurants all the time because our rent is so cheap and we both hate to cook.

Being married is awesome.

After a year in the basement, we've saved enough money for a down payment and we buy a condo right downtown. At eight hundred square feet, it feels palatial compared to the basement apartment and my little bachelor before it. And it's warm. We spend three years there, happy, comfortable, carefree. That is, until *the ultimatum.*

THE FEELINGS I DON'T FEEL

The ultimatum comes after a huge fight. We've had this argument before, but tonight he's even angrier with me. Tonight he has had enough, enough, of waiting for me to have "the feeling." You know, *the feeling.* The way women talk about how much they want to have a baby, how much they can't wait to be pregnant, to be a mom. The feeling I don't feel.

He says, "You said you wanted to have a baby!" And I say, "I do! I'm sure I do … but I just don't have the feeling yet. I'm only thirty-one, we still have time —"

He cuts me off: "We've been married for four years!"

"I know, and it's been awesome! What's the rush to have a baby? I'm just not ready yet!"

I'm not ready yet. Or actually sure I will ever be ready. I've never had the feeling or anything close to the feeling. Not even a twinge. I haven't felt the magical desire to be pregnant, to give birth, to care for a baby who will turn into a child and then into an adult, and for the rest of my life be tethered to me. And I worry. I worry that a baby will change everything between us; that once we have a baby, our carefree, comfortable, love-drunk feeling will be gone. We won't be able to go to the movies on a whim anymore, or eat in restaurants four nights a week. Or be able to sleep in, or sleep at all! We'll no longer be a nation of two.

But he wants to be a dad so badly. I remember when we first met, he said, "You are the mother of my children." The funny thing is, I had that same feeling about him, this strange biological imperative, that he was the father of my children. Even before we were a couple. But the idea was more romantic than real for me.

His jaw is so tight, and he grits his teeth at me in the way he does when he's angry. His face is so close to mine, his finger pointing right at my chest but not actually poking me, just close, so close, and he says through clenched teeth, "I *never* would have married you if I knew you weren't going to have a baby."

"WHAT?" I say. It comes out like a croak. And then tears, so many tears. He never would have married me? Does he mean he only did it so I'd make him a dad?

He asks me to get off the birth control. He says he's done waiting for me to have "the feeling." I cry and cry and say, "Okay, okay ..." because I think I will lose him if I don't do this. I reason with myself: I may never have the feeling, so what the hell, why not just get pregnant?

After the tears, the long awful night, he's back to his kind, funny self. I feel better, too. I've resigned myself to the idea that my body, mind, and life are all about to change forever. I'm committed to doing it. I mean, babies are cute, aren't they? Sure. And they become funny little children eventually, and I definitely like those. Maybe "the feeling" is bullshit; maybe all those other women are just making it up! Maybe this is just another thing I'm afraid of. But I never let fear stop me, so why would I now?

I go off the birth control. My doctor warns me that since I've been on it for so long, it may take up to a year to conceive. So, I approach getting pregnant like I approach most things in life — I produce *the shit* out of conception. I go online and learn how it all works — how long the egg lasts once it's released and how long sperm lasts once it's inside of me. I figure out when I'm ovulating next, plus or minus three days. Then, based on how long the egg and sperm are supposed to last, I come up with a plan: We need to have sex eleven days in a row, with my approximate ovulation date somewhere in the middle.

"As long as we do that, we've got to hit it!" I say, and The Husband is pleased with my calculations. He kisses my forehead, and I feel amazing because if he's happy, I'm happy. And I love when he's so admiring of my ability to estimate numbers quickly and accurately — how long it takes to get somewhere, the gratuity on a restaurant bill, the price of an item that's 65 percent off, and now, what the formula is to make a baby on our first try. Which is exactly what happens.

On the calendar in our kitchen, I plot the eleven-day sex-a-thon. And we have fun, excellent sex on each of those eleven days. One month later, we're driving in his parents' town, and suddenly I feel so tired. I'm a little dizzy, and I just feel weird. And then I know. I'm pregnant. Just like that. Just like that, driving in our little car it hits me: I'm pregnant. I don't know why I know it, but I do, and it's the most certain I've ever felt about something I have no proof of.

I see a drugstore and pull the car into the parking lot. "What do you need?" he asks, and I tell him. Fifteen minutes later, we are back at his parents' house, up in the bathroom together with the door locked like two teenagers hiding something. He sits on the edge of the bathtub while I pee on a stick. He reads the instructions fifty times, even though I tell him not to worry, I'm a pro at these tests.

He looks at the stick. He looks at me. I'm pregnant. I've just given him the thing he wants most in life. He looks happier holding that positive pregnancy test than I have ever seen him, before or since.

BUILDING

When I'm six months pregnant, we sell our awesome downtown condo and buy an old house in the north end of the city. People will dispute "north end" and they're right, but to this downtown girl? It feels like we've moved to the treeline.

The reason we're here above the treeline is me. Even though I've lived downtown since I was nineteen. Even though I love living within walking distance to everything and being in the centre of it all. Even though I love living in an apartment, I am the one who pushes us to buy a house away from it all. Me. I know. It's like I'm a totally different person now that I'm pregnant. A person who thinks "the right" thing to do is to live in a house because a baby is coming. Even though we could have made do in our condo, or just bought a two-bedroom. For some reason, I'm stuck on the idea of a house. *A baby needs a bedroom! A baby needs a house! And it should be quiet, so a baby needs a detached house! With a backyard! And a driveway. With a garage! Make it a double!*

So this is why we're here, in an eighty-year-old house, with a leafy backyard and a double garage, nowhere near downtown. Nowhere near any of our friends or favourite restaurants or parks. Nowhere.

There are only two things I enjoy about being pregnant — one is that my hair is as shiny and curly and healthy and beautiful as it's ever been or will be. The other is that I can feel her moving around inside me. And she moves a lot. "What's she building in there?" I always say, quoting a Tom Waits song and imitating his voice as I do it, which always makes The Husband laugh. I just can't believe how much activity there is in my own body! Sometimes, I'm lying down and part of my belly just changes shape as she jabs some appendage into the wall of the sack she's growing in, which just happens to also, miraculously, be part of my body. Beside me is her dad, as silly and adorable as ever. He grabs at the appendage and manages to hold it for a second, and I feel her fight to free herself from his grip. It's like they're playing together already, even though my body is between them, and I feel increasingly removed and lonely.

How can I be lonely with another human being inside of me? I mean, you can't get closer than that can you? I also have a husband who's wanted to be a father for so long. He's so jazzed by the whole thing, but my body hurts. It's uncomfortable, and now I can't play soccer anymore.

I play in a co-ed league every Thursday; it's the thing I look forward to most each week. I love my team and the way everything disappears while I'm on the field. Now that I'm pregnant and can't play anymore, I feel like a huge part of my life is missing. Instead I sit at home on Thursday nights with my uncomfortable new body, eating too much while trying not to think about soccer, or how once the baby comes, it will be my hormones that go wonky, not The Husband's, so no wonder he is so excited. It will be my body that will have to feed her, and before that, she'll have to come out of my vagina. I have no idea what any of that will be like. Let alone being a mother for the rest of my life.

I suppose you might be rolling your eyes at me right now. Go ahead. Being pregnant isn't always this blissed-out Earth Goddess Instagrammable wonder-show that it's often presented as. For some of us, it hurts and sucks to be pregnant — your body is stretched and pulled and your pelvis is actually tilting and your hormones are all wacky and you can't sleep. People give you all kinds of unsolicited nutritional advice about nitrates and soft cheese. Strangers touch you, because as a pregnant woman out in the world you are now somehow public property, like a park bench or a new city-approved sculpture. Everyone can just put their hands on your belly and congratulate you or comment on how huge you are. So I am here to say unequivocally: I don't like being pregnant. And I know I'm not the only one. Why can't we say that and still be good mothers? We can. I just did.

And yes, being pregnant is a beautiful thing, too. You're making a life. There's a body inside of your body! How crazy is that? It's like you're a human matryoshka doll. I mean, that's pretty amazing, even if it's uncomfortable.

One requisite of being a human matryoshka doll is reading parenting books and magazines. I flip through pages and pages dutifully, although they're filled with things and people I feel completely disconnected from. I'd rather be reading an article about the latest Radiohead album, not "The Top 5 Pregnancy-Safe Cleaning Products." But, I do happen upon one article that piques my interest, all about decorating the nursery. It suggests you paint your baby's room your favourite colour, since you're going to spend so much of your life in there for the next few years. Don't paint the room for the baby, paint it for you.

So that's what I do. I find painting very relaxing, and although I'm uncomfortably pregnant, I paint her entire room over the course of a few days; three walls mandarin orange, and one wall cream-coloured with giant hand-painted circles in mandarin, lime, and brown. When I'm finished, The Husband installs the mobile he bought to go above the crib: a complete solar system that orbits a bright sun. He's a scientist, what do you expect? It becomes my favourite room in the house.

I may not be in the best headspace while pregnant, but The Husband is really, really happy now. And he's been growing a beard. Or rather, trying to grow a beard, since he's one of those men who has zero body hair and not quite any facial hair either. It comes in scraggly and patchy, and the beard and moustache don't even touch in the places they should. Still, I find him impossibly adorable. I call it his "playoff beard," since he is determined to keep it until the baby is born. Just like hockey players vying for the Stanley Cup, he will not jinx the proceedings by shaving his face. It's quite a superstitious thing to do for a scientist, and I love him more for his contradictions. Still, part of me feels him slipping away from me. Everything is about the baby now, and it's like our relationship has shifted into a business partnership. The business of baby.

Almost every night now, The Husband rests his head on my giant belly and shouts "Hey!" She responds by jumping all around like an excited puppy in my uterus. He pokes my belly hard and says, "Whattaya at?" and she pokes back at him immediately, every time, and hard. They go back and forth like this, already communicating, and I feel more and more removed from things. More and more like a vessel, a host that will usher in his greatest relationship, making me insignificant. Which is exactly what happens.

FULL MOON, FIRST OF JULY

Dear White Shirt,

Tonight, we talked and talked, all the adults, once the kids finally fell asleep. We drank wine around a bonfire and then more wine and we talked about how the moment is life. How isn't it funny that the things you can't plan for often turn out to be the best things? If we let them.

We had more wine. We talked about death and fear. We talked about risk and love and gratitude. We talked about how our parents fucked us up and what ways we would inevitability fuck up our own kids. We laughed so much, even when what we were talking about was painful.

We smoked weed. We talked about how our lives are half over now — if we're lucky — so our goal is to have more fun and to feel more present in the now, in the *here*.

We talked about you, because everyone always wants to talk about you, and I always talk about you anyway because how can I not? You're so woven into my life in a way that I'm not always sure I understand but also in a way that strangely makes sense.

And I wished you were here. Because we're at a rented cottage on Canada Day and we ate ribs for dinner and homemade biscuits and beets and all that made me think of you and how you love to eat and would enjoy it — like, really enjoy it — and you'd say something quirky and funny because that's how you do, and I would look at you and be melty, because that's how I do.

I thought of Birdie's face and how it lights up around you. How she's always the kid with the single mom when we're doing things with my friends with kids. The other kids have siblings and two parents and she whispers wishes to me sometimes while she's falling asleep, things like "Mom, sometimes it would be nice to have a brother or sister to play with. But that's okay, I understand."

And I lie there very still beside her, because when I had her I wasn't sure I had "the feeling," you know? The right feeling I thought I should have about being a parent. But being her mom turned out to be the one truly good thing in my life. The one easy thing. And now that I'm approaching forty, "the feeling" is so strong in me I can't think of anything else sometimes. How my body seems to want another baby. Yours.

I would do it in a heartbeat now, no question, but time is running out, and you can only be occasional to us. You are not here lighting sparklers with her, or singing duets with me as I play guitar around the fire. You aren't worried that time is running out. You're trying to make sense of your own life. You're trying to be good and true to you. Your free spirit is what I love about you, even though it's the thing that keeps you from me.

And I crawled into bed now and I'm still wearing your Adidas jacket and it still smells like you somehow and it's like I'm flooded, but not with anxiety or sadness at what you will and won't be.

No, I'm flooded with good clear thoughts of all the things you already are.

xo,

mp

July 1, 2014

BIRDIE

Spring 2007. I'm eight months pregnant and I'm a giant, swollen mass. The doctor has put me on bedrest because my blood pressure is constantly through the roof. My feet have gone from a size seven to a size nine. For the last month, each night before bed, The Husband has wrapped my forearms in ice. He does it with such care and a lot of little jokes. I feel lucky to have a husband who wants a baby this much. The ice sort of helps with the agonizing pain, but nothing helps these ankles. I can't even see them anymore.

Basically, the last month of being pregnant totally sucks. When I'm thirty-seven weeks pregnant, The Husband drives me to the doctor for an ultrasound. The high blood pressure and swollen limbs have the doctor concerned I might have pre-eclampsia. She does an ultrasound and declares there to be very little amniotic fluid. She looks at us and asks, "You have any plans today? How do you feel about just having this baby?" and I am so relieved. Yes, please, take this baby out of me, please.

I'm induced. Thirty-five unbearable hours later, the next night, after so much pushing and no success, they wheel me into the operating room and do a C-section. The Husband has been at my side every step of the way, and neither of us has slept for what is nearing forty hours. I can barely see Birdie when he brings her to me. My eyes are crossing and I see two, three babies, all blurry.

"Is she okay?" I ask and he says, "She's perfect."

"Oh, good," I say, and pass out.

While I'm passed out, they finish up the operation. The Husband takes Birdie out into the hall where his mother, my family, and my best friend all meet her. Seven people meet my baby before I do. They all see her face clearly and touch her. I wake up an hour later to a nurse pushing the baby onto my breast, so I still can't really see her face. And I'm so full of drugs I can't make out anything that's happening, least of all that I am now a mother.

After five days in the hospital, we head home. My mother comes to stay with us at first, to help out. She argues with The Husband constantly. Every breath the baby takes is something for them to disagree on; they both have an opinion on everything, a low-level battle in the background of this new life. I'm too exhausted to have my own opinions. Not that anyone's asking me.

I feel completely dissociated. Like if anyone were to look at me, they'd know something was wrong. I feel like an alien. I'm sad, exhausted, and freaked out. I know nothing about babies. And this one is now killing me twelve times a day when she's meant to be fed by my body. There doesn't seem to be enough milk to satisfy her, so she's ravenous, and tearing chunks of flesh off my nipples. It's the most natural thing for a woman to do, we're told, but it's awful. It's the most physically painful thing I've ever experienced. I would rather have the thirty-five-hour labour again, or have my appendix burst again, or break my leg in two places again — anything, anything, would be less terrible than this.

The Husband and my mom fight all the time, but on this they agree: stop breastfeeding. But I feel like a failure of a woman. The Husband is understanding and kind about it. He says, "You couldn't have the baby naturally either, remember? So, don't worry about it." And he's right. The baby isn't growing; after three weeks she is still under her birth weight. So I give up. We put her on formula, and she becomes a plump, relatively happy baby.

The thing with maternity leave is, I'm alone. Just me and Birdie, a baby that never sleeps during the day. I pace through the house like a stranger, looking at everyday objects and forgetting the meaning of them. Wine glasses. Books. What are those for? I can't even imagine reading one book, why do I have so many? One day I open the bathroom cupboard and see a whole tray of eyeshadow I can't imagine ever putting on again. And I have so many big, shiny earrings. Where on earth would I wear such things?

Eyeshadow and earrings seem like relics of a life I will never have again. Instead, life now is just a series of endless days and nights with nothing but her crying and cooing and the vast empty sound of the vast empty house. There's no one to talk to, nothing to discuss. Each morning when The Husband leaves at eight, my heart sinks. I watch him drive away until I can't see him anymore, and everything collapses.

I'm looking forward to July though. He's a teacher so he'll be off for the summer and home to spend time with the baby. Home to help me get some rest, some bearings. And since this is the thing he wanted more than anything in the world, I imagine how excited he must be for the last day of work so he can be home to care for her.

But instead, he goes on a trip. As soon as the school year is finished, he goes to Washington, DC, with a bunch of co-workers. He says he has to, but I can't understand it — why would there be a mandatory work trip during the summer? Why would he go on a trip when it's his very first opportunity to be home with his newborn daughter and his wife? We have a huge fight about it. And then it comes up again, and again and again. For years and years, it just keeps coming up during arguments about other things, because I can't get over it, ever. I just can't.

When he comes back from the trip, there's finally some relief and I'm grateful to have a teacher for a spouse, so he can be there during the day to help carry the load. He changes every diaper, and shares the nighttime feedings with me. I'm able to get some sleep, and do things with both of my arms free. The help feels like a luxury after those long first months alone. But also, it's just more fun with him around. We sit out in the backyard under the trees together, the three of us, a little family, picture-perfect. We go to Wasaga Beach, and I'm able to lie in the sun and swim, unencumbered, because he's in his preferred spot in the shade with the baby. On a daily basis, he barbeques happily for friends and family who drop by to see the baby, and I feel more at ease in it all. New parenthood feels less of an effort for these two months. We are a team.

Once summer is over, it's back to being alone in the big, empty house. Winter comes early and stays *forever*. Time moves slower than I ever imagined it could. I play with Birdie, I sing her songs, I feed her, I comfort her. I look at the clock and it's only 9:30 a.m. God. I feel like maybe I will die from sheer emptiness, from the lack of people that aren't babies or on TV. I miss my desk at work. I miss meetings and creative conversations and writing and … work. I miss work. I know being a new mom is work, but I don't process it that way. It just feels lonely. I miss talking to my peers about music and art and books. I miss organizing and creating and discussing and laughing. I love my baby, but I don't love being home all day long with her with no one to talk to, only laundry and making baby food to break the monotony.

I know what you're thinking. You think I sound cold and distant, not like a mom is supposed to sound when talking about her newborn. Maybe you think it sounds like I don't love my child. That I'm too busy thinking about myself and all that I've lost, instead of bonding with her. But that's not what this story is about. I'm not here to convince you that I love her. Because I do. And that love grows with every year of her life. Every day, I watch Birdie become this funny, clever, kooky person. She fills my life with more joy than anything or anyone.

But right now I'm talking about The Baby. And I'm sorry if that seems cold, but sometimes, honestly, they're two different people to me. It's hard for me to reconcile The Baby and Birdie as one and the same. I was never diagnosed, because I never talked to anyone about how I was feeling, but looking back it seems pretty clear I had some form of postpartum depression. Maybe I just had what they call "the baby blues," I don't know for sure. But the pressure to love being a new mom, to somehow instantly know what to do and how to cope … it was real. We've all been fed the same *new mothers are instinctually amazing at it* propaganda, except I didn't feel amazing at it at all. A lot of women don't. Instead, I felt shame. And an indescribable sadness. So judge me, if you want, but I'm going to return there now, to those early days. Those long, endless days at home alone with a newborn baby.

I feel isolated. I've always lived downtown, but now I'm in this strange neighbourhood that seems so far from anything or anyone I know. Sure my friends and co-workers all came to visit me when the baby was first born, but after that initial rush, people stopped coming around. It's 2007, so social media is barely a thing. Even the internet is a thing I have to go upstairs, turn on a big ol' computer, and wait for. I don't even have a cellphone! I'm finding it hard to connect with my friends.

And I'm having trouble connecting with new people I meet, too. The women with babies in my neighbourhood all seem so put together. Like they aren't struggling with it at all. They probably are, in their own ways, but I feel like a disaster compared to them. They're such naturals at being mothers, and they all breast-feed like it's no big deal. They always talk about how they don't want to go back to work. They love maternity leave. I just can't relate. I'm so out of place with my bottle-fed baby and my tattoos. With my love of my job and the world downtown.

There is at least one thing I look forward to each week: soccer. As soon as Birdie is three months old, I return to my co-ed soccer team. I'm really out of shape, but I give it everything I've got. In that ninety minutes a week, when I'm on the field, I think of nothing but the game. I feel pure exhilaration — I'm competitive, physical, quick-witted.

For those ninety minutes, I feel like myself. Like the old me.

When it's over, I go back home, sweaty and happy. Each week it's the same: I come in the back door and The Husband is sitting on the couch watching TV. "How was the game?" he asks, and I excitedly recap the whole thing. He listens patiently and with interest. He knows I love playing soccer. He knows I'm mostly miserable these days and that once a week this is the thing that saves me. He goes back to watching his show, and I take a shower. The baby will wake up any minute now and will need my attention. I've got to go back to being a twenty-four-hour mom. At least until next Thursday and those blissful ninety minutes on the field.

Of course maternity leave and being a mom gets easier as the months go on. Sometimes, I even enjoy it. She's beautiful. Her head is so perfectly round and she's got these big blue eyes and straw-coloured hair, nothing like me with my brown eyes and dark hair. But she came out of my body, and that never stops amazing me. I sing to her. I play with her. I read her books and talk to her all day long. I get a bit better at it, the maternity leave, even though I'm counting the days until I can go back to work.

But exactly two months before my return to work, when Birdie is ten months old, something suddenly and unexpectedly starts to go very wrong.

SUCK IT UP

I'm in the middle of a soccer game when I first notice it. *Man, I keep missing the ball. That pass was so wide.* I keep misjudging the distance between me and the ball, between me and other players. *I must be exhausted. I'm seriously off my game tonight.*

It gets worse. The next day, I'm driving with Birdie, and everything in my field of vision just starts jumping around. The road looks like it's underwater. I call The Husband and say, "I don't think it's safe for me to drive, you'll have to come and pick us up." He drives me to a downtown hospital, Birdie asleep in her car seat in the back. It's way too expensive to park downtown, and besides, it doesn't make any sense to bring a little baby inside an emergency-room waiting area, so he drops me off with a casual "don't worry" and goes back home.

I sit in the emergency waiting room for over four hours. A woman is howling and cursing. A sad-looking man is pacing back and forth across the room, shoulders hunched. Another man across from me is attached to his chair with handcuffs, a police officer on either side of him. I can't read or see the TV very well, and my eyes hurt a lot, so there's nothing to do but close them and sit with my thoughts.

The hours pass slowly. Eventually, I see a doctor and he sends me to another floor for a CT scan. Then more waiting, more time alone, with nothing to do but worry. Nothing but endless blurry hospital life all around me.

And then I hear the voice of the doctor I just met with. I get up and try to sneak closer, hiding behind a post so I can listen in on his conversation. "Female, thirty-three years old" — I'm pretty sure he's talking about me now — "... need to send her to you for more tests ... could be, but ... consistent with multiple sclerosis ... more tests ..."

My heart tightens. Multiple sclerosis? What is that? My mind races to remember. Is it something to do with my spine? *No, no, dummy, that's scoliosis, not sclerosis!*

This makes me laugh for a second until it dawns on me. Is it that thing we used to fundraise for when we were kids? Yes! The MS Readathon! I might have that? What is it? I really have no clue what MS is at all, other than I was a top fundraiser for it in grade school, which is very unhelpful information in this moment.

The doctor does not say MS to me. He gives me a bunch of forms and says the neurology department will call me in the next day or so to make an appointment for an MRI. "Good luck," he says, and I detect something, like a hitch in his voice? But, why? I can't really see his face so I don't know if it's because things look bad for me, or because he's a tired ER doctor.

"Thanks, I'm sure whatever it is, it will be fine!" I say.

Practically blind, with my head reeling from the possibility that I have some disease I know nothing about, I stumble along the crowded street to the subway. My eyes kill. The buildings are moving as I move. Everything I see is vibrating, and I can't make out anyone's face. I stare down at the sidewalk and try not to fall over, try not to cry. I take the subway, then a horrible, bumpy bus. I feel so alone, so terribly and achingly lonely. Why didn't I take a cab? Or call a friend to come pick me up? I honestly don't know. An hour later I get home. The Husband is on the couch watching TV.

For the next few weeks, I take care of the baby every day with everything in my field of vision jumping around like our old TV set in the seventies. It's like watching *The Love Boat* on a glitchy channel. Except it's my life, not *The Love Boat* at all. I'm so afraid I'll drop the baby, so afraid something will go wrong. My eyes get worse. The jumpiness makes me constantly nauseous. And then, on top of it all, I develop double vision. I have to sew myself an eye patch, which helps steady me. How did I sew? I really don't know.

The Husband doesn't take a day off work. In fact, he begins teaching night school a few times a week and playing extra Ultimate Frisbee games, which means most days he leaves at 8:00 a.m. and doesn't get home again until 10:00 p.m. I'm sad and tired. I'm finding things difficult to manage, even though I have no choice but to manage. No one is offering respite. But maybe I'm not asking?

One night he arrives home after 10:00 p.m. and I ask, "Do you have to come home so late all the time?" Even through blurred eyes I can see his body stiffen, his jaw tighten. And then he says, "You need to suck it up, Parise."

Of course, I do. I go for MRI after MRI, test after test, doctor after doctor. And I go to almost every one of them by myself. Then, when Birdie is eleven months old, I'm diagnosed with multiple sclerosis. I'll give him this — he was there for that appointment at least.

The timing is terrible. My maternity leave is almost over, and I'm finally going back to work. But my eyes are still all screwed up, making it impossible to see, to drive, and to read and write. The neurologist prescribes a steroid treatment. "This should clear up the problem!" he says affably.

So, every day for a week, a public health nurse comes to the house and hooks me up to an IV drip. I sit in our spare room on an old futon with the IV in my arm. I can't read or watch TV with these stupid eyes, so I just sit alone, for an hour, doing nothing while the steroids flow into me, the taste of metal filling my mouth. It's the only hour of my day where I'm not caring for the baby, or doing laundry, or cleaning. I'm just sitting alone in a quiet room, with a bag of drugs that will hopefully make my eyes go back to normal.

They don't. And now my body is addicted to steroids. They have to wean you off them by giving you more, did you know that? So for two more weeks, I have to keep taking the drug, the taste of metal constantly in my mouth while my eyes bounce and shake. For two months, I lived as normally as I could with these crazy eyes. I tried to suck it up, tried to keep it together, but now that the steroids have failed, I'm freaked out. I'm starting to feel actually depressed.

I'm a journalist. How am I going to read and write all day long with these fucking eyes jumping around? How can I hide my diagnosis from everyone if I have to wear an eye patch all the time? Will I get passed over for promotions or cool special projects if managers know?

My good friend, The Practical One, sits with me one day and does what she does best — real talk. She's the only one who seems to notice that I'm getting sadder and sadder. She starts to tell me about a woman she saw on Oprah once and I roll my jumpy eyes, but she continues. This woman had some unimaginably horrible thing happen to her, she was like, dying or something, but she continued to be upbeat and positive, inspiring everyone around her with her lovely spirit. So Oprah says, "How do you *do* it?" and the woman tells her she wasn't always like this. When it first happened, she lay in bed all day crying and saying, "Why me?" But then one day, she just thought, "Enough." She decided to give herself five minutes a day to feel sorry for herself and that's it. Then she had to get on with it until the next day when she had another five minutes to scream and cry and throw things and then move on.

I love this idea. I say to my friend, "I can do that! I can only feel sorry for myself for five minutes a day and move on!" It really sinks into my head as the best idea I've ever heard. And so it's exactly what I do. I plan out five minutes a day to feel sorry for myself. And then after that five minutes I say, *It's only your eyes. What if it was your hands? That would be way worse. Or your legs! And besides you can still sort of see; maybe there's a modification you can do to your computer at work.*

I start to make a mental list of all the ways I can deal with it, especially since I won't be taking care of a baby all day anymore. I'll be making a radio show again, which is *nothing* compared to being a stay-at-home mom. I try walking around without the eye patch. I get my hair cut. I plan Birdie's first birthday party.

Then I wake up one morning and I can see again. Just like that.

I return to work after a year off, and no one knows what I've been through. I keep it at that. I don't tell anyone. I get back to work and it feels great. Months later, I begin taking a very expensive drug treatment, a needle I have to inject every single day. A nurse comes to the house to show me how to do it, and The Husband sits with me and learns, too.

I read a pamphlet about how there are actually several different types of MS, including the not-so-bad type I have, called relapsing-remitting. The other main type is called progressive, which, as the name suggests, is much, much worse. After reading up on it more, I realize how strange a disease MS is, in that it can take so many forms, and the range of severity is massive. It seems like every symptom is possible, or not possible. With relapsing–remitting, the neurologist tells me, I could have another attack at any moment, or maybe not for another ten years. Or ever. There's no way of predicting it.

"Attack" is what they call it, which sounds pretty dramatic and I'm not too sure it's a medical term. I learn that the attack I had, with the jumpy double vision, was caused by a huge lesion on my brain stem, which is basically the comms room of your brain, controlling the flow of information between your brain and body. It's also responsible for basic body functions, like heart rate, breathing, reflexes, and motor control.

I see the MRI of my brain and they aren't joking: the lesion on my brain stem is *massive*. That big blurry blob affected the motor control of my eyes, causing my jumpy vision (called nystagmus) and the double vision (diplopia). But those things have cleared up now. The attack is over, I'm back at work, and the neurologist is convinced that as long as I take the expensive drug, I will remain in remission.

And so, there's nothing for me to do other than continue on as normal. I feel confident that this will all be fine. I will inject a needle every day for the rest of my life and it will be *fine*. I could have another attack or I could be hit by a bus, the chances seem the same to me, and so I choose not to think about it too much. There is too much life happening, too much to do, too many other things to focus on. I push out any thoughts of wheelchairs and walkers, of tremors and degenerative tissue, of growing lesions on my brain. *That won't be me!* I say to myself after the allotted five minutes of feeling sorry for myself.

That won't be me.

CHAPTER THREE

RUNNING UP THAT HILL

FINISH LINE

I don't know where I get the idea or why, but one day in the spring of 2009, I decide I'm going to sign up for a 10K race. Other than during soccer games, and a few years on the track team in my youth, I haven't exactly been a runner. Or at least not a distance runner. Ten kilometres is a lot of kilometres if you've never really run, are supremely overweight, and have had a baby and an MS diagnosis in the past year. But this is a thing I decide I'm going to do. Run 10K. Alone.

I go to a running store and buy proper shoes for running on asphalt and concrete. The tiny woman who works there gives me tips on how to do "ten-and-ones," which is to run for ten minutes then walk for one, and repeat. I sign up for the 10K online and try not to be overwhelmed by words like *corral* and *best time*. I put on some yoga pants and a stretched-out old sports bra and wake up at 5:30 a.m. to run around the neighbourhood before work. I do this a total of six times before the race. To call that "training" would be generous.

On the day of the race, I'm standing in my corral alone. Well, alone in a crowd of two thousand people. I'm freezing, because it's seven thirty in the morning in early May. I'm wearing my ratty yoga pants and the free T-shirt I got when I registered. Even though it's extra-large, it feels really tight on me.

I'm not so much afraid as awkward. Everyone is with buddies or in big groups. They're all wearing sporty clothes that seem to fit them properly. I don't know why I thought this was a good idea. *What am I even doing here? By myself!* I put my earbuds in and adjust my iPod, which is attached to my arm on this iPod-attaching thing someone lent me. When the starting gun goes off and the crowd surges, I press play on the perfectly crafted race playlist I've made, and I surge, too. Maybe this is cheesy, but, in case you're dying to know, the first song on the playlist is Kate Bush's "Running up that Hill."

I'm not going to lie, it's not easy, especially considering the most I've ever run is four kilometres, and that was only on the last of my six "training" mornings. But I run. I do my ten-and-ones, passing the flags that mark each kilometre, through Kate Bush and Arcade Fire, K'naan and The Clash, Vampire Weekend and Magic System. I'm amazed at the people that line the streets, cheering us on, offering us water. The sun is out in full force now and it's a lot warmer. I'm sweaty and my lungs feel like they're going to burst but I push on. The last kilometre is the worst; it feels like another ten for some reason. My legs are rubbery and I feel like I'm looking at the finish line forever, like I will never actually get there.

When I do arrive, I see Birdie in the crowd. She's two years old now and on top of The Husband's shoulders, wearing her white sun hat, the one with little flowers embroidered on it. The Husband is pointing me out to her and as I'm running toward the finish line, her voice cuts through the noisy crowds' shouts and the ringing of bells. "Moooooooooooooooooooommm!"

And I think, *Oh my God, I have MS.*

I don't know why, but this is when it hits me most. Everything that has happened in the past two years just pummels me in this moment, the moment I cross the finish line. I burst into tears. Uncontrollable sobs. And the two of them run over, hugging me and cheering. The Husband's mother is there, too, and, ever the nurse, she starts quizzing me on my vitals. She hands me a banana and a bagel, which I scarf down immediately after I stop crying. I get my participation medal and although it took me an hour and a half to do it, I'm really proud of myself. I just ran 10K. And everything is going to be okay.

Time passes. Mostly I forget I even have MS. I still forget. I mean, other than taking the daily injections and pills, there's nothing much I can do about it, so I actually don't think about it that much. We go on with our lives, with this new phase of marriage, the one with a child in it.

I keep up with the running. I get up at 5:30 a.m. twice a week and run for an hour all around our neighbourhood. It's amazingly quiet, the city at that hour. There are hardly any cars on the roads and even fewer people. I sometimes pass young men, construction workers, sitting on their front porches sleepily waiting for the truck full of other young men to come and pick them up. I like that they always have a giant cooler at their feet, the kind you'd take on a camping trip, but they just have their lunch for *today* in there.

I also pass women, of all ages and ethnicities, standing at bus stops, going to whatever jobs they're going to so early in the morning. They hold their handbags close, look weary. I smile at them and sometimes they smile back, but not always. I wonder if they think I must be pretty privileged, to be jogging at this time of morning, instead of already dressed and on my way to work.

These early-morning runs are the only real time I have to myself. Just me and my thoughts, me and the quiet, me and my bursting lungs as I run down streets and through cemeteries and over streetcar tracks. It's not that I love running at all, or getting up so early, but more that I love the time alone that is so precious when you're married and a mother with a full-time job and a house to clean when you get home.

More time passes. The Husband is still so cute to me, even though he's changed a lot. He keeps his hair really short and spiky now, his shoulders are broader, his chest and body have thickened out with age and the diet of being married to an Italian. He's had laser-eye surgery so he no longer wears glasses, and when he had dental surgery to fix some damaged teeth, without asking they went ahead and straightened out his fangs, a feature I loved, the way they puffed out his lip. He looks good, but a lot different than when we first met. He still wears nothing but cargo pants and monochromatic T-shirts though, dressing nothing like the cool, stylish guys I work with, but I don't care. He is still the one I love, cargo pants or not.

Years pass. The house is a lot for us. Always a crack to fill, a carpet to rip up, a faucet to replace. Weeds in the backyard and big disgusting bugs in the basement. We're tired. Birdie is a handful. Every day there's a tantrum, a test of wills. We've become the stereotypical exhausted working parents. Our lives consist of work, the house, insane toddler, repeat. We take turns going out. He grabs drinks with his teacher friends or I hang with my media pals, while the other stays home with the insane toddler. We rarely go out together, if ever. But when we're at the house, we are together. There are always people coming and going, neighbourhood children running around, my dad dropping by, or cousins or friends. Barbeques, beer-making, board games, crafts, trivia nights. A house full of life and energy.

And always in the crowd, I hear his laugh, or I catch his eye across the room and he winks at me, or just gives me that smirk.

Our relationship like an inside joke between the two of us. I knew we would always be okay. We'd be the couple that would always be okay.

I was wrong.

ON STRIKE

Summer 2011. Birdie is four years old. The Husband and I are thirty-eight and thirty-six respectively. It's been eleven years since he first grabbed my hand and kissed me hard in the basement of that bar. The lanky guy who is now this man before me, creeping up on forty, with broad shoulders and a beer belly, tiny silver flashes across the night sky of his hair.

God I love him when I look over at him. He infuriates me and excites me, even now, when we are tired and run-down because Birdie at age four is like having three children all screaming relentlessly at once directly in your face. We work all day and she yells at us all night until she mercifully falls asleep. Then we go to bed together and talk in whispers because we're afraid she'll hear us and wake up and yell at us more. We add a tiny hook-and-eye lock on our door so we can have sex at night without me worrying she's going to walk in. We lie together and talk and giggle (in whispers) like teenagers until we fall asleep.

In the mornings I find him less adorable. He sleeps in while I get up and get ready first so I can then get Birdie up and get her ready. I look in our room and see him just sitting there on the edge of the bed, staring at the closet. Meanwhile, I get her on the toilet and wrangle her into clothes and beg and plead with her to brush her teeth and endure the screaming as I try to brush her hair or get her to brush it. I look in and he is still just sitting there, staring. And I want to scream, at him, at her, at everyone. Sometimes we do scream. It's a terrible way to start the day.

41

It isn't perfect, but what relationship is? What marriage is one hundred percent sunshine and roses? I love The Husband and he loves me, in spite of our exhausting hamster-wheel life, despite our differences and diverging interests. There is still plenty of common ground, and the foundation of our relationship is our similar spirit — the way we fight, hard, for the things and people we love. Our weird sense of humour, our own secret language. How he buys me the most perfect gifts for every occasion, a collection of necklaces and pendants that are unique and strange and so exactly *me*. How we still smirk at one another, still make out all the time and still have sex pretty much every day except when we're way too tired or grumpy. We are still, after all this time, totally into each other. I feel absolutely confident that no matter how we sometimes argue or annoy each other, we are a team. A dedicated couple who have each other's backs.

In the middle of July that year, The Husband goes away on a "guys' weekend" with his old pals from high school, a mild-mannered bunch who like role-playing games and pot-smoking. I love these guys, I consider them my own friends, and I'm glad he's getting a weekend away from our domestic life.

But when he returns, something is wrong. He's completely different, and I don't know why. He's sullen, a lot, and quick to anger. His jaw is tighter and it seems like everything I say is the wrong thing to say. He insists on enrolling Birdie in full-time daycare for the summer, even though he's a teacher and off, and even though it costs a lot of money and makes no sense. This makes me really angry, and we argue about it. I'm just supposed to go to work all day to pay for super-expensive daycare so he can stay home and do whatever he wants and not even hang out with his own kid, the kid *he* wanted so badly? But he doesn't budge. And so I reason that at the very least, he'll get some of the stuff around the house done — pull up the embarrassing weeds in the front yard, replace the screen door at the back of the house, paint the spare room.

He does none of it. He does nothing. All day long Birdie goes to daycare. All day long I go to work. All day long he ... I don't know. I don't know what he does. He plays video games, I can see that. He drinks a lot; the recycling bin tells me that. It's like he's on strike. He's become remote and absent even though he's right in front of us. He is done. And it's making me an angry, nervous wreck.

Summer turns into fall. The Husband turns into someone else completely.

It goes on like this for months. His jaw tighter, his eyes dull. Birdie and I chat at dinner and he's there, physically, but not *there* at all. I start taking her everywhere without him because he doesn't want to come to the park anymore, or to people's houses, or kids' birthday parties, or any of the other things we used to do the three of us, together. Birdie and I do art projects on the big dining table while he watches TV. We carve jack-o'-lanterns just the two of us, wrap Christmas presents without him, make a million valentines for her class. All while he sits there staring at the TV, beer in hand. (I guess I was being primed for single-parenthood. Funny to realize that now.)

During these six months, there *are* also good times. There are days when he is lovely and goofy and sweet and into me and into being a dad. There are days when we feel like a family. But mostly, things just get worse and worse between us. There are times when I look at him and it's like he's looking through me. We argue a lot, because I don't know what the fuck is wrong with him and he won't talk to me about it. Not knowing makes me angrier. I don't like him a lot of the time, even though I so desperately love and miss him.

He stops coming to bed at the same time as me, preferring to stay downstairs and watch hours and hours of TV. I start to take food to bed with me. Food fills the gaping holes of knowledge, the things I don't know, the questions he won't answer. I feel dismissed and invisible and I eat to quell the gnawing pain in my gut that isn't hunger, unless you count the hunger for a different life or the yearning to be seen again. Night after night in our bed alone, I eat cereal and toast and cookies and crackers, writing endlessly into my notebook: *What has happened to him? Where has my husband gone? Why did I ever agree to get married? This is such bullshit!*

As I put on more and more weight, he starts working out. He gets trim and fit and buys a bunch of new clothes — pants without cargo pockets, nice shirts, and shoes that aren't sneakers. He starts wearing a tie to work every day. He styles his hair for what seems likes hours every morning. He looks *good*.

I know what you're thinking, because in hindsight it's obvious and probably at the top of the "Top 5 Things to Look For If You Think Your Spouse Is Cheating" list. But I wasn't looking for clues because I didn't think he was cheating. I didn't even consider it. I mean, not *seriously*.

One morning, he's painstakingly choosing his outfit for the day (who *is* this guy?) and I half-jokingly say, "You're such a fucking dandy all of a sudden! Are you cheating on me or something?"

He spits back, "As *if*. When would I even have the time?" which seems as true a thing as he could say. Our lives are so busy, when would *anyone* have time to have an affair? I feel sheepish for even suggesting it. Of course he isn't cheating on me. Everything is falling apart, I know that, but this all must be a *phase*, a normal phase of marriage. Or he's just having a mid-life crisis or something. I mean, at least he hasn't bought a Ferrari.

Love as Torture

I grew up thinking love was torture. Love was passion, love was drama. I watched my parents fight in spectacular, telenovela fashion. I saw my aunt and uncle throw plates and punches while my little cousins and I hid under the kitchen table.

These couples loved each other fiercely. I'd sit at the top of the basement stairs, long after I should have been asleep, watching them dance close and call each other *darling*. A spark in their eye, an affectionate pinch of a bum, a laugh like a teenage girl.

So that's what love's always been to me: wild and sweeping. Changing from intense anger to soft care at any moment. Of course, my parents and most of my aunts and uncles all got divorced eventually, but by then it was too late, I'd sponged it all up. It's part of my very blood. Love is infuriating but worth every fight.

Which brings me here, to a place where love is only real if it can rage like a bonfire and also comfort like a fireplace. It's both, at once, the pain and the warmth.

It's why my heart is always cranked to maximum.

HE'S COME UNDONE

I just threw a vintage ashtray across the room in his general direction. It was made of glass, and when it hit the wall it sprayed everywhere, millions of tiny pieces all over the room. Some pieces even made it to the kitchen somehow, skidding across the floor.

I am howling, crying, begging him to stop twisting words. We've been like this before, but it's been worse these past few months, these months where something has happened to him

45

and I don't know who he is anymore. It feels like he's a ghost in this house, a ghost that stares infinitely at the TV. It makes me sad and then angry. And then, angrier. The more confused and angry I become, the more it leads us here, to a place where I throw a glass object clean across a room.

Suddenly, there's a tiny voice. "Guys?" the voice says. It's Birdie. She always calls us "guys" which is usually the cutest, but right now it is 1:00 a.m. and she is four years old and in her pyjamas in the kitchen, possibly standing right on top of tiny pieces of glass.

The Husband springs up like a saviour, shouting at me, "Look what you've done!" and scoops her up, cooing to her gently. He whisks her upstairs, comforting her like World's Best Dad, leaving me here, World's Worst Mom, I guess. I can only guess. I don't know why we are fighting like this, or what's happening. I'm so unhappy. I miss him and us, and I hate him and us, and I feel trapped, but not in a way that makes me want to break free. No, just in a way that makes me want to understand and fix, a trapping we can somehow transcend, together.

So I sweep up the glass. I sweep and sweep. He comes back. He holds the dust pan. He explains the properties of the glass to me, by way of explaining how something so small could shatter into so many pieces.

And then, we sit on the kitchen floor and talk. We stare at each other across this floor that only a few years earlier we put in ourselves when I was pregnant, tearing it up to reveal layer upon layer of linoleum in every pattern imaginable, decades piled on top of one another, an excavation of another family's life.

On this night, like all the others before it, neither of us storms off. Instead we talk. We talk and talk until we are calm again. Until one of us laughs. Until one person reaches out to the other and we are in each other's arms. Until one of us says, *Sorry, I'll do better,* and the other answers, *No, no, I'm sorry, I will do better.*

And so, like every single argument we have ever had, this one turns out okay. Exhausted, we go to bed together. We tangle our bodies up purposefully and kiss goodnight. We fall asleep pledging things will be different.

CHAPTER FOUR

THE BOMB

THE UMBRELLA

The umbrella is bright green, like a neon lime. I climb into the passenger seat of our car one morning when The Husband is driving me to the subway, and there it is, sticking out from under my seat. Clearly it's a woman's umbrella. But whose? And why? I lean over to get it, but it's jammed under the seat. You might even say purposefully jammed, in hindsight, but you just don't know, do you? I question The Husband and he seems unfazed, saying it must belong to a male colleague of his that he drove to a football game. I point out it's a pretty fancy, feminine umbrella but he just shrugs.

All I know is there's a woman from work he told me about a few weeks ago. It came out of nowhere, that revelation, like a scene in a David Mamet play. Something we were just speaking about, as an idea, not actually talking about, you know?

INT. BEDROOM — NIGHT

The HUSBAND and WIFE are lying in bed. They have just had sex and are looking up at the ceiling, legs in a tangle.

HUSBAND	What would happen if I was unfaithful?
WIFE	Um. What? Uh … have you been?
HUSBAND	No. No. But, what if there was someone I was interested in sleeping with?
WIFE	Is there?
HUSBAND	Yes.
WIFE	Who is it?
HUSBAND	A woman. At work. We've been friends for years. We go for tea every day. We talk about work and Ultimate Frisbee.

The WIFE takes a deep breath.

HUSBAND	She propositioned me once. I thought about it, but of course I didn't.
GREEK CHORUS	Oh yes, but he did! He did and did and did!
WIFE	Well, I get it. I mean, you're friends, you can talk about work and she understands and cares about it. And besides, you have no baggage with her. She sits across from you and laughs at the things you say. She doesn't ask you to take out the garbage, you don't hate that she never stops cleaning.

The HUSBAND sighs. He looks uncomfortable.

WIFE	Has anything ever happened between you two?
HUSBAND	No. No, nothing has ever happened.
GREEK CHORUS	But it was happening. It had probably happened that very same day!

And ... scene.

A few weeks later, the car ride, the green umbrella. *Maybe they drove to the coffee shop that day because it was raining.* But even though I know the umbrella is hers, I don't push it with him. I honestly think that we're going through a rough part of our marriage, and that he was finding missing pieces in this woman. I thought he was tempted, but would never actually go through with it. I thought we would work it out, that things would get better.

Am I the dumbest wife that ever lived, or what? *KABOOM!*

AN EDUCATION

Several times a year, The Husband would go out drinking with other teachers, sometimes after a school play or a colleague's retirement and always after a long evening of parent-teacher interviews. On these nights, I knew not to expect him home until 1:00 or 2:00 a.m., and I was fine with that. But in the past few months, these nights have become more frequent, and he has started arriving home much, much later, at 4:00 or 5:00 a.m. Sometimes I wake up to the sound of him crashing around in the kitchen downstairs. He's such a big, clumsy man at the best of times, but drunk and stoned, he's an elephant, and all household items beware.

Sometimes, I wake up in the middle of the night in a sudden panic. *Is he dead somewhere? Did he drink so much that he got in a fight with someone and is now lying in an alleyway somewhere, hurt?* My heart races and I call him and text him, but often there's no answer. Those nights are the worst. I lie there and worry, tossing and turning till I hear the lumbering giant come up the stairs.

I honestly only ever imagine that something horrible has happened to him. I never once think he's with a woman. Can you believe it? But that doesn't mean I'm not angry. By the time he stumbles in, I'm near-hysterical.

"You are a married man! A father!" I shout at him. "You could have answered me — I thought you were dead!"

And he mumbles, "Sorry, sorry ..." Always so sorry after the fact.

The best times are when I sleep soundly and don't wake up in a panic or hear him when he comes crashing into bed. Instead, I wake up in the morning light to find him lying beside me, his breathing heavy, his adorable but drunk face so sweet looking, so calm.

And this is how it is one morning in early November 2011, when, at 5:00 a.m., he returns from the grade 12 commencement. He crawls into bed and doesn't realize I'm awake. Turning onto his side, away from me, he lets out a huge sigh. Reflexively we wind our legs together as always. I watch his freckled back as it rises and falls with his breathing and I wonder, *What are they doing, these teachers, till 5:00 a.m.? Where do you go?*

He senses I'm awake and sleepily turns and looks at me, eyes half-open.

"Hi, Love," I say.

"Do you think your psychologist could recommend me a psychologist?" is what he says back.

THE THING WE'RE IN

"I can see where this is going. I can see we're going to fall in love," says The Man with the White Shirt. "You think we're going to fall in love?" I ask, and he says, "Of course! Look at us. Look at how we feel already!" This conversation is his attempt to explain why we should stop seeing each other. Again. He says he will never be in a committed relationship. He doesn't believe in labels.

It reminds me of a conversation with The Husband, a month before The Bomb. It was day one of what I like to call The Blitzkrieg, five mini-bombs, dropped on me one at a time, starting on Christmas Day 2011, and ending the night before we got on a plane to go on a trip to Jamaica. The Blitz lasts five days before the big finale, atomic in scale and efficiency, drops on me and changes everything, irrevocably, for the rest of our lives.

With all the surprise of a lightning war, I am hit on that Christmas Day as we're driving to his parents' house. As soon as Birdie falls asleep in the back seat, The Husband says, "So, I'm not really sure I believe in this whole modern marriage thing."

Modern. Marriage. Thing.

We have an abstract conversation, about marriage and the whole *modernity* of it. We talk about men and women and gender roles. He says men have no idea how to be *men* anymore, since they've grown up with no role models. I mention that our female role models were just as bad, but my heart is beating so loudly maybe he can't hear me. He just goes on and on and on. Eventually, I say, "Is there anything *specific* you want to talk about?" And he says, "Sometimes I'm not sure I want to be married anymore."

Just like that.

He stares out at the endless grey highway, hands fixed hard on the steering wheel and says, so quietly, "Who am I? I don't know who I am." At this, I give the most impassioned impromptu speech of my life. "Who *are* you? You're *you*. You are the *you* you were before and the *you* you're going to be. You're thirty-eight. You're funny and weird. You're really tall but you always bump your head as if you have no idea how tall you are. You always want to help strangers, and you do. You laugh at the stupidest movies and that sound is my favourite thing in the world. *That's* who you are."

I say a bunch of other things, too, things I love about him or admire, things that make him who he is. And I realize I've just managed to give a two-minute description of him without saying anything negative. This gives me hope.

He's so quiet. He puts his hand on my hand and squeezes it. I stare at the side of the road as it whizzes by. I close my eyes and brace myself for whatever comes next. I believed my speech, but all I keep hearing is "modern marriage thing." He's not sure he believes in it. Marriage. The thing we are in.

A few years later, when I fall hard for The Man with the White Shirt, here it is again. A thing he doesn't believe in, even though he's in it. Here he is, White Shirt, back in my bed one morning, staring at me the way he does as if I am the dreamiest thing. And that's when I say to him, "Have you thought about what you're going to do when you fall in love with me anyway?"

"Yes, I have," he says, "and I think it will destroy me."

I throw my arms up in the air, I roll my eyes, I do all the motions of exasperation because *come on*. I say, "But love should be the opposite of destroying!" because it should, it really should. What is the matter with everyone?

He has no response, and we just look at each other across my white sheets. His eyes are the best eyes I've ever looked into. They're like the master switch for me, turning all the lights on at once. I run my hand slowly down his face, ending at his chin, where I scratch lightly at his beard. We lie there, limbs interlocked, still looking into each other's eyes, endlessly searching for what, I don't know. And I want to just shake him and everyone, all of you, for being afraid to love because it might hurt.

BLITZKRIEG

It's no wonder we so often use military terminology when describing the breakdown of love; anyone who's been through it knows it feels just like war. A civil war more specifically, the way a nation once together suddenly finds itself divided and at arms. And so, it's no different for me. I have told you there was a Bomb, and before it, there was a Blitz.

Day One as you know, was the "modern marriage thing" conversation. *Kaboom and Merry Christmas!*

Day Two, Boxing Day, we're lying in the too-small bed of the guest room at his parents' house when he quietly and very seriously tells me that he's been "emotionally distancing himself" from me since the day I was diagnosed with MS. I'm stunned.

"You don't understand how many times I've buried you," he says, and I call him a drama queen. I say, "I'm not *dying*. It's not cancer or anything! Why would you *bury* me? I'm going to live longer than you probably, you idiot!" I am pissed off and really do think he is an idiot in this moment. I can't stop myself from calling him names and being awful because I can't understand what he is saying to me. *Why would he purposely distance himself from me because I got sick?*

"Self-preservation," is his only answer to my confused tears. A quiet, simple answer to my angry questions. Self-preservation. He pulled away from me to protect himself. *But from what?*

After he falls asleep, I lie awake for hours and I feel like Alice falling down the rabbit hole, looking at things that used to make sense in the real world but now float by me, past me, over me, like they were never mine to understand or keep.

Day Three of The Blitz. We are thankfully driving away from his parents' house and back to our own. The second Birdie falls asleep in the back seat, kid-drunk on so much Christmas, I immediately ask him, "Are we breaking up?" and he says he doesn't know.

I stare out the window at the cars filled with other families on their way to and from somewhere. *Are they as miserable as us?* I wonder. I'm so tired of being confused. I close my eyes and wait.

"All I am is three things," he finally says, matter of fact. "I'm a teacher. A husband. A father. And only one of those things satisfies me. Only being a father brings me satisfaction."

My heart sinks into the passenger seat. My twenty-five-year-old heart, the one that fell in love with him, the one that twelve years later still thinks of him as so much more than just "husband" or "father" or "teacher." My thirty-seven-year-old heart hurts, too. It's sustained the sturm und drang of the past six months of our marriage, and now this. *This.* The anger rises up in me, hot like a kettle about to boil, ready to scald him if he isn't careful, and me for certain.

Day Four. The Day I Learn She Exists. You know this story: the post-sex conversation about a woman at work he's friends with and how she propositioned him once but of course he didn't do anything.

Of course not, *of course.*

Day Five. The night before we're getting on a plane to go on a trip. We're packed and ready and have actually gone to bed at the same time, for the second night in a row, when in the darkness, he says quietly, "I hate this house. I hate living here. I hate having to fix things and cut the grass and shovel the snow and paint." And I say, "You've never painted a thing! I painted every room in this house!" As if that's the point I should be making.

The truth is, I also hate our house. And so I turn on the bedside lamp, sit up and tell him. I tell him I hate that no matter how much we fix it up, there's always something else that needs to be fixed. That the only things we spend money on are things for the house. That most of our "down time" is spent on the house, too, something always to be swept or moved or mowed or dug up or built or painted. And honestly, I hate the neighbourhood, it's just too far from downtown for me, my commute is unbearable, and I miss the culture of downtown living. Mostly, I tell him, I miss living in an apartment; I've *never* liked living in a house.

We look at one another and smirk. Here we are with common ground and we didn't even know it. We both hate living in this house! When I got pregnant, it had been our shared dream, to have a house we'd live in for the rest of our lives, but it wasn't right for us, it wasn't *us.*

"We belong downtown!" I say and he smiles. He leans over and grabs me, wrestling me into his arms shouting, "We belong in a condo again!" and I laugh. We kiss hard and long, like we just remembered who we were.

"Fuck it, let's sell the house. Let's buy a condo and start over again!" we say, and all the air comes back into our relationship in that moment, as if we really believe selling our house will fix our marriage. We have sex all night long and talk about condos during rest periods.

The next day we get on a plane and on that plane, we're excited, like everything old is new again. We kiss and laugh and talk about which downtown neighbourhoods we want to live in. We reaffirm our marriage, we hold hands, we say, "This is going to be the year," and "Let's try this. Let's try this. I think it's going to work! So do I!"

The Blitzkrieg is over. It's ended on a high note, if you can believe it.

We go to Jamaica with Birdie and two other families and have a week like no other together. Every moment is sexually and emotionally charged, his shiny dark eyes alive again and always looking right into mine, his hands all over me. The laughter and warmth is back, the goofy charm and the sexy roguishness. It feels like 1999 again. My friend The Bright One is with us and she and my cousin keep teasing us, calling it our "second honeymoon." It feels like it, it really does. On New Year's Eve we kiss on the beach while a crowd of people party around us, Birdie and the other children asleep on chairs pushed together. We dance and he tells me this will be the best year of our marriage, and I almost believe him.

When we get back home, the "second honeymoon" feeling lasts about two days before he freaks out on me. I cry and scream, "Nothing has changed! Nothing has changed!" and he spits back, "Of course not! We've tried, but things are not getting better!" None of it makes any sense to me. I feel crazy and confused, insecure and unsure. Everything I say or do could be innocuous or could throw him into a rage, and I never know which it's going to be.

We fight and then make up. We try and then fail. We look at condos, and our real estate agent comes over to assess our house. I'm as confused as ever, walking on eggshells. He says things like, "I despise the term *husband*, and the things you have to do as a husband," on the exact same day as he says, "I love you, I love you, I want to be your husband."

Another day, he says, "This is done. I am a shitty husband. This is done. I am not a good husband." And I protest, "I'm willing to fight for you! For this marriage!" which I am, although he's right, he is a very shitty husband and has been for a while now. This flip-flopping, this uncertainty, I don't know how he can vacillate so wildly or whether I can withstand it.

I won't have to for long.

One night we're making dinner and it suddenly erupts into a *huge* fight. This time, it's The Husband who throws an object clean across the room. The object is a cutting board with a pile of freshly chopped parsley on it. The parsley flies everywhere, green snowflakes on our kitchen floor. On my clothes. All over Birdie. My father is there and he scoops up Birdie and runs out of the room with her, shouting, "Calm down!"

The Husband does not calm down. I run upstairs crying and scribble furiously into my notebook: *All I said was "Why aren't there serviettes on the table?" What is the matter with him?! Why is this happening?*

Later, we will jokingly say to people that our marriage ended over serviettes and parsley. No one else finds this funny.

We go to bed that night not talking. And the night after that, a Friday, he goes out for drinks after work with his colleagues and he just doesn't come home. For the first time in twelve years together, I wake up in our bed. Alone.

The following afternoon, he shows up and we sit together on the edge of our bed. We hold hands. He says he wants to talk about how we can make our marriage work. We go for a drive and spend hours in a crappy pub talking about our relationship. He says over and over that he wants to make our marriage work.

I say, "You have to be in it. Are you *in* it?" and he says, "Yes."

As we drive back home I feel hope again, like maybe we are coming through the fire. And then he casually mentions the woman from work. *Her.*

I say, "Was she there at the bar last night?"

"Yes."

I don't know if I can even tell you this next part. God I wish I had a glass of gin right now, but I said I would do this so here's what happens next:

I say, "Is that where you stayed last night? Her place?"

He drives, staring straight ahead, and as flat as the road we're on, he says,

"Yes."

HERE'S WHAT I CAN TELL YOU

I can tell you this. When The Bomb first drops, it feels like the hand of God reaches down and pulls everything out of me — entrails, guts, what's left of my heart, my breath, all sound. I am motionless, airless, frozen, everything has exploded and yet, I am in some kind of cryogenic state. Life is an instant blurry, swooping mess, like I'm underwater.

I open the car door and run out into the thick snow. We've pulled over to the side of the road, into the entrance of the cemetery where my grandmother is buried, and my uncle, and my cousin who died too young. The weirdness of this is not lost on me, even in the shock. It's freezing out, my coat is open and I have no mitts or hat or scarf, but I just run and run to the cemetery gates. They're locked.

I feel like throwing up into the snow. I can't stop shaking, or crying, or screaming. Alternately I just stand there mute, thinking, *it's not true, it's not true, this can't be true.* It is so unbelievably cold, the two of us like that, ankle deep in the snow, facing each other beside the massive iron cemetery gates, surrounded by tall twisty trees that sway in the wind, scratching the sky with their bare branches.

This isn't happening.

But it is. Scattered all over the snow is everything inside of me, torn up and then spit out by this hyena of a man. Right there, at the most awful moment of my life, I suddenly recall a dead moose I saw in a national park once as a teenager — it was nothing but bones in the snow, and fanned all around the bones was its hair.

"Why is it like that?" I asked, and the Park Guide said the wild dogs tore into the moose fast for meat, spitting the hair out while they were tearing it to shreds. This is the image I think of in those first few moments of shock. *I am just bones in the snow, everything has been torn out.*

The next day I call our real estate agent. Staring right across the dining table at The Husband, I say into the phone, "We need to sell the house. We need to sell it this week."

CHAPTER FIVE

FALLOUT

THE KINDNESS OF STRANGERS

It's been three days since The Bomb dropped. I'm driving home from work. I've slept maybe two or three hours the past few nights, and then only with the help of sleeping pills and whiskey. The pain in the place where my heart once was is something awful. I drive straight to the liquor store and buy a bottle of Southern Comfort.

I'm thirty-seven years old and this is the first time I've ever bought a bottle of booze for the express purpose of drinking it alone. I'm pretty sure everyone in the store can tell there's something wrong with me. I carry the bottle out by the neck, no bag, nothing.

Even though it's February, there's some kind of freak weather system happening that's mirroring the freak weather system in my marriage. It's really warm out, and everyone is walking around in T-shirts looking slightly confused and unsure. The windows in my car are rolled down as I pull out of the parking lot, making a right turn onto a major street without looking first.

I cut a car off, and the guy is not impressed. He immediately starts honking, and since his windows are also down I can hear him screaming at me. For the next few minutes he follows close behind me, honking the horn and yelling. I am shaking so hard. I can't handle his anger because I am nothing but thin threads of a person over here. The bottle of Southern Comfort rolls on the passenger seat. The liquid sloshes along with the angry horn-honking. I can't wait to get home so I can drink it. I think of how only one month ago The Husband and I were on vacation, on a beach dancing close, talking about how we were going to do better, how this year was going to be ours. We kept calling it our "second honeymoon."

At the next light, the guy I cut off pulls up beside me, tires screeching. He's about sixty years old, with long dreadlocks that hang past his shoulders, his car covered in a thin film of winter. He leans out of his window and practically into mine, shouting, "You want to kill yourself or something? You want to kill *me*? You don't have a family? You don't care about *my* fam—" He stops abruptly. I see his face fall. He can tell something's wrong with me.

"I'm so sorry, I thought I had enough time to turn ..."

He shakes his head to stop me, his face now completely softened with empathy and concern. "Little lady, are you all right?"

"No. No, I'm not all right."

The light turns green but we continue to sit there, our cars blocking the only two lanes as we look at each other through open windows. The cars behind us start honking but neither of us moves. His face is so kind and he says, "Lord, look, whatever it is, little lady, whatever it is, it is going to be okay, I can tell you that. Can you hear me say this truth?"

I nod my head. I'm shaking so hard and I want to just rest my head on his shoulder and cry. I want to ask him what I should do.

I want to ask him if he knows why we have the capacity to be so cruel to the ones we love. I want him to tell me I will survive this, and how. The cars honk angrily but he doesn't even flinch. He looks me right in the eyes and says, "Believe me, you are going to be *okay*. You are going to be okay. Say it, too."

"Okay," I somehow manage and at this, my heart is reminded of its existence and begins to pump a little. I will be okay because he said so, and look, now my heart started working again! He drives off slowly and so do I.

Life is unpredictable. Sometimes, it can be so cold your bones can't stand it, and then there's a freak warm spell and next thing you know you're walking around in a T-shirt, confused. Sometimes you dance on a beach with the one you love and he tells you this will be the best year of your marriage. But a month later he won't come home because he spent the night with someone who has already been a part of your marriage for a long, long time, just no one thought to tell you. Sometimes a total stranger believes in you more than the person you love most.

I go home and play house with my daughter and The "Husband." When he puts her to bed, I take the bottle of Southern Comfort into the backyard with me and drink it in the freakishly warm February air. "I am going to be okay," I say out loud to the patio table and chairs. "I am going to be okay."

STATIC

It's still the early days of the shock and awe. I'm numb inside. I'm electrified and not in a good way. I'm numb and electric all at once. I'm the way your finger feels when you stick it in an electrical socket, that buzzing tingle alongside the dull pain.

I don't eat. I don't sleep. I can't do anything but walk around like a zombie, the kind that's being slowly eaten by a human, the human she loves most in the world. I drink alcohol. Lots of it. As soon as Birdie is asleep I open the cabinet doors and take whatever there is and drink it straight up. I do this over and over, every night for two months until many bottles are drained. I smoke cigarette after cigarette in our backyard, staring out into the night. I've never been a smoker or a drinker, but suddenly here I am, an old country song come to life, drinkin' and smokin' my heartbreak away.

Let's be clear, this isn't just heartbreak. For those of you who have felt it, you know the word *heartbreak* doesn't even scratch the surface. You know like I do that there's no word that comes close to describing what happens to you in that moment when you first find out about betrayal.

The way your mind and body are just a piece of paper the person you love has casually tossed a match onto. The way they stand there as you burn, staring, dumbly, as you turn into a heap of ashes. The way they blame you for being paper in the first place, when all along you should have known they were fire.

In a heap of ashes, I go to work every day. Instead of an hour on the bus and subway, I start driving our car downtown, and paying for ridiculously priced parking. It cuts my commute down to only twenty minutes, and this, my friends, is my first post-apocalyptic gift to myself. I drive each morning in a hung-over, sleep-deprived daze. Sometimes when I park the car I can't remember how I got there. Sometimes I cry the entire way there. Sometimes at a stoplight I stare blankly at the human life going on around me. Everything I thought was real, isn't.

My head is messed up, my guts are rotted. The place in my chest that used to house my heart feels like it's collapsing under the weight of a woman I met fleetingly once. A woman who knew my husband so much more than I ever realized or could have guessed. Now she's like a thousand-pound weight on my chest, squeezing every ounce of blood out of my heart like it's a tomato.

Still I go to work every day. I sit at my desk but I don't actually do any work at first. I cry in front of my computer, even though I am the boss. My co-workers stand around helplessly offering me Kleenex. I make them cry, men, women, young and old, the single ones and the coupled. They're all devastated to see me like this, to hear my grief. Sometimes I sleep in people's offices, sometimes an endless parade of people come to my desk to see me, a receiving line of pained expressions. It's as if my husband has died. But he hasn't. I hate him and love him in such desperate, equal measure.

All day and night, I think about them having sex. I can't get it out of my head. It's on a sick and tortuous loop that makes me wince, that twists the inside of my empty stomach into knots, makes me bury my fingernails into the palms of my hands. I'm losing weight so fast that people notice after one week. By week two I've lost almost twenty pounds, a thing I didn't even know was possible. One day I run into a woman who works in my department. She sits far enough away that she hasn't heard the crying or seen the parade of concerned people. She stops me in the hallway and shouts enthusiastically,

"What ARE you DOING lately? Whatever diet it is, I NEED to do it!" I can't get a word in, and she continues, "I don't care WHAT it is, you HAVE to tell me! Because you look FANTASTIC. Like, AMAZING. You are totally GLOWING! Every time I see you, you are SKINNIER and SKINNIER! So what is it? I HAVE TO KNOW!"

Finally, she stops and I say, "Well, it's the Shock and Grief Diet, just whiskey and cigarettes. I really don't recommend it." I feel awful when I see her face fall as she quickly apologizes for intruding. There's no way she could have known. I say *it's okay* a hundred different ways and then right there in the hallway at work, I spill the whole story, beginning a sustained period of oversharing that yes, *obviously*, continues today.

Fifty times a day I say "My husband had an affair" to anyone who even looks at me. Co-workers, the ladies at our daughter's daycare, other parents in the neighbourhood, a homeless man, the pharmacist. I just say it, plainly like that, the same way I would say, "I've had a cold for a few days." I can't stop telling people. I want them to know what's wrong with me. I want them to know this shell of a person used to be vibrant and real, and now I'm a ghost and this is why. This is why. *My husband had an affair, you see?*

By the way, I really don't recommend the whiskey-and-cigarettes diet. No matter how effective it is.

One of my colleagues is a lifesaver; she sits right beside me. A long time ago the man she loved hurt her badly, and she hasn't been the same since when it comes to men. The Husband's behaviour only strengthens her conviction — if he could do this, then it's true that all men are selfish assholes. This breaks my heart. I don't think all men are assholes. *People* can be assholes. Some people lie to themselves, so much so that after a while it becomes easy to lie to others. I say this to her, but it sounds like I'm defending him.

Meanwhile, she's a godsend at work — picking up all the tasks I'm not doing, leading the team for me, acting as my proxy in meetings and taking care of things so I don't have to. I'm eternally, shamefully grateful. She tries to make me eat solid food, but I just can't. So each day she buys me one of those giant smoothies that have protein and fruit in them. It takes me all day to finish one, but that juice basically saves my life. She saves my life. She frets and cares for me until I can function again. I feel blessed that the HR gods have given her to me by chance, sitting her next to me when I need her most.

In my spare time, I obsessively Google my husband's name and the name of the woman. I try to find out everything I can about her. But frustratingly, she's a digital ghost. I don't know what I'm trying to find, but I keep searching anyway. Nothing in my life makes any sense and I want to understand it, I want it to come together in front of me like a completed puzzle so I can say,

"Ohhh." So I spend hours trying to piece together the events leading up to the end of our marriage, pinning down dates and times using calendars. I hack into his phone to look at texts and emails. I don't know why I'm doing this now, *after* The Bomb has dropped. And anyway, there's a very small trail to go on, but I triangulate events like a good journalist, writing them all into my notebook, trying to piece it all together. An expert in emotional forensics.

Everyone, including my psychologist, begs me to stop this behaviour. "Even if you could get all the dates right, you will *never* have the whole picture," she says to me. "It doesn't matter if he slept with her on December twenty-third or not. You have to let this part go."

I say to her, "I know, I know." But inside I think, *It does matter, it does! It matters if he slept with her on December twenty-third. He was married on that day, and all the days. So it does matter.* Why can't anyone understand that?

One of my aunts, who I'm very close to, writes to me every other day. Every time I see her name in my inbox, I feel a tiny bit closer to reality. Her emails have the linguistic effect of the healthy juice my friend brings me. She writes short messages to say she's thinking of me, to say she understands the complexities of what I am feeling, to remind me I am strong. She's the only person who consistently checks in on me this way and she keeps it up for almost a year. In these early days it means the most to me.

One day later that summer, she tells me a story about a friend of hers who caught her husband right in the act. He'd gone alone to her family's cottage, which was isolated on a small island. She decided to surprise him and meet him there a day earlier than planned. She rowed the boat from the shore to the island cottage and walked inside. There was her husband, completely naked with some woman, on their cottage bed.

In the ensuing confusion and shouting and tears and everything else we can all imagine, my aunt's friend did the best thing

I have ever heard. She took the mattress right out from under them. *The mattress!* She hauled it right out the door, over her head, and onto the rocks. Then she poured kerosene on it and lit it on fire. Right there, right then. They were on this small island, remember? So there was nothing to do but to stand there, all three of them, and watch as that mattress burned.

I do nothing quite so dramatic. I don't take him to court, we don't have a custody battle, no bed on fire, nothing. I just slowly spiral down, away from myself, deeper and deeper into grief and straight into the arms of that monster, Loneliness.

SCISSORS

I don't light a mattress on fire, but eventually I do find a way to burn myself. Grief hits me hard. And it's the kind of grief people aren't comfortable with. Everyone understands you if you're grieving the death of a loved one. We're patient with that sorrow. But grieving a marriage? No one has time for that. The grief of betrayal? Everyone expects you to just get over it. *So your husband cheated on you. You have to let it go and just move on.*

Let it go and move on. If only it were that easy. Instead, grief consumes me. I walk around with a bullet wound that never heals and bleeds another woman's blood. Months later, after we move out of the house and into separate places, I grieve the life I suddenly have, abandoned and alone. The life I didn't ask for, the life I never wanted. And I grieve in a way that still surprises me. I turn to men to fill the emptiness. I turn to strangers. I go out all the time — dancing, drinking, and going home with hot young guys I will never see again.

I want it that way. I've only ever been in long-term, monogamous relationships. I've never had, or wanted, a one-night stand. Sex has always been tied to love for me. But love made a fool of me. Love betrayed me. So I throw love into the trash, and myself along with it. I seek out sex. Only. But I am lifeless with these guys. I feel nothing when we're together. It feels the same as washing dishes, or slowly cutting out a difficult pattern with scissors — blank mind, concentration on task, and absolutely zero human emotions. A flame might flicker sometimes, but only for a second, and then it's gone.

There is nothing fulfilling about having one-night stands with strangers. It fulfills the *objective*, sure, and sometimes it is amazing or surprisingly sweet in the moment, but my heart is always doing something else while it's happening. My brain is also gone. I imagine I'm just a blow-up doll. Or a corpse. I don't look or act like one, but I am dead inside. Afterward I think, *That's it, that's the last one, I can't do this, I can't do this. I can wait until true love comes again. I can stop all this and try to heal.*

I think, *Maybe I can get into watching a TV show like a normal person. Instead of going into bars to find temporary affection, I can wear yoga pants and binge-watch seasons of* Scandal *and eat ice cream. Or whatever it is people do alone at home.* I resolve to start being present in my life again. So I write a list out on a cue card:

1. Stop feeling sorry for myself.
2. Find comfort in something that isn't sex. There must be something, right?
3. Stop wishing for things and people I can't have.
4. Start taking care of myself.

It doesn't take. I carry that cue card around with me, but I don't do any of those things. Instead, I keep meeting new guys and cutting out difficult patterns with scissors, feeling nothing. All of that nothing, to dull the something that once was.

Above my bed is a piece of art I bought at a coffee shop soon after the separation. The Ex-husband and I would meet there to "hand over" Birdie. She'd arrive with one of us but leave with the other. And although we didn't need to, we'd always linger, drinking espresso and flirting.

The shop had all this art for sale on the walls, these beautiful line drawings on blocks of wood. One of them was just a big pair of scissors. It was called *Because of Love*. I bought it immediately and hung it over my bed. You know, of all the men that have passed through this bedroom — no one ever said anything about those scissors. Until, of course, The Man with the White Shirt.

One day soon after we meet, he's lying there looking at it, his dark eyes heavy with the afternoon. So I ask him what he thinks it means, these scissors called *Because of Love*. The Man with the White Shirt doesn't hesitate. He says, "The scissors are so you can cut away things left behind. To make room for love."

And my heart burns bright white heat for him.

THE DEER

In the immediate wake of The Husband's destruction, a disturbing trend emerges. All of the coupled women we know suddenly become suspicious of their husbands and partners. They snoop in drawers and hack into cellphones. They look for clues on Facebook. Some even go so far as to point-blank question their men.

I tell them all the same thing: "No, no, your guy isn't like that. Your guy wouldn't do this to you." But they all shake their heads and say, "I've never known any couple more into each other than you two, so if he did this to you, then anyone can!" It's a losing battle. I feel awful that our horrible situation has caused a ripple effect of suspicion.

"That's not my responsibility," The Husband says with a dismissive shrug when I point this out to him, and I shrink back from his finely sharpened edges, his refusal to see his actions as having any impact. But listen, if a deer walks out into the road, and then just stands there because it's too stupid and afraid to do anything, when someone hits it and causes a huge multi-car pileup, it isn't the deer's *responsibility* that cars were smashed and people were injured. But it is the deer's *fault*, isn't it? The deer in fact *caused* all of the harm, can we agree on that?

The deer is, we all know, a lucky bastard that somehow came out of it unscathed, but still just as stunned. So, the deer can go right ahead and lie to itself all it wants about the damage it caused. That doesn't make it untrue.

WHY I'M TELLING YOU THIS

The Deer believes he has no responsibility for the impact of his actions, but he does want me to know it will be *my* fault when Birdie finds out he had an affair, because I told our family and friends. But what was I going to do? Lie about it? A fact is a fact. When Birdie finds out, it will be because there's something to find out.

Maybe you think it's wrong for me to talk about it so openly like this. That sharing this story is selfish and indulgent and will cause her harm. But I want to tell you this story, share these ugly truths alongside the beautiful ones, because life isn't one-dimensional. It's nuanced, and subtle, and full of contradictions.

We surprise ourselves constantly, all of us. I want Birdie to know that. Her parents are fallible. Her parents have darkness and light. Her parents love her more than anything and continue to raise her together. We bought homes across the street from each other, for her.

We didn't go to court, for her. She deserves to have her father in her life, and that's why I made those decisions. When Birdie finds out about his affair, it will be because he had one, not because I've told this story.

Birdie will learn about the bad choices I've made, too, the way I dealt with the grief, but I'm not ashamed. She'll know I'm proud of who I am. I've considered it. A lot. What it means to tell you all this. What it is to talk about life, the messy and stupid as well as the beautiful. Regret and redemption. The dark moments don't have to define us, but they do help shape who we are. And that's why I talk about it.

CHAPTER SIX

LEFT AND LEAVING

NEIGHBOURS

Every night after The Bomb, I go see our close friends who live up the street. We met when our daughters were babies, and now they're about to have baby number three. We jokingly call ourselves "The Commune" because of the way we share everything — tools, dinners, kids' clothes. The husbands, both scientists, make beer together, with elaborate setups in our cold cellar. We take vacations with them, and weekend camping trips; we spend every New Year's Eve together, and all of our birthdays and kids' birthdays.

They take the news especially hard. I cry and cry in their living room, drinking all their wine, while my friend The Chemist, paces. He can't understand how The Husband could do this to me. He's so angry. And he gets angrier each time I protect The Husband, each time I justify the things he's done. His wife, The Practical One, my dear, dear friend, sits beside me in tears and so pregnant. The due date was the same day The Husband dropped The Bomb, but the baby hasn't come yet. I am shamefully grateful for this, because I need her more than anyone else right now.

Each day passes and the baby holds out. On the fifth night, as I cry on the couch, I apologize for the millionth time for bringing my sadness to their house just as they're about to have a baby. The Practical One shushes me and says, "I think she's waiting so I can be here for you." I whisper to her giant belly, *Thank you.*

Once she *is* born, I don't want to infect their house with sadness, so I move on to other neighbourhood friends. I go out almost every night, crying at the house of whoever will take me. I sit in their kitchens and drink their rum, their gin, their anything. I go through all their Kleenex. The husbands all have angry tight jaws as I cry with their wives. He was their friend, but he maybe was really just a stranger.

Meanwhile, for the whole two months until we move out, The Husband stays home every night. I will lose my mind if he goes out and he knows it. That I have already lost my mind is beside the point. That he managed to have an ongoing affair mostly in the daytime? Also beside the point. We never discuss it, but we both seem to know it — The Husband is living in undeclared martial law.

IRISH BLOOD, ITALIAN HEART

"I'm selfish," he says, for the fiftieth time, and she smashes the dining table hard with her hand and yells, "Fine, but is that good enough for you then? Because if not, what are you going to *do* about it?"

I want you to meet my best friend in the world. She's at the dining table with us, and she's angry. Her boyfriend sits beside her, and we look at each other with the same arched eyebrow that says *holy shit, she's good.*

Let me just pause for a second to tell you that my best friend is one of the toughest women I have ever known. Irish blood, Italian heart. She takes shit from no one. She's passionate and loyal, fiercely so, but she's also sensitive. It's as if The Husband has done this to her. And she's letting him have it, crying as she says, "What. Are. You. Going. To. DO ABOUT IT? Because you can't just keep saying you're selfish, but also say you're a good father. You can't just say you're selfish, and be fine with that while your wife gives you joint custody, lets you stay in this house, doesn't take you to court. So what are you going to do for her?"

For her? For once in his life, it looks like someone has genuinely given him an idea he's never thought of before. He turns and looks at me, but I am so scared of what is happening at this dining table, so shocked that someone is defending me, that I've become a small, airless thing and I can't even look at him.

I feel like I'm back in grade 6 when I was the new kid at school, and a group of girls circled me at recess to beat me up because a popular boy liked me. At the time I thought I could take one of them for a bit, but I had no chance against four, when out of nowhere strides Irish Blood, Italian Heart, at twelve years old, already a head taller than the other girls. She walks right into the circle and stands in front of me like a giant shield. She tells the girls that if they want to beat me up, they need to go through her first. They back away, and the two of us have been friends ever since.

Now here she is, twenty-five years later, defending me again, only this time with tears streaming down her face. "You *owe* it to her," she says, pointing across the table, jabbing the air in my direction. "You owe it to her to do something *now*, not just sit there with your hands in the air saying, 'I'm selfish, oh well!'" Her words hang there for a few seconds, her finger still pointing at me, as she stares at him, blue eyes blazing.

When they go, my heart sinks on the driveway. My defender is gone. I stand there and stare at the grey March sky, the giant trees in our backyard bending with the wind, the years. I go back inside and he is there, still at the table, like he's been freeze-dried. He looks up and says, "She had a lot of good points. *A lot*. What *am* I doing for you?" I look right into his shiny dark eyes, and I see him for just a moment, at twenty-six years old, staring across a café table, telling me he loves me. I see all the joy and pain we shared for twelve years.

I see now in his eyes: remorse.

This affair was something he did for himself, so yes, he was selfish. And so far all he's been saying is, "I was a shitty husband," so it's still been about him. But from this moment on, over the next month until we move out, he actively tries to make this easier on *me*. Irish Blood got through to him, somehow. Protected me again.

LEAVING HOME

All of the boxes have either red or blue stickers on them. So does the furniture. Blue sticker — his moving van. Red sticker — my moving van. The Husband hired the same company to move us both. *Do I still call him my husband?*

Finally, after two months of living in the house together, the day has come to move out. This is really happening. We are really, truly separating. We greet the movers together, and explain the red and blue system. We joke and talk with them and give them bottles of water. After about an hour, one of them asks, "You're moving to two separate places? I *never* would have guessed that." Then he shrugs his shoulders, commends us for our organization ("I love this sticker system!") and goes on with his work.

Our two separate places are actually across the street from each other, but it's a big city street. We've decided to live no more than a five-minute walk apart, for Birdie. But it's for us, too. We still think of ourselves as a team. We even went to Ikea together to pick out furniture for our new places. It must have looked like we were moving in together, but we were moving out. As the men come in and out, emptying our home, we stand together in the kitchen. With every box, every chair, they clear out our life together until all of our things, divided carefully into red and blue, are in two separate trucks outside.

When the trucks drive off we stand there on the front porch for the very last time together. We hold hands. We hug. "I'm starving," he eventually says, and kisses my forehead. We get in what is now designated as my car (no red sticker though, haha) and go have lunch together.

It's a chain fast-food place — the sun outside blazing, uncharacteristically hot for April. Not a person in the place would guess that they're looking at a couple whose marriage is over, a couple that has just separated all their things into two trucks. No one would know that one betrayed the other so deeply and unexpectedly, it sent the other one into a state of shock so severe she has stopped eating food altogether, started drinking and smoking, and is now dependent on sleeping pills to get her through each night.

Here she is though, that ravaged wife, having a laugh with him as he tears into a hamburger, king of the world. She pretends to eat french fries. For a few minutes she's forgotten the eviscerating pain. She's at the point now where for at least five minutes of each hour, she doesn't automatically think of him having sex with the other woman. This is a huge improvement over the preceding two months, where any time her mind went even a little bit idle, images of the two of them would flood her brain, stab her in the heart, and shred her insides.

Every day for those two months, lacking sleep and basic nutrients, she went to work, and then came home. He would have dinner waiting as always, and the three of them would sit at the table just like they always had. The evenings were status quo — bath time and books and tucking in. Once their little girl was asleep, they would meet at the big wooden dining room table, the one they had dreamed together of having one day. The one they bought on sale after they were married, the wife sitting on top of it to ward off other bargain hunters while The Husband tried to find a store employee.

Every night for those two months, they'd meet at that big wooden table. They'd have a drink together, or three. They'd talk or cry or fight or fuck, sometimes all four. They'd go through files, make lists and assign tasks. They'd pack and pack and pack, the boxes climbing alongside the heartbreak. For two months, that dining room table was ground zero.

Together they'd mythologized that table, imagining how one day their daughter would spend evenings doing her homework on it, how as a teenager she'd bring her first young love there for dinner. The Husband and Wife liked to do puzzles together on that table, host dinner parties at it, do their taxes on it. Each Hallowe'en she laid newspaper on it and they would carve pumpkins and talk and laugh while separating the seeds for roasting. And it was there, against the rustic teak, that they divided twelve years of accumulated possessions, dismantled twelve years of love and memories, unearthed twelve years of lies and secrets.

It took two months to sift through twelve years, to separate, to say goodbye. To put red stickers on, to put blue.

The only piece of furniture we fought over was the table. Everything else we divided up easily. But oh, the table. I held onto that piece of wood like it was the marriage itself.

THE THING ABOUT TRUTH AND TRUST

Did I really, truly, trust my husband when we were married? I've wondered myself; you aren't the only one. The answer always comes back to me as yes.

When we met, I knew — because he told me — that he'd cheated on each of his serious girlfriends before me. He knew that although I hadn't ever cheated in the traditional sense (sex), I *had* fallen into deep emotional relationships with other people while in each of my serious relationships. I always had someone else lined up and ready to go. But here's how we rationalized it: those days were over. We were young then! We were wilder, we were still experimenting, we weren't mature. *Now,* we rationalized, *now we're in our mid-twenties and this is different.*

Most importantly, *now* we were making a vow. A vow of marriage, of solidarity, of unity. A contract that not only implied trust, but was predicated on it. Without trust, there was nothing. This is how I saw it anyway. After I found out he had been lying to me, all of that evaporated. I didn't know what was real. That's the thing about trust. It's only good until it is broken.

That he broke it was a fact. The details remained — and remain — fuzzy. He lied a lot that day when he dropped The Bomb on me. You can't blame him; he was in a panic. He lied on top of his lies, trying to minimize the hurt, not realizing that lying more wasn't the way to do that. At first he said it was only one time. He'd only slept with her one time, the night before, the night he didn't come home to me and Birdie. Then he said actually he'd slept with her two times, the other being the night of the grade 12 commencement three months earlier. He maintained it was only those two times. Finally, he settled it. They'd been having a full-blown sexual relationship for three months. Not a one-time mistake, but a series of deliberate choices.

Over and over again, they would get into our car and drive to her condo. They'd walk together from our car to her building, go inside, and have sex. His wedding band, her free spirit. He'd shower, because of course later that night, he'd be having sex with me. He'd leave to pick up Birdie from daycare. He'd get dinner started. I'd come home from work. Over and over again, for three months he says, he went between her place and ours. The place that was his wife and daughter. Three months.

I didn't know what to believe. I had already departed from this world and was lost in a vortex of unmanageable pain. He spoke to me but it was like I was floating above us. I could see me crying and shouting. I could see us fighting and fucking and calling the real estate agent.

Nothing was real. Those days and weeks and months were underwater. But this is where we left it. My husband had an affair for three months because that is what he says is the truth. The trouble is, how do you trust the truth when it comes from a liar's mouth?

And this is the thing about truth and trust. The thing I have to live with every single day. *Was the affair really three months long? Was it a year? Two? Was it the whole marriage long? Were there other women and other times?* Twelve years is a long time for a really good liar to lie.

How do I trust anything he says ever again? How do we raise our daughter together if there's no trust? The only way to co-parent effectively was to trust him, right away, right after his string of lies was revealed. I had to trick myself into trusting him so that we could raise Birdie together. But I wonder sometimes if trust has a different meaning for me now. Now, it's a lot less about certainty and more about faith. Now, I have to just go on what he says. I have to *believe* in him. I have to. That's the only way any of this works.

PAIN SCALE

"Why are you doing this to yourself?" asks almost everyone. Why do I put up with the not-boyfriendness of The Man with the White Shirt.

The way he says he loves me, the way he acts so crazy about me, the way I am his best friend and he's mine. The way we seem like the most matched couple except we aren't, because he can't, he doesn't know how, he doesn't think he wants it, even though he says he can't live without me. So yeah, they ask me why I put up with this, because they're worried. They don't want to see me get hurt, be crushed again. I get it, but they don't have to worry. Let me tell you a story.

One night I had a really late soccer game, and we had no goalie, and since I'm the captain, and also a defender, it made sense for me to play in net. Except I'm, like, barely five foot two, so it really *doesn't* make any sense for me to be a goalie. On this night, a guy shot the ball so hard that when I made the save, it dislocated my thumb, bending it in the most unholy, unnatural position. I howled so loud that everyone playing stopped. It was excruciating, excruciating pain.

When I got to the emergency room, the triage nurse took a look at it and asked me to rate the pain on a scale from one to ten, where ten is the most painful thing I've ever felt. "Uh, four?" I said. She looked at me with disbelief. "*Four?* Are you sure?" The thumb looked like a swollen, twisted Joshua Tree dangling off the end of my hand.

I said to her, "Well, I've had a child, so if going through labour is ten, then this is just a four. Maybe five?" Boy did that nurse laugh! She laughed and laughed. "I'm going to go ahead and write nine," she said.

So this is why, when people worry about me getting hurt again, when they say I'm compromising and that I'm going to get burned, I say, "No, no, don't worry, this is just a four. On the pain scale, you know? If The Husband having an affair is ten, then nothing anyone else can do will ever hurt me more than a four." And I believe myself. You can't keep breaking a shattered glass. So I don't stop putting myself in the way of hurt. I don't stop calling The Man with the White Shirt, or texting him, or seeing him.

I mean, I stop for a bit, and then I don't. We manage a few days, sometimes a week without contact, and then we're right back where we started. And we go on like that, until he pulls away again and it feels like a four. But it's nothing compared to The Husband's ten.

So I don't care. I'm not afraid to love because it might hurt. I will take the pain because it comes with moments of beauty. I know when it comes to love, there's no such thing as zero on the pain scale. I'll be fine. *I'll be fine.*

CHAPTER SEVEN

PROTECTION

AT NIGHT

For the first few weeks that I'm alone in my new place, I wander around it like a ghost. At night, I can't sleep at all, even if I take two sleeping pills with three rum and cokes. I try all kinds of combinations, all kinds of things, but the emptiness of my bed is too much for me. I toss and turn, I get up and pace. I cry and cry. I arrange two big pillows beside me so it will feel somewhat like my six-foot-two husband is there beside me. A pillow husband. I'm pathetic.

The nights Birdie is here with me, I don't drink or take any pills. But then no amount of pacing or husband-replacing pillows helps. And it is on those nights, in those early days of the separation, that I eventually go into her room and lift her into my arms and carry her, heavy as a sleeping child — which is *heavy*, by the way — and bring her back to my big empty queen-sized bed. I tuck the blankets around her, and make sure her stuffed dog,

Pasta, is in her arms. I look at her small face, brush the sweaty hair from her forehead. She has only just turned five, and she will not remember any of this. She won't remember what it was like to live with both her parents.

In our new life together as just the two of us, we've been exploring our new neighbourhood. Picking wildflowers under the expressway, having picnic dinners in the park. Even though I'm sad and in shock at my sudden part-time family of two, these moments with Birdie are unexpectedly wonderful.

And I'm grateful. I know I'm lucky. To have this beautiful child, and this nice apartment. So many people have it much harder when their marriages end. They don't have the support system I have. The good job with good pay. I recognize what I have. That I'm able to grieve with a roof over my head, the sky-line outside my window, my child who still has two parents who love and care for her.

In my bed, Birdie breathes heavily beside me, just like her father did, and finally, *finally*, I am able to fall asleep.

PREPARE YOURSELF

The very first night I'm alone in my place, really alone, without Birdie, makes me unhinged. I am crazy crazy crazy by 8:00 p.m. *Why am I here, alone in this weird condo? Where is my husband? Where is my child? Why aren't I with them?* That they're across the street is making me more insane. She's so close to me, but I can't see her, can't kiss her forehead goodnight. My baby. My own baby. It feels like everything has been taken away from me, and now so is my own baby, half the time. I am near hysterics now. I didn't think it would be so bad; I thought I would just unpack and it would be fine, but instead I am pacing, shaking, crying, crazy.

I decide to call my friend The Bright One. She's been through it. The difference is, she never really let on how bad things were or what was happening. She was proud and guarded, in stark contrast to my oversharing, tell-anyone-who-will-listen strategy. Right now, she patiently listens as I bawl my eyes out and then even though it's late on a Tuesday night she offers to cab over to my place. I'm practically begging her to, let's be honest. There's a caveat though: "My hair is only half done," she says. "I wouldn't just leave the house like this for anyone, all right?" I laugh and say thank you a million times over.

When she gets to my place, we go straight to the washroom so she can finish putting her hair in. I sit on the toilet freaking out while she calmly listens, twisting the small braids in, one at a time, slow and deliberate, just like the way she speaks to me. She isn't going to be easy on me.

"You need to prepare yourself for this," she says. "*Prepare yourself.* You need to have these nights full of things to do. *Planned.* Because you will always feel the hole when she's not here. You've got to fill that hole with other things." She's twisting her braids, and everything inside me is twisting with them.

The Bright One can be tough sometimes, but she's also one of the biggest-hearted people I know. She's funny and smart and everyone loves her, *everyone.* But I understand the difference between what we project, and what we harbour. Everyone loves her, but still her heart was split open, still she battles the monster Loneliness day in and day out. She's the only person I know that really has any clue what this feels like for me.

So no matter how tough she is on me, on this night or for the next few years, I listen. To her, I always listen. From here on out, I plan. If Birdie's not with me, then someone else is.

Sometimes that someone else is The Husband. *The Ex-husband*, I mean. We still sleep together. A lot. For a long, long time after we separate and divorce. *Yeah, I know.* Remember the red and blue stickers? The day we move out and end our twelve-year relationship? It doesn't really end that day. It will never really end, maybe.

All of my boxes, with the red stickers, aren't being delivered until the next morning because I want to paint. A few of my friends come over to help. We order pizza, paint the bedrooms, and talk about relationships. The Husband is across the street moving into his own apartment and Birdie is staying with close family friends for a few days until both our places are set up and ready for her.

When my friends leave around 10:00 p.m., I'm alone in my new empty apartment. I have one of our old camping mattresses and I'm trying to blow it up, but it keeps going flat. I just stare at the thing. *What the fuck am I supposed to do now? Just sleep on the hardwood floor?* Right at that moment, my phone buzzes. It's The Husband. His move has gone well and he's wondering about mine. I say the air mattress is fucked. Five minutes later, he's at my door with beer and a mattress pump. There's no fixing the thing though, and we sit on the floor with our backs against the wall, drinking as the mattress slowly deflates in front of us. He tells me to come spend the night at his place. And I do.

Just this morning, two moving vans took away all of our things, and now here we are, the two of us, walking across the street from my new place to his new place. Here we are, climbing into our old bed together, surrounded by boxes with blue stickers on them. Here we are, spending the first night of our separation. Together.

My boxes will be delivered and unpacked the next day, and over time we'll make two new homes for our separate lives and for our now-divided daughter. But we will keep finding ourselves in each other's beds. For years. Our legs, like our lives, still wound together.

I know. It's not the Empowered Woman's Clean Break you were hoping for. But it's us.

SUPERCONNECTORS

It's June 2012. I've lived alone for two months, and my place is coming together. I love it here actually, set up how I like it, neat and tidy, no cupboard doors left open, no toilet seats left up. Out every window you can see the city, and out the bedroom windows, the CN Tower looms huge in front of us, all lit up with different colours at night, the rumble of commuter trains a new melody.

It takes me ten easy minutes to walk to work each day, thirteen in heels. Not having to take public transit anymore improves my life by a million percent. We are *downtown*. In this way, I feel normal again. I'm in the right place again. Physically, anyway. Mentally, spiritually, I'm still trying to figure out which direction is up.

I was domesticated for so long that I have no idea what people do for fun, which bars or cafés are cool, where to go dancing. My reference point for all that is, like, 2002. So I start to hang out with The Superconnectors. You know them? Those friends you have that are connected to all kinds of people and different scenes, because they're open and fun-loving and curious and just totally, completely *great*. I'm lucky to have a few of those friends.

One is a woman with a big laugh. She's always laughing, and you can hear it from miles away. She's like walking electricity, powering up everything and everyone she touches. So I hitch myself to Big Laugh as much as I can. I recognize an old me in that energy, a me that once was. The other superconnector is a guy I've known for a long time, the one I call Forever 21. He's freewheeling and fun-loving and seems to know everyone in the city. His stories are always about crazy adventures in far-flung places with interesting people.

Forever 21 always knows what's happening on a Friday night, and he will take me there, throwing me into all kinds of spontaneous situations. The best thing about my friendship with him is that we're just friends. There's no expectation of romance, no drunken fumbling we'll regret later. As the year goes on, there are plenty of times we will sleep in the same bed like cousins at a sleepover. He's my pal, my brother.

In these early days of June, the weather is already really hot. One Saturday afternoon Forever 21 texts me saying he knows a bunch of people that are hanging out in the park, *so let's go!* We hop on our bikes, stopping at the beer store on the way. Then we sit in the park with a collection of people I've never met. We drink, we talk, we throw a Frisbee around. We smoke and eat and drink some more. All. Day. I'm really confused by this. They all seem to be in their thirties like me; don't they have anything to do today other than drink in a park for seven hours, just hanging out like we're twenty-one? But no. They don't. Or if they do have errands to run or laundry to do or other *shoulds*, they don't care. They'd rather enjoy this first real hot day of summer.

Enjoy. That's not something I've done in a long time. Enjoy something. I know that sounds crazy, but honestly I just spent, oh, *all of my life* not enjoying things because of all the other things I should be doing. To just sit in a park at age thirty-seven instead of crossing things off a list … this is big for me. *Huge.*

Forever 21 is beaming. That's what he does. He looks like he's enjoying himself all the time. Being around that kind of energy is powerful for me. I grew up with a lot of negativity, in a culture and in a family where *should* was the primary driving force, where criticism and advice, followed by complaint, was the main style of communication. And then there was the guilt. It's on this day, in this park, with my friend and this group of total strangers, that I start to realize the importance of having positive, bright forces in my life. People who are enjoying things.

The rest of the summer is an awakening for me, and I'm not just talking about when I finally, in late July, begin to sleep with random men for the first time in my life. It's an awakening that

I can let my list-making, constant planning, and guilt fall away a bit. I go with the flow a little more.

Forever 21 says, "Let's just go to a soccer game!" and I say, "Right *now*? But I'm not prepared!" and he says, "Whaddaya got to be prepared about? Let's go!"

And we do. We just up and go see a game with two of his friends I've never met, after we just spent seven hours hanging out in the park, and you know what? I have the best time. One of his friends at the soccer game, The Lawyer, becomes one of my friends, too, after that. A few of the other people from the park that day become my friends also, especially one woman, another superconnector, The Traveller, who sparks an epic trip to New York City. I meet so many wonderful people over the next year all because of her. Eventually, she will be the reason I meet The Man with the White Shirt. She's a tough cookie who's soft on the inside, and she becomes a confidante and coach and sister to me. These superconnectors remind me how to have fun again. They teach me how be to be spontaneous.

And that spontaneity is also making me a better parent. The more time goes on, the more relaxed I've become, and Birdie relaxes with me. I'm a lot less *do this, do that*. We ride the ferry out to the city's islands while she wears a Supergirl costume. I teach her how to use chopsticks in the noodle place up the street from her school.

She shouts "U-turn!" pretty much every time we're in the car, because I always manage to drive in the wrong direction, or get lost, so used to having The Husband as navigator. But instead of stressing it, I laugh at myself. She laughs with me.

I leave dishes in the sink at night and play with her instead. If she takes forever to get dressed in the morning, I make a game of it instead of yelling at her to hurry up. We are feeling breezier. Her temper tantrums disappear. She becomes more of a little pal and less of a little pain in the ass. I don't want to make too big a deal of it, but being around the three superconnectors has taught me something that's totally cliché, but no less amazing — don't sweat the small stuff.

There's a moment that symbolizes this awakening period of my life more than any other. It's 2:00 a.m. on a hot June night. We are leaving one dive bar to go to another. It's me and Superconnector 1 (Big Laugh), as well as Superconnector 2 (Forever 21) and one of his friends. The two guys have bikes, but Big Laugh and I are on foot, wearing summer dresses.

"Hop on the back!" shouts Forever 21. So of course Big Laugh just bunches up her skirt in one hand and hops on to the back of the other guy's bike like that's just a normal thing to do. I stand there dumbly, worried I'm too heavy for my friend to pedal. Worried about weaving through the traffic of the downtown streets. Worried about the logistics, since I'm wearing a dress. Like he senses it, Forever 21 shouts, "I got ya, no worries!" with a smile as wide as the continent. With trepidation, I sit, side-saddle on the back of his bike. I tuck the skirt of my dress up under me, put my arms around his waist, and off we go.

And this is the image I will have in me forever, the feeling: the dark 2:00 a.m. sky, the cars going by, the streetcar rumbling past. Behind me, my friend is cutting the night with her big laugh, enjoying the crazy moment. Wind on my face as the bike weaves through it all, heading to somewhere, I don't even know where, and it's okay.

It's okay not to know where I am going.

Still,

sometimes I miss seeing a man's razor nestled in beside my toothbrush.

YOUNG AGAIN

When you have a kid, this thing happens where you start making friends with other people who have kids. Being a parent is the common denominator. Your single friends become these frivolous people who talk about completely abstract things like dancing in a bar until 4:00 a.m. Or all of the movies they've seen *in movie theatres*. And they always seem to be complaining about how "tired" they are.

To them, you've become a boring shell of the friend they once knew. A parent-zombie who posts three-hundred identical photos of your baby on Facebook and pushes a ridiculously huge and unnecessary stroller around, and talks about the cutest thing your kid said for like, a *half hour*. This is why the natural progression of domestic life is to allow your closest single friends to fall away while you quickly make friends with people who know the real meaning of tired. People as boring as you. People with kids.

Now that I'm single, the strangest thing has happened. Although I'm still a mom, I'm only an on-duty mom for half of the week. The other half it's like I'm twenty-five again. Part-time parent, part-time partier. Most of the new friends I'm making, the people I spend my spare time with, are other single women. *Oh, you had your soul ripped out by the love of your life? Me too! Let's drink and work on each other's online dating profiles!*

I also hang out with a bunch of single men. We all trade stories and advice, commiserate, drink. A group of us go to New York City together and stay in a tiny East Village apartment. We sleep a combined total of seven hours over three nights, go to amazing restaurants, art exhibits, plays, bar after bar after bar. We shop. We smoke. We do whatever we want. It blows my *mind*. This is how it is with childless people in their thirties, I've discovered. They live exactly like I did in my twenties! And now so do I, half the time.

The other half of the time I'm with our old friends with their intact marriages and multiple children. And I'm the single one with my only child. My parents' generation had a word for women like me — *divorcée*. Whatever you call me, I feel like an outcast now, a fifth wheel. I'm a pity party, table for one.

Everything in this scenario is familiar — here we are in my friends' house just up the street from the house we once lived in, that one there, the one with the red door. We were a family there once. Now I'm a divorcée over here. Don't look at me too long or you'll turn to salt.

The kids are going wild, running all around the house. The adults talking and laughing in the kitchen. Wait though, something's missing, what feels different? Oh yes, The Husband, The *Ex*-husband. He would have been here. He *should* be here. Instead this scene is like a "Spot the Difference" photo at the back of an old magazine. I overhear the kids in the other room. "Where's your dad?" asks one of them, and Birdie's voice, tough yet nonchalant, "Oh, I don't know. At home I guess." The kid, unsatisfied with Birdie's response comes to me and asks, "Where is he?" I answer honestly — "I don't know" — and my heart sinks into the ground. That's the only thing that's different here — the absence of him. Well, I'm different, too. I'm a shelled-out version of who I once was, a shadow. Look at me here breathlessly recounting dating stories, regaling the room with all of the cool places I've been going and the things I've seen now that I'm a free agent with joint custody. Now that I have all the time in the world.

It's a funny thing, actually. Before the breakup, every moment of my life was taken up by Birdie or The Husband, or my mother, or my job, or ... well you know. I know you know. There was no time to think, no time to rest, no time to take care of myself. I'd dream of having an hour to myself, an afternoon. And now, here I am with so much time I don't know what to do with it.

You can only drink so much. You can only sleep with so many men. And that only fills the time between 11:00 p.m. and 5:00 a.m. Don't get me wrong, it's been an incredibly liberating experience, this new phase of my life I never wanted. For the most part, the guys are good-looking and oh so young, with hard bodies and lovely faces. They have energy. They're generous. They haven't had a chance to be bitter yet. I never give them the chance. My bed smells wonderful for a day or two after they leave. I inhale the pillows like a schoolgirl wearing a boy's sweater for the first time. The smell of a man is something I miss a lot, so I appreciate the lingering of it for as long as I can. Thanks to The Husband, I'm young again, rah rah.

And so I tell the stories with relish, as if I need to prove to my married friends that I'm constantly turning lemons into lemonade. Sometimes I am, don't get me wrong, but here with this familiar crowd, I feel like even the best of my new experiences are still just more lemons. It feels like there's nothing sweet about the life I've constructed in the fallout of my marriage, not compared to their lives. All I feel here is partner-less and glaringly alone.

YOUNGER STILL

"I don't think we'll ever run out of things to say to each other," says The Man with the White Shirt. He says it, softly, like a fact. And wistfully, like a fact he's already resigned himself to. It's early May 2014. The sun is coming up over the city, and we're watching it burn through the sky. We didn't wake up to watch the sunrise, it's just that we haven't gone to sleep yet. We've spent all night like this, lying in his bed, talking — about music and our childhoods, about this funny story and that. There *will* always be this much to say, he's right, because we're on the same wave, we have the same enthusiasm, the same curiosity, and it feels like we even share the same past, though we've only known each other for nine months.

"I love you, I love you, I love you," he says, so many times I lose count.

As he makes us coffee and eggs, I walk around and look at things. His things, things I love and that make me feel more connected to him, even in this cramped and untidy space. The way he's turned a vintage briefcase into a nightstand and how that mirrors the little retro suitcase in my apartment that I use as a tool box. The massive art deco Absinthe poster he has on the wall, similar to the one in my apartment, except I spent a lot of money to have mine framed and his is held in place by big peeling chunks of packing tape. And look at all his tiny trinkets and keepsakes, arranged just so.

Some of my things are in his bathroom now. Just a few, in a drawer, no big deal. I know I'm not the only one in his life, but I don't find evidence of anyone else here. There is only my toothbrush, my comb, my hand cream. Not even his other not-girlfriend, Rockabilly Redhead, seems to leave her stuff here. I wonder if she knows about me, if she cares. What does she think about him seeing both of us at the same time and maybe some others in between? I wonder what she wants, is hoping for. I know what I want. I want to be able to think about him and not have it hurt. Over time I get bolder, leaving more and more of my personal things in the bathroom and other parts of his apartment, too. Marking my territory, even though it isn't mine to mark.

Later, I wash all the dishes as he naps. I love doing this. I mean, I can't really explain it, why it feels so good to be washing his dishes while he sleeps or why I am here at all, accepting his half-love in return for my full. But there's an electrifying comfort in this moment, this normal I feel in the most abnormal of situations. When I'm here, in White Shirt's apartment, I have to be honest, I really do feel young again. Here there are no responsibilities or demands. There aren't even any clocks! Here I don't think about mortgage renewals and ex-husbands and missing my

Birdie so much it hurts. I don't think about car payments and insurance expiration dates or what to make for dinner or office politics or my parents.

His apartment is a cozy cocoon of just the two of us and no sense of time. A stark contrast from my real life *out there*. In here, I can be twenty again. We can fall asleep when the sun comes up. We can talk all day and smoke weed and drink coffee and never put clothes on. We can pick up guitars and sing songs together. We can get creative ideas and both have to dash to grab our notebooks and furiously scribble things down in them. We can laugh and lounge around and have sex four times in as many hours.

In here, I am relaxed. In here, with him, I feel the most like me.

CHAPTER EIGHT

FORZA

WHAT ARE YOU FIGHTING FOR?

One after another, people start telling me how they found out their fathers cheated on their mothers. One woman was fourteen when she found out. She wishes her mom would have waited until she was older and mature enough to handle it. At that age, she felt like she didn't have the tools to process it properly. She says that it fucked her up about men and trust and love. Another cool young woman I know tells me that she knew about her father's affair since the second it happened, when she was five years old. She's relaxed about it. Sure it made her think differently about her dad, but she loves him and they've always had a good relationship.

And then there's my friend with her mom's name tattooed on her arm. It's Canada Day, four months since The Husband dropped The Bomb on me, and we're sitting out under the stars at her parents' cottage. We're drinking and talking. Fireworks in the distance. The hot night air. The mosquitoes. The gaping hole in my chest. I drink more alcohol so I can reach the point where the hole doesn't hurt so much. *Where is he? Why isn't he here with me?* Over and over in my head.

I tell my friend that a week ago, The Husband came to my place late at night unannounced. He asked me if I wanted to go see a marriage counsellor for what he called a "possible reconciliation." Possible reconciliation. This is how he talks sometimes, like a law textbook more than a living, breathing human. Still, I tell my friend, "I'm willing to try. I'm willing to believe him when he says he's still in love with me, that he's remorseful. I'm willing to try to reconcile, to do whatever it will take to save my marriage."

And she says, "You're fighting so hard for him. But even if he were to turn around tomorrow and come back to you one hundred percent, would he be able to give you all that you need? Would he really love you enough, the way you need to be loved?"

I'm quiet. This is a real fucking question I haven't considered. But I'm considering it now, here, Wasaga Beach, first of July. "No. He wouldn't."

"So then what are you fighting for?" she says, and I see it in her face. The pain of growing up knowing her dad had cheated on her mom. The pain that her mom had decided to stay. She tells me the reason her mom's name is tattooed on her arm is as a reminder. "The strongest woman I know, and the stupidest," she says, matter of fact.

I'm not sure how I feel about this. That her mother was stupid for staying. I think there's something admirable about trying to rebuild a marriage after an affair. But I can't help but wonder, *What* am *I fighting for? A man who only sometimes loves me? A man who treated me with less respect than anyone in my life?* No matter how much I love him, I want to be loved the way I love — open and huge and real and without limits. That's a marriage worth fighting for. *I'm done fighting for us.*

After this night, I never once think about getting back together with him. There will be no "possible reconciliation." From now on, I know that will never happen, and I don't want it to.

ACROSS THE SEA

I have to go to Italy. I can't explain it, I just know it's a fact. I need to go to Italy. I need to see my childhood friend, to be with her and her family, to feel the warm air of the seaside and the cool air of the mountains. I need to drink wine under a pergola as the sun sets while we laugh and cry together over the shit-show my life has suddenly become. I've been cut loose, adrift. In Italy I will feel grounded again, I just know it.

I need to bring Birdie with me, since no one in Italy has ever met her. I need to bring my sister's daughter, too. I *want* to. She's thirteen now, and she's travelled with me before — The Husband and I used to take her everywhere with us. I often feel like she's my other daughter. I want them both to come with me to our homeland. To feel the sand and the warm Tyrrhenian Sea one day, and walk among two-thousand-year-old ruins the next. So I book three tickets for the beginning of July.

Everyone thinks I'm crazy. It's only been a few months since The Bomb and even fewer since we moved out on our own. "You've had the worst six months of your life!" my friends say. "Why would you take two kids to Italy with you after everything you've just been through?" But I just know this is what I have to do.

And so we go, three girls across the Atlantic. My tornado of a five-year-old daughter. My thirteen-year-old niece, who packed nothing but identical pairs of extremely short cut-off shorts. And me, a functioning pile of pain. I'm already in withdrawal from booze and cigarettes, since I won't smoke or drink while I'm with the kids.

Right from the start, the three of us have the best time.

LA TAVOLA

Here I am, staring out at the Tyrrhenian Sea. It's a blinding blue with white flashes, and the sun is as hot as it gets, and the sand burns your bare feet in seconds. Birdie is along the water's edge, scooping sand into piles that get washed away faster than she can make them. My niece is nearby, idly placing shells on the piles and allowing Birdie to order her around. Neither of them has siblings and so they are like sisters, which is why I couldn't imagine coming here with one and not the other.

My childhood friend is beside me. We've known each other our entire lives. *We met in our mothers' tummies!* we always say, even though we've never done the math to bother to see if it's true. I've travelled all the way across the Atlantic to be with her, specifically, because she is the anchor my unmoored life needs. Italy is the anchor.

The sea before us is unbelievably flat. It looks like a painting, the edge a perfect line, not even a ripple as far as the eye can see. I've never seen anything like it. "La tavola," my friend says, like she can read my mind. "We call it la tavola — the table — whenever the sea is as flat as it is today." We sit quietly and look at it.

I've spent the past five months in rubble, a shaky, confused mess. We will talk about it all, in every detail over the days to come, whenever the kids aren't around. But for now at least, just being here with her has calmed me. Without the drinking and smoking, my head is clearer. And with the warm sun on my face and The Husband an ocean away, I feel like I can breathe.

TREADING WATER

The trip to Italy is only ten days long. I've planned out six days in and around Rome, with my childhood friend and her family, and the final four in my dad's hometown in the south. Ten days. The

Husband and I have never been apart for more than three days, not in the entire twelve years we've been together. And in that time, we have never, ever, gone even one full day without contact, even since the separation. We are the least separated separated couple ever. This will certainly be a test.

As each day passes, the pain of what's happened diminishes. I feel less like a trauma survivor and more like a regular person again. I take the girls into Rome and we spend the day sightseeing, getting on and off subways, walking up steep hills and tiny, crowded streets. We go into little shops, eat tons of pistachio ice cream, and marvel at everything around us. The Colosseum blows my niece's mind, just like it did the first time I saw it when I was fifteen. Just as I remember it affecting The Husband when I brought him to see it. Standing inside something so big, so majestic, so ancient, so barbaric. It's like looking at the inside of love itself.

We alternate between days in the city and days at the seaside. In the evenings we stay in my friend's town, south of Rome, having dinner with her husband, her teenage son, and her parents, who've known me my whole life. Whenever the kids aren't around, my friend and I do nothing but talk talk talk. We talk about love and heartbreak, faith and duty, right and wrong, choice and independence.

I wish we didn't have to live on different continents, that the years between visits weren't always so silent between us. But I love how as soon as we're together again we're connected at the hip, and it's like no one else is there. That's the thing about girlfriends sometimes: our bonds can be lifelong and intense. It's no wonder men are always disappointing us.

Her father and I talk a lot, too. One night on their balcony, after everyone else has gone to bed, I sit with him and stare out into the night sky. He talks about how heartbroken he is about the separation, how shocked. He, like everyone else in our lives, thought the world of The Husband and can't reconcile the man he thought he knew with the man that ripped my heart out. There are tears in his eyes as he talks, this big man with a voice like gravel, who was like another father to me when I was a kid, and a friend to my own father.

As his wife clears the dishes away, he lights a cigarette and makes an observation about The Husband that is so astute, it will remain with me for a long time.

He says, "Your husband's life before you was like a leaky, unstable boat. He didn't know how he could get off it, this stupid boat that everyone around him was going crazy bailing out the water all the time. Bail, bail, bail. Until he saw an island — you — and he knew that was it, that was where he could finally stand. So he jumped off and he swam to you. And it felt good to stand there, so he did. But after a while, he got restless. He kept seeing boats go by and he forgot how much he hated it out there.

"He only knew he didn't want to be standing anymore, so he jumped back in. He swam and swam, and that's where he is now. Treading water sometimes, swimming sometimes. Then treading treading treading. But he never lets his island out of sight. He'll always keep you in his sight, but he just feels like he can never come up on the shore again."

The sound of an engine kick-starting on the street below punctuates the end of the story. I cry and he says, "Hey, Mich, it's okay because at least you still have you. You are always going to be you, which is the beeesssstt, okay?"

CALABRIA

After six days, the girls and I say goodbye to my friend and her family and get on a train headed south to Calabria. My dad has been touring Italy with his lovely girlfriend, and we've arranged to meet up with them in his hometown. They're there at the train station when we arrive, along with his cousin, the one with the exact same name as my dad. I love this man, this cousin with my dad's exact name. I burst into tears the moment I see him. We hug on the platform for a long, long time. It's so cool, so strange how you can have these inexplicable ties with some people, a magical, indefinable connection. He is one of those people for me.

The town is small, and high in the mountains. It's more rugged here compared to Rome, more pastoral. The air is fresher, the people a little rougher around the edges at first, and the food is out of this world. My dad is overjoyed to have his two granddaughters here in the place he was born. He makes us do all the things you have to do when you're with my dad in Calabria — go to the cemetery, pass by the church my grandparents were married in, sit on the bench outside his aunt's home and listen to her and the other old ladies from the town talk and talk while drinking the world's strongest caffè.

Here's the house he was born in, and look, in the sitting room there's a trap door that leads to the cellar where the goat and the chicken would go each night so they wouldn't get stolen or eaten by dogs. Here's the five-hundred-year-old chestnut tree where young lovers like to meet. And here's "the world's *best* water!" at St. Angelo, my dad's favourite spring high in the mountains above his already-high-in-the-mountains town. It tastes just like water, but he thinks it's the best. And now we have our feet in the sea. "Isn't this *the best*?" he says, over and over.

Everything is *the best* to my dad, which makes this part of the trip all the more awesome. I'm so happy to be here with him again, to have the girls be part of it. He wasn't always this way. There were years after my parents' divorce that things were not *the best* at all. My mother left him, and in the depths of his heartbreak he made a lot of mistakes, and his relationship with my siblings and me suffered. For almost ten years, we kept our distance.

Many years later, my dad returned to us a completely different man. My sister and I called him The New Dad because he was so much less judgemental and hard, so much more involved in our lives and in our children's lives. It's such a gift to have him back. To have The New Dad shouting, "Isn't this *the best?*"

We go to our family's farm, a place that is actually, to me, *the best* in every way possible. It's one of my favourite places on earth, and the girls fall in love with it, too. We pick figs and yellow plums off trees. We pluck flowers off zucchinis, gathering them in our skirts for me to fry up later for a snack. I imagine all the generations of women in our family doing this exact thing in this exact spot.

And it is here that I'm finally able to think of things other than my husband's betrayal and the splintering of my heart. Here I am able to enjoy how my daughter, a city kid through and through, is expertly picking figs by twisting them at the base before pulling. Or how my niece in her too-short shorts is carrying a basket of vegetables on her head as she traverses the steep countryside, as if it could be fifty years ago, or even a hundred. At the farm I feel like there is a purpose to all this, like there is a reason to love even if it means loss.

On the very last day, The Husband phones. As soon as I hear his voice, everything becomes choppy waves again. Every word he says to me is like I'm being hit by those waves, pulled under where I can't breathe. I hear him saying he's been busy and hasn't actually missed me that much, and I say, "What?" and it sounds hysterical. I'm pulled under again, gone with the undertow.

I cry. Not just regular crying, but the kind that comes from another time and space altogether. The kind that is so deep and hard that you feel like you will never stop, ever. I can hear the uncomfortable clinking of cutlery in the next room where my family sits, trying to eat lunch while I explode from my insides out. I know the girls can hear me, but I can't stop. They're just kids and they shouldn't have to hear this. But I can't stop. Nine full days without him, and with this one sentence he's cut me again. *He was busy. He didn't miss me.*

I pull it together enough to sneak out the back door, grabbing my purse as I do. I walk around to the other side of the house, and sit on a stoop facing the mountains. I light a cigarette, even though it's daytime and anyone could catch me. My breathing slows. The hysterical wailing stops. I take in the cigarette smoke and the fresh mountain air. I look at the blue sky and for the first time in my life, I don't want to go home. I want to stay right here, with my dad's cousin, with the old sad dog that's looking at me, with the mountains and the sea. I want to sit right here forever and turn to dust.

And then my dad rounds the corner. He mercifully says nothing about the cigarette in my hand. He just sits beside me and stares out at the mountains, too, the sun beaming directly into our eyes. Here's my father, talking to me about heartbreak. Talking to me in what might be the most tender tone I've ever heard him speak in, since he's usually well-meaning but often brusque and unemotional. Here's my dad comforting me, tears in his eyes. I lean my head on his shoulder.

Suddenly, I realize he knows what this feels like. This grief, he's felt it. He had his heart shattered by my mother, and he fell down the well of self-pity until he was out of reach, even from those of us who loved him most. Now here he is with me on this stoop, telling me as much, telling me how he let his pain devour him. Reminding me that I'm strong and don't have to be devoured by what The Husband did.

With my head on his shoulder and the sun in our eyes, we stare out at the mountains in silence, that same vista people in my family have looked at for generations. How many of them sat here like this, their hearts in a million pieces, with no choice but to keep moving forward? Did my grandmother ever feel this way? Is it inevitable that one day Birdie will feel like this? *God, I hope not.*

We sit and stare, and, with his arm still around me, my dad says, "You're not smoking now are you? Because it's no good."

A few weeks later, back in Toronto, I go to my favourite tattoo artist in Kensington Market. She designs a beautiful font for the Italian phrase I want tattooed on my right wrist. I need it there, where I can always see it, inked into my skin to remind me where I'm from and also what I'm made of.

I have mettle. Fortitude. I come from the soil and the sun and the sand and the ruins. I come from war and poetry and invention. In my blood run the seas that flow out into the Mediterranean.

On my wrist facing up at me, she tattoos *forza e coraggio.* Strength and courage.

I'm going to need it.

PART ♥ TWO

*I think about how I was once part of love,
and now I am apart from it,
standing on the sidelines in wasted
sexy underwear.*

CHAPTER NINE

VOYAGE

WE BECOME OUR OWN WOLVES

It's January 2013. I am alone in my apartment at 6:00 p.m., eating a fried egg and having a drink. A Dark 'n' Stormy; it's become my signature. Imagine — just one year ago, I didn't even drink at all, and now I drink so much, I have a signature! That's progress, baby. Let's do some more inventory, shall we?

I'm thirty-eight years old. I feel like I've lost everything, and therefore I believe I have nothing. Oh sure, I *own* this apartment, so that's something. And I have things in it, and a cleaning lady I've never met who comes every two weeks and cleans it for me because somehow I can't. I used to clean an entire house top to bottom, a house I owned with The Husband — excuse me, *Ex*-husband — but now I can barely keep nine hundred square feet clean.

This boy I was seeing for a while could not get over the cleaning lady thing. I don't even know how it came up, but after it did, he always found a way to use it against me, this completely bourgeois thing about me he found disgusting. I tried to explain to him that when people used to tell me they had cleaning ladies, I would judge them, too, but after my worst year ever, can't I give myself this one thing? I felt as ashamed of it as he felt suspicious, both coming from lower-class immigrant families and all. But it was a waste of time to explain myself to him. And I didn't care to. That wasn't what he was there for.

Anyway, the fact that I cooked eggs today is kind of amazing. Usually, I have a bowl of cereal, or just rum for dinner. That's all I can manage when Birdie isn't here. If I don't have a "date" lined up and I'm just here, alone, it can be pretty bad. But look at me, cooking! How's that for personal growth?

At this moment, it's been eleven months since The Bomb dropped, and Birdie and I just got back from a trip to the Bahamas. When The Ex-husband picked us up at the airport, he looked cuter than ever, his hair going silver now as he approaches forty. He small-talks me, but I feel like punching him or kissing him ... both in equal measure, sue me. It's all I can do not to break into hysterical tears in the car, our old car, but the psychologist says I have to stop crying in front of Birdie.

As he drives, The Ex-husband pokes at me, jokes, then notices enough to stop and wipe a tear from my cheek. He looks crushed, but free. Sad he's hurt me so much, but so happy to not have to miss NFL games anymore because of my family's events. Or something. Of course I'm oversimplifying, but this car ride is exhausting.

We pull up to my apartment building and Birdie, in her old-soul way, says, "Mom, I just wanted to say that I hope you have a really good night tonight," as if she's an empathetic woman in her thirties, not a five-year-old at the end of a long trip. Tears shoot out of my eyes like unexpectedly burst pipes. The Ex-husband squeezes my hand and makes a face that says *hold it together.*

I do. I always do.

So I've started the new year pretty much the same way I ended the last — alone, sad, angry, drinking too much, sad, angry about being alone, repeat. It's cheesy to make a resolution at a time like this, in January along with everyone else, but goddamn it, I need to do something. I can't sit here being proud that I made myself a fried egg for dinner for fuck's sake! Or that I didn't cry in front of my daughter this time, where's my gold medal. I mean, *honestly.*

You have to believe me: I want to stop feeling sorry for myself. I really do. But I don't know how. I don't know how to be okay with these empty spaces, the physical one here in this apartment with no husband in it, no daughter. Just the sounds of the fridge buzzing and ice cubes clinking in a glass. Just me and the vast emptiness inside of me where love once was. I don't know how people combat the loneliness, how they push through the space without having to fill it up with anything they can find like I've been doing. But I do know that something's gotta change. I can't keep blaming The Husband for throwing me to the wolves when I've become my own wolf, devouring myself because I can't take the pain when the night comes.

Oh, God, sorry. It's always the rum and sometimes the tequila that makes me this way. Ah, fuck it, really, I can't keep blaming it on the booze when we all know it's just my heart — the world's worst and most broken record. Look, I know that since the beginning of time people have been betrayed and deserted by the person they love and trust the most. This isn't the first time in history someone's had a hard time being alone.

But this is my story.

THE BABIES

Let me tell you about The Babies. That's what us single women call the seemingly only available men in this city: babies. All the single women I've talked to in Toronto from age thirty-five to forty-five have slept with men much younger than them for most of their dating lives. Oh come *on*, you say, none of you can find a guy your own age? Where are they all? We talk about it some-times — *Are they all married or in relationships? Are the ones that aren't married sleeping with twenty-six-year-olds themselves? Does a woman their own age look like a walking piece of baggage?*

It's all very mysterious and it means in this city, there's a giant group of single, super-educated, well-dressed, great-careered, home-owning, vacation-taking women in their thirties having fun, casual sex with guys ten or more years younger than them. Getting no closer to finding the one — or anyone, really — to have an actual relationship with.

Okay, so they aren't *all* babies. Every once in a while a guy our own age will come along, but they're even worse. They're trying to *find* themselves. They aren't in a *rush*. They say they're into polyamory. I mean, why not? They've got all the time in the world without a built-in biological expiry date.

Look, I'm not saying every single woman in her thirties wants kids, but for the ones that do, time's ticking. They *are* in a rush. They don't have the same luxury that single men have to stop and find themselves. To casually date and not commit to any one person because there might be something bet-ter out there. Someone *more right*. In a big city like Toronto, there's endless choice. Everyone can just stay at the sampler table for as long as they want until one day they're ready to make a decision. Which is cool if you can, but for the single women I know who want to meet someone *and* have a baby, the endless sampling sucks. All these choices means no one ever has to choose.

So they come and go, in and out of our lives, and because they're hard to keep track of, we give them nicknames: *Shy Banker. Hot Actor. Crazy Guy (formerly Cute Guy). Snaps. The Giraffe.* It's a dating shorthand, a way to quickly catch each other up.

"Whatever happened to Billable Hours, anyway?"
"We just had no chemistry at all. I gave him three dates and was like, movin' on!"

"You won't believe who asked me out, now that I finally met someone else."
"Tall, Stupid Lawyer??"
"EXACTLY."

"Okay, don't be mad but Crazy Guy is back ..."
"Oh my GOD ... WHY are you doing this to yourself?"
"I just think awesome in bed trumps crazy, don't you?"

I'm really not sure how my life became an episode of *Sex and the City*. It's the weirdest thing.

HOW IT HAPPENS IS THIS

It's hot. July 2012. I've just returned from the trip to Italy. The first thing I do when I get back is have sex with The Ex-husband. Even though he didn't miss me. Even though I never want to get back together with him. It's funny being human sometimes, isn't it? We've been having sex consistently, several times a week, ever since we moved out of our house and into separate apartments. It's masochistic maybe, but it's easy. He lives across the street, and we get each other.

Look, I *know*, okay? But for the past twelve years I've only slept with him. And I've never been on a date, ever. I've never had a one-night stand. I've never picked up a guy in a bar. I've never given my number to someone I just met. I have no idea what to do or how to do it, now that I find myself thirty-seven and single for the first time. But I know this — I'm not interested in finding a boyfriend or a new relationship. I just need to have sex with someone other than The Ex-husband. I need to have sex. Simple as that. I just don't have a clue how.

So I ask my friend's husband for advice. He's the quietest person I've ever met. Mostly in contrast to her I suppose; she's Big Laugh, after all. Big Laugh's Quiet Husband has never said more than a few words to me before this night. But here eating dinner on their balcony in the hot July air, I ask him because he's a man. And because I don't really know what else to do and I'm embarrassed to say what I'm about to say. I say, "I need to have sex. But how do I find someone to do that with?"

I say, "I tried to seduce a couple of guys I know, but they totally turned me down. Is there something wrong with me?"

Big Laugh's Quiet Husband sighs and then quietly says, "There's nothing wrong with you. They turned you down because they're good guys who know you and what you've been through. What you need to do is find a *stranger*. You need to go to a bar and pick up a stranger and have sex with him."

I stare at him. "I can't do that. I can't do that! I can't even imagine *how* to do that."

And he says, "Make an online dating profile and be totally honest. Trust me, if you want to, you'll get laid by tomorrow."

I hate the idea of having to go online, it freaks me out, but at the same time, it seems like a good way to solve my current problem. So I make an online profile on one of the most popular dating sites in Toronto in 2012. I put up some tasteful but hot photos of myself. I write a bunch of stuff about me that of course no one will read, it's all about the photos anyway. Within an hour I have more than fifty messages. And I see that Big Laugh's Quiet Husband was right — I will get laid by tomorrow if I want. And that's exactly what happens.

FIRST GUY

The First Guy is memorable for being the first. The whole day leading up to us meeting I'm a bundle of nerves. It feels like it's prom night and I know I'm going to lose my virginity. I kind of am, in a way. I mean, I haven't even kissed a man other than The Husband since New Year's Eve 1999. And here I am in July 2012, about to go for drinks with a twenty-six-year-old magazine editor.

He was one of the first to start talking to me on the dating site. He was charming and smart, and we chatted a lot and agreed to meet. *Twenty-six is a baby. What am I doing?* He said he had lots of experience with online dating and that he loved older women. I told him I had no experience. "So if I chicken out that better be cool!" "Absolutely," he said.

I do not chicken out. It feels like it's a thousand degrees out, so I throw on a light dress and a pair of heels. I fan myself on the streetcar the whole way over. I'm early and see him first. He is dressed really nicely and has an incredibly fit body, but his face isn't *quite* as cute as in his photos. Undeterred, I walk up to him and we go inside the bar.

We have beer and easy conversation. We talk about where our families are from, about our parents and our siblings and how we were raised. We talk about school and careers and how we each got to where we are professionally. We click, there in that loud downtown bar, and my nervousness slips away. He seems harmless, and into me, and a good candidate to be the first guy I'll be with after my husband broke my heart.

He also has the same name as my teenage boyfriend, my first love, the one I dated for several years and was the first person I ever had sex with. Two firsts, same name. He was a wonderful boyfriend, my teenage love. Caring, sweet, and loving. In contrast to most of the stories I've heard from women about their first sexual experience, mine was awesome because of him. Now here, this young man in front of me is about to usher me into a new sexual phase of my life, and he has the same name as the boy who ushered me into the very first sexual phase of my life. I take it as a sign.

As we talk and drink, I become more sure. This is the right thing to do. For the first time in my life, I am going to have sex with someone I don't know or care about at all. Despite his age, The First Guy seems pretty mature, with a career and his own condo. We go to that condo.

I text his address to a friend, as well as his cellphone number and his first and last name. *If you don't hear from me by 9 am tomorrow, I'm dead*, I text. *Oh, just have fun!* she texts back. The whole thing feels crazy. Only five months ago I was bored and resigned to my domestic family life, unhappy with the stranger that my husband had become. Now here I am, in a fancy loft conversion with a man with abs like I've never seen. It is insane. It is amazing.

Let's stop for a moment and reflect on this sweet boy and his hard, hard body. I've never seen anything like it, except in movies maybe. But here it is in front of me, lean and smooth and undeniably beautiful. He's incredibly lovely and generous throughout the whole thing. I just can't stop giggling because I can't believe this is happening. If he finds this unsettling, he doesn't let it show. When it's over, I'm in awe. *I just slept with a complete stranger!* And I didn't think of The Ex-husband even once. It's the greatest feeling. But poor First Guy! He tries to cuddle with me and I have no interest. I say, "Thank you so much!" with way too much enthusiasm. He seems confused, and why not? He has no idea what he's just done for me.

When he asks me when he can see me again, I say, "Why??" Honestly, I never want to see him again, even though it was so great. Without having articulated it to myself or anyone, I know my one-and-done policy is now in place. I have no interest in having a boyfriend, or any kind of casually permanent thing. I know I don't want to get to know anyone enough to like them, enough for them to lie to me, enough to have them break my barely mended heart. I know I just want to do this whole thing over and over again: meet a stranger, have sex, then go home.

Sailing

For me, talking to a guy in a bar and then going home and having sex with him is equivalent to just walking down to a marina, picking out a yacht, and then sailing it around the world. Without a map. Or knowledge of the sea. Or even a fucking clue about boats at all. *That's* how foreign a thing it is to do. *That's* about how prepared I am. But Life said to me: *There's a yacht, go sail it or something!*

So damn it, am I ever gonna try.

THE CAKE

One morning in that first year of separation, The Ex-husband comes over to my apartment to help me mount the TV on the wall. Birdie's at my mom's for a sleepover. After the TV is hung, we sit and work on the parenting calendar for September and October. There are a bunch of upcoming days that hurt just to look at — the day we got engaged, the day we got married, the day he says he first slept with *her*. I start to cry.

Usually this is the point where he gets defensive, or angry, and gets up to leave. Instead, he tries out this new thing he's been doing lately — "I'm going to be a good ex-husband because I was such a shitty husband." Good Ex-husband holds me. Good Ex-husband kisses me. Good Ex-husband lies down with me on my bed in the morning sun. *I swore the last time would be the last time.*

We still touch each other constantly. He looks down my top or grabs my butt, I run my hand under his shirt — all absent-mindedly. We hang out at his apartment, and I say something sassy. He chases me and I squeal, running, darting around furniture until he finally catches me and throws me on his bed, or couch, or just pins me against the wall and kisses me hard, like it's 1999 again. Then we just pull apart and continue on like nothing's happened. But I feel lighter, if only for another half hour.

One day at the end of this first summer, we're swimming with Birdie, and the two of us splash and jump on each other in the pool same as we always have. Reflexively, I wind my legs around him in the water, and he swims around with me on his back, like always. At one point, he turns back to look at me and smiles. It's the most real moment of happiness I've seen on his face in almost a year. I kiss the back of his neck. *I'm the cake. But he's my cake, too.*

Yeah, The Cake. As in *You can't have your cake and eat it, too.* In The Ex-husband's case, he has it, he's eating it, he's *king* of the fucking cake.

"Don't be the cake!" my friends keep telling me when I tell them I'm still sleeping with him. "I know, I know," I say, but deep down I don't mind being the cake. I want to sleep with him because I want to feel him close to me. His familiar scent, movement. It has nothing to do with getting back together, everything to do with the physical intimacy I crave. Also, it's way too easy living across the street from each other. Part of me knows they're right. He's getting everything out of this arrangement, while I get the scraps. But I'm not ready to stop yet. So yes, I'm his cake and he's mine. We can't let go of the constant ignition that exists between us, regardless of the harm, the heartbreak.

Meanwhile, I continue to make my way through half the twenty-six-year-olds in this city. Twenty-six. The same age The Ex-husband was when we met and fell in love. Yeah, even without a degree in psychology it's pretty obvious what's happening there. But The Babies, they're all over me! Maybe they can see that I'm a wounded gazelle easy for the pounce. Maybe that's the same reason guys my own age don't come near me. I don't know. I don't know what it is or what's happening.

But I'm learning some things. I'm learning how easy it is to make shallow, sexy talk with a complete stranger. How easy it is to line up a time to meet for drinks and then how easy it is to bring them home with me, get what I want ... and kick them out. When they leave I cry, but not for them. I cry for whoever this is I've become, this opposite of a wife.

CHAPTER TEN

HALF-LIFE

DUALITY

I'm going out tonight and packing my smaller purse. My "dancing purse," as I call it. It's the same items every time — lip gloss, cigarettes, gum, a couple of condoms. *Who am I? When did I become this person?*

The next day, before I go pick up Birdie at The Ex-husband's place, I dump it all out onto my bed and get my bigger, non-dancing purse. I remove the cigarettes and the condoms, replacing the single-lady things with single-mom things: snacks, a pack of hand wipes, a bottle of water.

Duality. My new middle name.

CRAZY GUY (FORMERLY CUTE GUY)

Oh, boy. Let's talk about him for a moment. Cute Guy is twenty-six, gregarious, ridiculous, hot-headed. A Scorpio like me. In every other way, not like me. We meet online, and we start a silly email exchange that goes on for days. His grammar and punctuation are awful, but the banter is charged and fun. Eventually, he suggests we meet at La Hacienda, an old dive bar on Queen West. I haven't been there since my twenties. It seems fitting.

When I walk in and see him sitting there, my insides do a little dance, which is new. He is impossibly cute and tall, with big arms and shoulders that he instantly wraps around me in a big hug, even though we've just met. There is an instant spark, a real click. We sit on the back patio and drink and drink. We smoke cigarettes and laugh so much my face hurts. He can keep up with me, my digs and jokes, and it reminds me of The Husband and I when we first met all those years ago.

When we leave, we walk through the crowded summer streets, still laughing. We don't say it but we are walking to my place. He puts his arm around me, and I'm surprised. I can't imagine a guy like this would want to be seen with his arm around me — *me*, an old and damaged lady. I'm guessing you know what I'm talking about, the way we sometimes think the world can see the way we feel on the inside.

So it began with Cute Guy.

After our first fun night together, I actually do want more, I do want to see him again. So for the first time, I lift my one-and-done policy. As summer ends and into the fall, he comes over once a week, and at least there are those three or four hours where I'm actually having fun, feeling good, talking and just goofing around like I'm twenty again. He calls me *kiddo*, which I adore, since I love nicknames. He breaks into song at odd moments, his smile is great.

When I'm with him I forget all about The Ex-husband. But when he's gone it's no big deal either. I don't even think about him until he texts me five days later and we repeat. Sounds perfect right? But it doesn't last long. You know it doesn't, since at some point Cute Guy becomes *Crazy* Guy. Here's how.

One night, bored, I search his name on Twitter and find that he tweets at least twenty times a day. I scroll back to the dates we were together, and lo and behold, each time on his long journey home on public transit, he tweeted about me and the things we did. I chalk it up to typical millennial behaviour, and since he didn't mention my name I figure what's the harm? The tweets are complimentary at least, and make me laugh both for content and enthusiasm. But it's still a little weird for me, you know?

I don't bring it up. We go along as usual. And then he starts to get a little defensive, accusing me of wanting more from him, of liking him more than I'm letting on, of wanting a relationship. I don't know why he thinks that. I love the arrangement we have. I adore him but only when he's around. He is not relationship material for me. He's a wonderful escape once a week, a respite from my crumbled marriage and my role as mother to a demanding five-year-old. I mean sure, I like him, in that he is so good to look at, to smell, to feel normal-ish with for a bit each week. None of that means I want anything more, but the cute starts to get a little crazy.

One night, after we text back and forth for a long time and the conversation gets confusing, I decide to just phone him. He doesn't answer. But immediately he texts, *WTF? Why are you phoning me?* like *I* am a crazy person, like we haven't been talking through texts for the past hour! He breaks it off with me. A week later I convince him to stop being an idiot and come back. He does come back one more time, then flips out again. He writes me a crushing email that says he has no regrets but that this thing "has run its course."

I let it go, although I *am* disappointed. And, shamefully, sometimes I still scroll through his Twitter account. Look, these Friday or Saturday nights as a single parent are alienating. While everyone else I know is out having fun, or with their partners, I am just so alone, Birdie asleep in her room, me staring at the wall, or my phone. So I check out Cute/Crazy Guy's Twitter account. Sue me.

And then I realize that he has a blog. A blog where he writes, a lot, about anything that comes into his head. He writes about stupid customers that come into his store, or how he lost $100 at a blackjack game. He writes about women, women he *names*, and what they do together, and how they misunderstand him, the games these women play, the drama. My heart stops when I see the first post about me. There, on the internet, a fairly detailed description of me and my *assets*. What he liked about me, the things we did together. And how I was *obviously* in love with him, and how *obviously* messed up I was. He wrote that I was a walking contradiction and more trouble than I was worth.

For some reason, I'm the only woman he hasn't named, which I guess should give me some solace. Instead, he's given me a nickname, a thing I normally love, but in this case not so much. Because he refers to me as the MILF. It makes me feel a hundred years old. It's like I get sober in that exact moment. I suddenly stop and question everything about myself and all my actions leading up to this point. All the drinking and sleeping around. What I've been through with The Husband has made me into the kind of woman that can now be reduced to an acronym — *a joke* — on some Baby's blog.

I Smoked Six Cigarettes Today,

and ate a chocolate bar for dinner. God, it's like I've become Bridget Jones or something.

RUDDERLESS

"Hi honey, I'm home!" I say to no one, any time I walk in the door of my empty apartment after a long day. It's a little joke I have with myself now. I throw my keys on the counter and say it out loud to the nothing. And then I turn around and just head back out. Anything to not be in that cold, quiet space with its lack of living, breathing beings. I just get the fuck out of there as fast as I can.

"You do too much," says my father, pretty much every time we speak. He's right. I do a lot. I fill up every space with busy. Any moment without Birdie, any moment that is now the absence of what was once my little family, without the promise of a new one, I fill with booze or men or workouts or friends. I stay up all night writing. Reading. Moving furniture.

There's so much space now so I fill and fill and fill it. I do too much and I don't stop. I can't stop. I know if I do I will stay frozen like that forever, unable to move, preserved this way in amber, a curiosity for future generations. I'm a woman out to sea, nothing solid to tether herself to for miles in any direction. Rudderless.

THE BEAR

We were on the edge of a cliff. This isn't a metaphor for our marriage — we actually were camped out on the edge of a nine-hundred-foot cliff in the summer of 2004. Below us was the Atlantic Ocean, dotted with wild and beautiful things I'd never seen before — sea stacks, pillow lava. But I couldn't see them. For the first time in my life, I was having a panic attack.

I'm an experienced camper, but I'm also from a flat place, so pitching our tent on this cliff with a raging sea below really freaked me out. Also, there were steaming piles of bear droppings, very fresh, all over the place. But there was no turning back. It had taken four hours to hike in and now it was getting dark. We were staying the night.

The Husband was a good husband back then, so he tried to calm my panic on the cliff. We'd been married for almost two years at that point. It was a beautiful time in our relationship — the time after the wedding but before we had a baby. We were best friends, we did everything together, and we hardly ever fought. This edge-of-a-cliff camping was in the middle of a month-long road trip in our little car from Toronto to Newfoundland, the island of his birth. It had been an amazing month, except for this panic attack, me standing frozen in the wind, breathing so heavy, eyes wild.

The Husband coaxed me to sit down. He got out my old transistor radio and tuned it to the only station we could get out there — CBC Radio, the public broadcaster I work for. He made a fire and cooked up some toutons, this traditional Newfoundland bread. He poured molasses on the warm bread and gave me a cup of tea. He tucked my hair behind my ears, kissed my eyelids, one, then the other, and then the first one again. He made jokes about "false advertising" since I was supposed to be an experienced camper. He had it all under control in this crazy place on the edge of the North Atlantic. My anxiety started to disappear, my breathing slowed. He made me feel safe.

That night, we slept in a tent that had to be tethered to a platform so we wouldn't blow away. I slept hard. The next day when we were back in civilization, he told me why he hadn't slept nearly as well. In the middle of the night, he'd woken up to the sound of loud sniffing at the wall of our tent. It was a bear. A bear so close he could feel its hot breath on his face. Slowly, The Husband turned on his side and put all six foot two, two hundred and twenty pounds of himself on top of me, completely covering me as best as he could. His heart was beating so loudly, he worried the bear would hear it or I would wake up. After what felt like an eternity to him, the bear eventually ambled away. I slept right through it all.

Five-year-old Birdie loves this story. She loves how he says to her, "Imagine the tent wall is right here," and puts his hand in front of her face. "Now, I'm the bear, aaaand … snufffff" — he blows a gust of wind into her face and they both break out laughing. This is the part where I say, "And your dad just put his whole big body right around mom's body to protect her, so the bear would get him first."

"That's right, I did!" he shouts.

That's right. He did.

THE SWINGS

I never feel more divorced, more alone, than when I'm at the playground with Birdie. Especially in this first year. It doesn't matter which park I go to in this city, it's always the same — each child seems to have two parents, one with another, smaller child strapped to their body.

Hon? Can you please get some sunscreen on Pilot or he'll burn.

Banjo! Come here and get a seaweed snack from your mom.

God, I am being such an asshole right now. But honestly, sometimes I hate these people with their intact families. I hate that I sit here on a bench, alone, pretending to read a book while Birdie plays happily with the other kids. Every once in a while, she looks up from what she's doing and gives me a wave. I wave back from behind my giant sunglasses, hungover from spending the previous night dancing and drinking and doing karaoke, only to make the sharp one-eighty to motherhood by this afternoon.

Here I am, sitting alone in this park watching blissful domesticity as it buzzes around me. Cool fathers with their beards and skinny jeans chatting easily with their lithe and stylish wives who hold lattes and complain about the quality of Mandarin being taught at the daycare. *Why do they seem so effortless? Why are they just married and doing married stuff and that's* okay? *If it really is that easy, why couldn't my own husband do it?*

I study them. These couples don't *look* any happier than we did. Some of them look less happy even, and all of them look way less into each other than we were. I mean, some of the women sound brittle and exasperated every time they say anything to their husbands. Most of the men seem distracted and uninterested. Hang on, no, *all* of the men seem distracted and uninterested. Not in their wives necessarily, but in life in general maybe? They all look like they want to be someplace else.

I recognize these ghosts. *I do not miss that part of marriage.* The way you sink into those roles whether you ever believed you would or not. Now I'm sitting on this bench with less longing, remembering instead the fun I had last night, how I woke up giddy and satisfied this morning. How I spent the early part of today lounging around my apartment, reading magazines and making espresso, napping, writing … all before The Ex-husband dropped Birdie off mid-afternoon.

It's not too bad a life. I may be settling into it even. But oh, *damn them*, shit, will you look at that couple? They're sitting on two swings side by side, holding hands and laughing. They look so into each other, don't they? And now everything inside of me starts to crumble, crumple. I miss The Ex-husband so suddenly, so painfully, so desperately. I feel the hot tears as they flash-flood my eyes. God, I miss the swings, the swinging part of love.

Just ... Different

Before the breakup of my marriage, the number of men I had slept with, including The Husband, could be counted on one hand with room to spare. As you know, I was in a long-term relationship with each of them, so that means until The Year of The Bomb, I'd never had sex with anyone I wasn't in love with and who wasn't in love with me. But now I've forgotten what it's like to experience it that way.

I'll amend that: I haven't forgotten, I just miss it.

It's amazing how different it is when you don't love the person you're with. Not bad, just *different*. The term *meaningless sex* really does a good job explaining it. It just becomes a function you perform, a function with great immediate results, obviously, and it is fun and exciting, sure. But nothing beats that feeling, the one where you are so full of love and desire *at the same time*.

This is why when I meet The Man with the White Shirt, everything and everyone else becomes insignificant. When we're together, it is finally that thing I crave, that thing I miss, that perfect, heady mixture. It isn't just sex with him, it's *sex*, the way it's meant to be. Or, at least the way I want it to be. I can still have fun, exciting, excellent sex with others, but desire without love just doesn't feel substantial enough. It leaves me hungry. Wanting.

Other men are just candy, but he's an entire meal.

CHAPTER ELEVEN

THE SADDEST OPTIMIST

A PRETTY SAD GIRL

I'm getting an MRI. It's midnight, in the basement of this old hospital, the one I was born in thirty-seven years ago. I'm alone, about to slide into a tube while magnets crash around me like a symphony of instruments all made out of garbage cans. There's nothing more cinematic than this moment maybe, me walking down dimly lit hallways into a basement reception area at midnight to get my brain scanned for a stupid disease no one seems to know very much about.

I'm filling out the form I have to fill out every single time I get an MRI, once a year. *No metal filings in my body, check. No shrapnel, check.* Shrapnel. This makes me laugh every time, as though since last summer I've been out to the front lines or something. The admitting nurse is staring at me. She's old, too old to be working this late if you ask me. I look up from the form and she says, in this gorgeous East Indian old-lady voice, "You are so pretty I can't help but notice. But I have never seen such a pretty girl look so sad inside of herself."

She's looking at me expectantly so I try to respond, but I've got nothing for you, lady. I can't think of anything to say. I'm a pretty girl. A sad girl. A pretty sad girl. Yeah, I know. "I'm thirty-seven and I'm alone," is what I finally say. She pats my hand and it's all I can do not to fall into the deepest hole.

In a small room, I take all of my clothes off and stuff them into a locker. I put on two hospital gowns, one forward and one backward, as instructed. I remove all five of my earrings, and the rings on my right hand. The locker needs a four-digit passcode, so I punch in my childhood address. Freezing, I sit on a plastic chair in an empty waiting room, alone. TV news on top volume for no one. My socks on the cold floor. Soon enough, I'm sliding into the MRI machine.

Here I am, lying on this table. It's really snug. Dark. And there's this cage-type thing holding my head in place. The technician tells me not to move. You aren't allowed to move or else the pictures they're taking of your brain will be ruined and you'll have to start all over again. I don't want to start all over again. It is *snug* in here, remember? And I'm going to be in here for the next forty minutes. *Don't move don't move don't move.*

And then it begins. *Clang clang click click click!* Holy *Lord* it's loud. But quickly, it gets really rhythmic sounding to me. Really *musical.* I hear … music. Each time the machine takes a picture of my brain, it sounds like a different "song" to me. The songs are actually called "pulse sequences" and they are as deliberately composed as any sequence in a piece of music. What, I've done my research, okay?

It's cool, this magnetic techno I hear. And after awhile, I forget about the lonely empty hospital and how pathetic — and cold — I feel lying in this tube. My breathing starts to lock in time with the high-pitched whirring and clanging of the magnet's coils.

Rhythm is all about movement. But here, inside this giant machine, I experience rhythm in the very absence of movement. Lying very still, in a cold room in the basement of a hospital. Tuning in to the pulse sequences like songs on a radio. Songs that create images of my brain. And make me forget about my heart. For a little while.

When it's over, as the two MRI technicians help me out of the machine, I crack a joke about them having magnetic personalities. In the change room, there's a young woman putting on a blue hospital gown. I tell her she can leave her socks on *and* her underwear, even though they told her to take everything off. "Oh! *Thank you*," she says, and then, "I've never done one before." So I give her a spare pair of ear plugs, as well as my old sleep mask. "Trust me, it's super-creepy to watch yourself slide into a tube so you'll want your eyes covered. With your forehead held down by that clamp it's a little too *Clockwork Orange*, you know?" We laugh and I see her whole blue-gowned body relax.

When I leave, I smile at the sweet old nurse still sitting at the desk. That's just me, I guess, The Saddest Optimist. A pretty, sad girl who never gives up hope.

Two years later, when I have to go in for an MRI, The Man with the White Shirt is with me. He has packed an entire bag of supplies, as if we're going away for the weekend. He's got his laptop, loaded with episodes of the old TV series *Lost*, which we've been bingeing together obsessively, two sets of earbuds and a splitter, a two-litre bottle of water, two sandwiches, and a chocolate bar.

He covers my cold, exposed legs with his jacket.

He tells me I look sexy in my hospital gown and, even though I roll my eyes and say "Okaaay," we both know I like it. He does a little low growl in my ear and pretends to try and get under the gown, slowly running his fingers along my thigh. I pretend to push his hands away and we laugh, sweetly, the way joking lovers do. He nuzzles my neck, he tucks my hair behind my ear, he kisses me. And it is all just as it should be. This. This is the way love used to feel, this is how I want love to feel.

Love sits with you in the basement of a hospital at 2:00 a.m. Love tells you how much you're adored, even when you've got bags under your eyes and are wearing a hospital gown. Love keeps your bare legs warm. It comes back here with you, year after year, with varying arrangements of snacks, so you never have to do this alone again.

Love waits with you. It waits.

TRAINING

The personal trainer looks at me with concern. It's 7:00 a.m. and we're in a park and she's about to put me through a full hour of serious workout. It's a Tuesday.

The personal trainer is twenty-six, beautiful. I am thirty-seven, still drunk. God, I remember that once upon a time *I* was twenty-six with my shit together, looking at drunk people with concern. But hey, I'm here, aren't I? I didn't cancel on her! I never cancel. I always show up no matter what state I am in, two, sometimes three, times a week. I've committed myself to being pushed hard by her. Some guy left my bed at 3:00 a.m., and here I am at 7:00, doing an unbelievable amount of lunges, squats, and sprints. Jesus Christ.

It's early September 2012. Back when The Bomb dropped, I gave myself a six-month time limit on feeling sorry for myself.

So here we are, six months later, and I have to get on with it. The beautiful personal trainer is the first step. She says her first priority is to get me to stop drinking, then smoking. She wants me to eat again, properly, but I'm still not that into eating. My whiskey-and-cigarettes diet has given me a body like I've never had, but I want to be strong again. I need my body to get stronger so that *I* will get stronger.

From this point on, I push myself. I get lines in my abs I didn't even know you could get. When I run, I'm faster, less winded. My soccer game improves because I'm more agile thanks to Beautiful Trainer and her crazy regime. Everything tightens up. I buy clothes in sizes I've never bought clothes in before. And then I buy more. So many clothes, I can't stop, because for the first time in my life, I actually fit into everything I try on. I get stronger and stronger. I can lift my fifty-pound daughter now without any trouble. I can carry her sleeping body plus a thousand bags all the way from the car to the elevator then down the long hallway to my apartment and I don't huff and puff or even crack a sweat. I feel awesome.

Beautiful Trainer is changing my life. Sure sure, *I* am, but really it's her. She says, "Ten more," and I do ten more. She says, "That's okay," when I burst into tears, sobbing through abdominal crunches, crying through squats, saying over and over to her, "I don't know how I got here. Why am I here? I don't know why my husband did this to me. Why did he do this to me?"

Something about pushing myself physically is pushing the words out of me, pushing the confusion right out with the sweat. Beautiful Trainer nods her head, her eyes fill with tears. "You are amazing and strong. He did it because he's a jerk. And you're going to get better. Now do that set from the top." And I do. I do every set she tells me to, twice.

By the end of the first month of training, I've cut down on the smoking and I ease up on the booze. *A lot.* It isn't daily anymore, and it will never be again, thank God. I put some weight back on because without all the drinking I'm hungry for food again, and anyway the weight is good because my muscles are strong.

I actually stand in front of the mirror now, and see something I like. Everything is leaner and tighter but still super curvy, still lots of meat. It looks great. For the first time in my life, I love everything about my own body. It's an incredible achievement, to stand there in your skivvies and say "Damn, I look good."

All these years later, I still do this. No matter how much weight I've gained, or how many rolls I have, I continue to look at myself in the mirror and say "Damn, I look good!" even if I'm not totally feeling it. It's one of the best things I've learned to do. The best gift I've given myself. Because I do look good, and so do you, goddamn it.

PAST IN PRESENT

In this first year since The Bomb, The Ex-husband and I have settled into our complicated relationship. He comes over and fixes things for me, brings his drill and hangs pictures and wall lamps. He listens to the water heater and tells me why it's making that clicking sound.

When I go to his place, I straighten out the clothes in Birdie's closet. I counsel him on the finer points of dressing a five-year-old girl. I secretly marvel at how put together his place is, how exactly *him* it seems, even though it has all *my* furniture in it. I oddly feel good that he has his own space, his own sense of style in it. I don't tell him this.

One day when I'm there, I go into Birdie's room and notice that he's hung two big frames over her bed. One is a collage of a bunch of different photos of him that I took before she was born. The other is a collage of photos of me from the same time period. The two of us in our twenties, all smiles and swagger. As soon as I see them, I freeze. I can hear Birdie: "Mom? Mom?" but it's like she's at the end of a tunnel. My head is swimming. *We were so young once.*

In a sad trance, I lie down on her bed but can't stop looking at the photos. Birdie runs to get her dad and he rushes in and immediately grabs my wrist (which is so him, you know?) to check my fucking pulse as if I've had a heart attack instead of knowing these happy photos of us would tailspin me.

When he realizes what's wrong, he crawls onto her bed beside me. He curls his arms around me, his right leg folded over mine, in the exact way we slept each night for the last twelve years. Birdie jumps into the bed with us and looks so happy she could burst.

His hand on my face, gently. He says, over and over, "Should I take them down?"

"Of course not," I say, once I return to earth. I tickle Birdie and kiss her goodbye. Then I walk across the street.

WHEN SHE'S HERE

When Birdie's gone I feel emptied out. There's no other way to say it. It's like I have a phantom limb — I can feel her here with me even though she isn't.

She's with her father, she's fine. She's happy and healthy and getting everything she needs from him during the 50-percent-of-the-time she's there, and not here. But it eats away at me, this part of the loneliness, this walking past her bedroom with its purple walls and stuffed animals, here, right here in my apartment, but empty. The place where a child once was and now isn't. But will come back to.

So many goodbyes, so many reunions. It takes adjusting to. Mostly for me. Birdie's unfazed by her two homes. She acts like it's all completely normal. We've been parenting her, together, every step of the way since we separated, and it's paying off.

Just look at her.

She's wearing her Supergirl costume … *again*. It's nowhere near Hallowe'en. I don't care. I let her wear it whenever she wants, what's the difference? Right now she's putting together an Ikea stool, and has all the parts laid out perfectly on the apartment floor. She studies the manual thoughtfully, as any Supergirl would. I take her orders: *Hold the legs in a cross pattern! Use the star screwdriver to put in the long funny little screwy things!* Her orders are all shouts. She *is* half-Italian. Together, we make a pretty good little stool. It's still in her room all these years later.

She's starting Senior Kindergarten at a new school in our new neighbourhood in our new life. She's got a brand new pair of white sneakers. "So *plain*," she says, so I hand her a black Sharpie. "Go for it!" Her blue eyes wide with excitement, she tricks out those sneakers like she's a five-year-old graffiti artist. They look so cool.

Now she's six. She wants to get her ears pierced. No, her *ear*. Just one. "That's my style," she says, so I hold her little hand as she gets it done. She squeezes me hard and says, "Holy, that hurt!" but she doesn't cry out or cry. We walk back home swinging our arms, trying to guess how many windows are in each tall building.

Birdie at every age slips tiny notes into my purse and sometimes my lunch bag for me to find later when I'm at work.

Oh hi mom! Have a GRAT day! says one.

Oh hey Mom do you NO you are totalle the best? says another.

I keep them all. In my purse. Any time I feel like a sad lonely loser, I pull them out to remind myself I'm the luckiest loser that ever lived. I may have loved and lost, but at least I loved and lost. And this unbelievable little human is the result.

Here's Birdie at seven. We're walking in a big downtown park and we see a hip-hop artist I know. He's making a music video in the park and Birdie and I get pulled into the fun. Dancing and lip-synching along to the track in a little ramshackle booth. Afterward I say, "Wasn't that the coolest? We're going to be in a video!"

"I really liked your friend's dog," she says. "And the song I guess." She takes off to play with the other kids in the playground.

In these moments with Birdie, I'm whole again. I'm relaxed. I'm relaxing into being a part-time parent to her, not having her dad to defer to or negotiate with about what happens in the small moments. We're just two people here, me and Birdie. We create our own space, develop our own rhythm. I try not to worry about how other parents parent. I run on instinct. I don't put her in any classes or extra-curricular activities. When she's with me, the city is one big adventure.

Birdie's with me every other weekend, and that's when we make art together — collages, paintings, drawings, sewing projects, elaborately decorated cupcakes. I refuse to make plans for us on Saturday mornings. I want us to have this one time, every two weeks, where we don't have to rush off anywhere. The not rushing is what brings me closest to her. Carving that space out for us is the best decision I've ever made as a parent. Every Saturday morning is a master class in just chilling out — staying in our pyjamas and making things and making a mess of the place. Who cares? I don't look at my phone, I don't answer calls. We become remarkably in tune, doing our own things but still interacting. Mother and daughter in parallel play. It's wonderful.

When it's time for Birdie to go I say, "Don't forget about the invisible thread!" and she says, "I won't, Mom!" The invisible thread that's always connecting us, whether we're physically together or not.

When she's here, we're both learning and growing, everything's new for us both. So we design our life together, over the years. We redraw the lines of parent and child, woman and girl, human and human. We make it all up as we go along. In pyjamas and taking no calls.

RINGS

I only ever think about them when I'm on public transit. Engagement rings. On a crowded streetcar, they're everywhere — on fingers gripped around poles, tapping on cellphones, or curled around a book, their diamonds twinkling and taunting me. Oh, there's another one, look as she absent-mindedly twirls it with her left thumb, the way I once did with my own, this girl who looks too young, all edges, all high-pitched complaints, as she shout-talks to her friend.

For months after The Bomb I would twirl the space where my engagement ring once was with my thumb, minutes passing before I'd realize it wasn't even *there* anymore. It would never be there again. Now it sits in a little box beside my wedding band, both nestled together on soft black cloth. Closed away forever.

I never wanted a ring, you know. I never imagined owning a diamond or wearing one, never looked at them longingly in a shop window. It just wasn't my thing. But once he gave it to me, that beautiful ring he designed himself, I never took it off. Never, not till the bitter end. Not even during my pregnancy, until I was so swollen I had no choice. The Husband used butter to try to get those damn rings off my enormous finger. We killed ourselves laughing, there in the kitchen of the house we had just bought, and teasingly I said, "Couldn't you just have used hand cream like a normal person? Why *butter*?"

"But I love butter!" he said, and we laughed some more.

Once the butter did its magic, I immediately put the wedding rings on a chain I wore around my neck day and night, the platinum and the white gold pressed to my heart as I slept, swishing across my skin while I was at work, something for me to fiddle with while riding the bus home. I didn't take that chain off until after Birdie was born and my fingers went back to normal size. And then I put those rings right back on.

I think about his ring. His wedding band, which he also never took off. I think about the day I bought it for him, how I had it inscribed with my nickname for him: My Rogue. (*I know.*)

I think about him touching her face, her body, while wearing the ring I put on his finger on our wedding day. I think of the cool platinum running along her skin, through her hair. Touching her in places and in ways I don't want to think about, places and ways I used to need booze and sleeping pills to eradicate.

Rings. They're just objects. They're just symbols. We just give them to one another in front of all our friends and family and in front of God, that's all. We say *eternal* and everyone reaches for the Kleenex. But what we mean is *for as long as I can stand it.*

He had my wedding band inscribed with *Me Vision.* That was his nickname for me, the lilt of his Newfoundland brogue, the dialect that replaces "my" with "me." Sometimes he'd call me his demon. Vision, Demon, Vision, Demon. It's hard to say what he meant by these things. I never really knew. Anyway, he had long stopped calling me either of those names by the end. The end I didn't know was the end.

And yes, I called him My Rogue. A strange nickname, I know, and in hindsight is almost like calling him Heartbreaker or Soul Destroyer or Goddamn Liar Cheater. That would be even weirder to put on a wedding ring. But to me, My Rogue was a rascal, with that devilish smirk, that dark stare. He was Han Solo to my Princess Leia.

Fun fact: they were the two figures on top of our wedding cake, in place of the traditional bride and groom.

You know, my wedding band was also my mother's wedding band. I mean, who thinks it's a good idea to use the wedding band of her divorced parents? But I thought our love transcended superstition. The ring was from the sixties, just like my vintage wedding dress, and I loved it, the design on it so different from anything I'd ever seen. So I didn't think it was bad luck. I didn't think an object could hold such currency.

Now I put more weight in objects. Now I'm no dummy.

CHAPTER TWELVE

ADRIFT

October 2012. I'm walking with a tall, smart musician. He's really great and we've been talking non-stop all night. Right now, we're headed to his apartment and as we get closer, I realize something. *Holy shit, we're walking right up to her place.*

Yeah, her.

When I first found out my husband was sleeping with another woman, I became obsessed with finding out everything I could about her. There wasn't a lot to go on, but The Husband had let slip the intersection she lived at, and my journalist-brain knew just what to do. I drove to that intersection. The neighbourhood around it was densely packed with houses, condos, lofts, and apartment buildings. I went to each and every building. I got in and out of the car, over and over again, looking for her name on the front door directories. And then, at an old mattress factory that'd been converted into lofts, I found it. The way it made me feel just to see her name there I can only describe as a cliché — my blood boiled.

I pressed the buzzer. It was March Break, and because she's a teacher, I imagined her to be home, still sleeping, probably lying there beside someone else's husband. I pressed the buzzer again. Honestly, I had no plan. I knew if she said hello, no sound would escape from my mouth. I knew I would do nothing, her voice echoing in the glass doorway. She didn't answer. I got back in the car and bawled my eyes out. I shook and cried the whole drive to work. I wanted to drink so badly.

Now, cut to seven months later and here I am, walking on her street with Tall Smart Musician. *There are tons of places he could live. There's no way it's going to be in her building.* But, oh. Oh yes, it is. It's the biggest city in the country and yet there I am, about to sleep with a man I barely know, right at the scene of the crime. I decide to take it as some kind of a sign and resist the urge to pick up rocks and hurl them at every single window until she sticks her head out. I resist yelling her name at the top of my lungs. Instead, I go inside the apartment of the super-nice, super-smart musician. And when he gives me an orgasm, I make it extra-loud just in case.

Then, I do something I've never done before. It's late and Tall Smart Musician says I should just sleep over. Now, I have a rule with men — no sleepovers, never. But it seems right to break that rule, to sleep overnight in the very building where earlier that same year my husband spent the night, as our daughter and I slept in our beds at home. I want to take the power of that place away. So I do. I sleep with a cat on my head that night, in the bed of an incredibly sweet man who will go on to become a true friend of mine.

When I walk away the next morning, I feel a little lighter. I have no impulse to buzz her door repeatedly, or shout her name, or throw rocks. I light a cigarette and walk. Eventually I hail a cab downtown to my place, change my clothes, freshen up, and go to work. It's Wednesday morning after all.

HOT ACTOR

Friday night, that same week, I'm sitting on a bar stool in a very hipster bar in a very hipster part of the city. A friend of mine is DJing. Another friend is sitting on a barstool beside me, talking to a guy, and I'm trying not to be rude as his friend talks at me, small bits of spittle hitting my face.

The place is packed, but all the men look the same. Same jeans, same haircuts, same beards. I am so bored. *I'm totally not getting laid tonight. What a waste of a Friday.* In five days I will be thirty-eight years old. I hate this bar, I hate these guys, I hate The Husband for throwing me out into this world to make a go of it alone.

And then, the most gorgeous guy in the world walks into the bar. You can almost hear the angel chorus above the hipster din. It looks like the crowd parts for him. I wonder if he's some singer or a model or an actor or something. He comes straight through the crowd and holding my eye edges himself in at the bar right beside me. He orders a drink, then turns his shiny brown eyes back to me and smiles. I smile back and he says, "Well look at that," and points to the tattooed words on my right wrist.

"*Forza e coraggio?* Huh. What's that, like ... strength and courage or something?" and I say, "Wow. Yeah exactly."

Neither of us touches our drinks, we just sit there and talk. About Italians and Jamaicans, about our moms and dads, our brothers and sisters, how we'd both grown up in little run-down towns side by side out by the airport. *Remember this? Remember that?* we keep saying, as if we grew up together, and in some strange way it feels like somehow we did. We talk about our careers, and it turns out he *is* an actor. He's only in town for a few months shooting a film. He's twenty-seven years old and smart and articulate and eloquent and gorgeous. At last call, I say a thing I've never said to a stranger before.

I say, "Do you want to come home with me?" and he says, "Yes I do."

We get into a cab and go to my place. And although he's a total stranger, I feel completely comfortable with him. He smells so good in the cab, I'll still remember it years later. That night is a turning point. The point where I realize, *I don't need dating profiles. I can do this, in real life.* I mean, if I can pick up Hot Actor, then I can meet anyone.

A few sweaty, incredible hours later, as we lie in my bed talking, I realize it's 4:00 a.m. So I say, "Kid, why are you still here? Time for you to go now." But soooo casually, soooo confidently, he says, "Nah, what's going to happen is this. We're going to fall asleep talking, and in the morning, we're going to do all that again, and then we are going to go get some breakfast." He kisses my shoulder, and I say, "Okay, sounds good!" because it sounds *amazing.* And it is.

Over the next several months, Hot Actor comes in and out of my life. He shows up at my birthday, and my friends and colleagues marvel at his hotness (and so he is crowned). We go dancing. We go for food. We hang out in my apartment. We have *fun.* One morning while I get ready for work, he just sits on the edge of my bathtub talking and talking … man, he talks so much. He's goofy and gorgeous and always compliments me, reminding me that even in daylight he still thinks I look twenty-nine. Even if it isn't true, it doesn't matter. It's funny, but I have absolutely no romantic feelings for him. He's like my pal — you know, the kind of pal with a six-pack, who I just happen to have sex with.

I know this sounds fun and exciting and like I'm living the life, but believe me, I would trade all the hot actors for one kinda-handsome husband. I'd give up every six-packed, late-night lover for one loving partner to fall asleep beside while doing a crossword. I have to believe that one day I will have this again. I live on hope.

Somewhere in the long stretch of November of that first year, I'm at a bar watching an old friend of mine, The Singer-Songwriter, perform. He's on stage with his wife, a brash, beautiful, warm-hearted firecracker of a woman. They've been together for more than a decade and here they are tonight, singing songs they've written together. At this moment they're covering a Johnny Cash/June Carter duet and if you could see them now, as we all do from the audience, you would believe in love, too.

They are *that couple*, the kind that ignites creativity in one another, the kind that operates like the most beautifully symbiotic machine. You look at them and you see it — that electrical field that flows between them, and then when they look at you, you feel pulled in, magnetized.

I've come here alone tonight and it feels awkward, sitting by myself in a bar, so I down drink after drink, hoping to feel less like an island, and maybe more like a lake, lapping so gently no one really notices me. Their performance is awesome and heart-crushing at the same time. Meanwhile, Hot Actor is texting me from some theatre party he is at. *See you soon,* he promises. Then an hour later, *Prolly in an hour or so?*

They come off stage and I congratulate them on their beautiful existence. They hug me tight. They're only in town for a few days, then back to their Vancouver Shangri-La. While Singer-Songwriter goes off to talk to other admirers, The Firecracker holds my hand. She says she knows how hard this has all been for me.

I wince, I fight back the geysers. It's a losing battle, again. She launches unexpectedly into her own story, one I didn't know, the story of her before she met my friend, before their magical pairing burst into existence. She was basically married, she tells me, together with the same man for ten years when she found out about his affair. She said it cut her life in two and she thought she'd never recover. She thought they'd be together the rest of their lives and then, poof! I listen, I nod, I am so stupid drunk and I wish I wasn't because I can't handle this story, I don't want this awesome woman to have ever felt what I've felt.

"But then I met the handsome singer-songwriter!" she continues, "and he was so into me, and I couldn't believe it was true, he was so talented, this handsome young thing. But what happened was that he was perfect for me. And I was perfect for him. We found each other when I didn't think such a thing was possible."

She smiles at me, her eyes two kind pools she entreats me to just go ahead and jump into. I cry. I cry and cry and cry there in the bar like the dumbest drunk girl in the world. She tells me her point is that the man she thought she'd be with the rest of her life wasn't the one. The one came after. Some people hit it on the first try, she is trying to tell me, but some of us just don't.

I hear her. I hear what she's saying. I want it to be true for me, too, holy shit. I've already figured out by now that The Husband was not the one for me. I already *get* that. But the string of boys that have come after, and my fear of letting anyone really in, has led me to believe that this *will* be it for me. This lonely me, getting grammatically indecipherable texts from young actors, this was it, prolly forever.

Her swimming-pools-for-eyes tell me not to give up hope. To still believe in love. So I hug her tight. I do still believe in love, and I won't give up. I know that, intellectually, but I'm not emotionally there yet. My heart is still slowly corroding, the wound in my side still too fresh. And my phone is beeping. Hot Actor, all twenty-seven-years-old-and-six-pack of him is texting me with excuses again.

When I get home I fall hard onto my bed — shoes, coat, and all — and try to read his text. *Still wanna see you, doe* … I see through spinning, blurry eyes … *but this party, you know, I gotta stay a bit more. I'll leave soon as I can.* I close my eyes to stop the spinning. It is midnight on a Tuesday, I have to work tomorrow, I have responsibilities, and what am I doing? When did I become this ridiculous mess? I fall asleep like that, in my dress and heels with my phone in my hand. I wake up at 6:00 a.m. and immediately check my phone. He never did text again, he never did show up. I don't even care, I realize. I only wanted him to come over so that I could fall asleep, but the booze and heartache had done the trick.

For months I think about The Singer-Songwriter and The Firecracker and what she said to me that night after the show. I think about it still. I cling to the hope, the belief in love. I have to. I have to.

At the end of December, Hot Actor's film shoot wraps and it's time for him to leave the city. We make one last plan to get together, on a snowy afternoon at the dead end of the year. He comes over and is his usual positive self, checking out the globe and magnifying glass Birdie asked Santa for, talking about his family and the presents he got, asking me how my first Christmas without my husband went, and then kissing me softly while leading me to my bed.

Our goodbyes are sweet but unsentimental. It's just "see ya," and then one deep long kiss and he's out the door. That's the end of that. I never see him again.

When He's Here

When he's here with me, I feel calm. There are no waves, the sea is as flat as a table, the sun warm on my skin. His scent in the room, I would bottle it. The way he fills the space like he was part of the original blueprints. Like he's always been here, just one of the many treasures I've accumulated over the years. My apartment like a curio shop, filled with objects that each have their own story to tell— seashells, rocks, coins. My grandfather's camera, my first guitar, framed postcards. The Man with the White Shirt, eyes blazing.

When he's here I can breathe out. I can throw out my line and there's actually something to catch it, something to be tethered to, strong and real. I'm not lost or seasick anymore. I'm docked for the night in the world's best port town. I'm the happiest tourist, it'll be the trip I talk about for years.

When he's here — here — in my bed, I feel so much I forget it wasn't that long ago that I did everything I could *not* to feel anything. When The Man with the White Shirt is here, I'm awake. I watch him sleep, tracing his dark eyebrows with my finger, then traversing the ridge of his nose, my God have I ever loved a nose? Not till now.

When he's here, everything is poetry to me.

PG24

An easy nickname, just his initials and age. Although I never tell anyone about him, and I never see him again, so a nickname is useless in this case. Still, this is how I think of him in my head, a little magical secret, a mirage. You can't get more impossibly young than twenty-four. I mean, *honestly*. But here he is, hanging on my every word. He is adorable and funny and smart and we have a lot of tequilas. It is almost Christmas.

Someone buys a round of shots, and down they go. He introduces himself. There's another round. We talk about music, and it's so easy to impress him. He works in a record store and thinks he knows everything about music, but I best him more than once.

My knowledge of Springsteen albums — of all things — is the clincher. But I keep walking away from him.

I'm in a fog of booze and this strange internal cocktail of high-confidence and low self-esteem. I'm amazing, I'm pathetic. I feel real and invisible all at once. The world is underwater with a reggae soundtrack. I'm trying to dance with uninterested men my own age, but PG24 is beside me again, asking why I keep running away. I give in to the underwater world, the tequila in my heart. We leave the bar.

"Let's go to your place," he says.

"We can't. I have a kid there tonight. And my mom's with her."

He looks surprised. And then says sheepishly, "Well, we'll go to mine, but … it's … it's not very nice, it's kind of a mess." I laugh and he takes my arm in his. We talk and walk, the December air strangely warm, no snow on the ground. And then we turn onto his street. *Oh my God.* It's the very street that I lived on when *I* was his age. Only three doors up from where I lived, with my boyfriend The Musician, fourteen years earlier. The universe is indeed mysterious.

Holy Lord, I'm drunk. How is this even a thing that is happening right now? My new life still astounds me. We walk in the door and a group of guys are in the living room packing up instruments. I feel like I will die from embarrassment. Surely in the bright lights of the house they can see I'm a hideous old lady. Surely they can see that their friend made a drunken mistake in a dark bar. But they're friendly and he's excited to introduce me. I'm mortified but try to play it cool. They're in a band I know really well, I love their second album, but I don't tell them that. I can't believe I'm in their house.

PG24 takes my hand and we climb up staircase after staircase, to the attic room at the top of the old house. His room is like a dream, like I'm floating in my own youth, like I've gone into a wayback machine, transported to my twenties. The unmade bed, the Christmas lights strung haphazardly across the ceiling, the milk crates for furniture, the David Bowie and Smashing Pumpkins posters on the wall. I'm in heaven.

Like so many of The Babies, PG24 did not disappoint. At 4:30 a.m., I say I have to go. He watches as I put all my clothes on. I tell him I had fun, that I'll never see him again. "How do you know? What if *I* want to see you again?" he says, but I shrug at the suggestion. He's served his purpose. He helped me make it through another night. Now he'll be a memory of a time where for a few hours I forgot I was a grown up, with all its attendant responsibilities and heartache.

I like to remember the two of us sitting on the beat up old couch on his front porch waiting for the taxi to come and take me back to my regular life. How he lit me a cigarette. And kept looking at me, kept smiling, kept his arm around me like I was his new girlfriend as we argued about which Springsteen album was the best. (*Darkness on the Edge of Town*, obviously.) How he kissed me long and hard while holding my hands on that porch. When the cab arrived. I ran down the path shouting "See ya, PG," saying his full name like one name, as I had done the whole night.

"Goodbye, Beautiful Dream!" he called back. As the cab pulled away, my head swam from the tequila, lack of sleep, and the general giddiness from the experience I just had. I rested my head on the seat, smiled and closed my eyes for a bit, arriving home at 5:00 a.m. At seven thirty, my daughter and my mom were both awake, crashing around in the kitchen. I woke up, too, and went on with my thirty-eight-year-old life.

THE BAD ONES

I'm not telling you about The Bad Ones. Or even about how sometimes the good ones can be bad. In this story, I'm only telling you about the sweet and memorable ones. The good-in-bed ones. The ones that didn't hurt me. Or scare me.

I wrote almost all of this story as it was happening. In the time before the Me Too Movement. This is important. In that less-woke time of only a few years ago, I was like a lot of women. I didn't report the bad things that happened to me on dates. Or at work. Or in life in general, starting way back when I was a little girl. It was just a normal part of life. A thing to get around or get past. A thing about being a woman in the world. Just status quo.

So in the time after The Bomb, the time I'm telling you about, where I meet handsome young men and have wonderful and wild experiences … some of those experiences were not wonderful. They were not all easy. I didn't write about The Bad Ones in my notebooks, where I always write everything. It's like I erased each one the minute it was over and I was back on safe ground. Sometimes, I didn't walk away from The Bad Ones. There are a million articles you can read now about why so many of us do that. And still, even now, some of you wonder: Why don't women say anything? Why don't women just walk away when things are clearly getting bad? Why do women sit through a bad experience, and then text the guy "Thanks for the date" even after they were treated terribly?

I'll tell you why. I just figured there was no point. Or that it was my fault for going on a date in the first place. Or for being drunk in the first place. Or for being single. For being a woman who likes having sex. For being a woman with low self-esteem. For being a woman whose husband had an affair and now here I was in some messed up situation with some messed up guy I just met, and *Phew, good thing I fought him and got out of it.*

But report it? Why would I report it? Talk about it? What would I say? That I drank a lot and went to the home of a man I barely knew and then halfway through he got crazy and not in a good way? That he was one of the smartest, most interesting men I'd met after my marriage ended, but he was also the one who held me down with his arm across my neck. He wouldn't stop, no matter how many times I yelled at him to get off me. It was like he was in a trance. He was a big man and I knew I'd be no match but eventually I said, so quietly in his ear, "I will fight you." That worked, I don't know why. But did I report it? No. Did I write it down? No. But I remember.

I remember that for some reason I sat there on his bed and talked with him for another half hour, about religion, soccer, true love, and the concept of forever. And then he walked me home and kissed me goodnight and this all seemed perfectly normal to me somehow. This all seemed to be just part of dating. This is what it is to be a woman who goes on dates. This is what it is to be a woman who enjoys sex, and wants sex, but doesn't have the safety of one committed partner.

When this story took place, I was resigned to a sad truth that to be a single, sexually active woman meant sometimes things are great, and then here and there things get really bad. And those times, I'd just suck it up and keep living and keep on dating and keep waiting for a unicorn to come along and be my boyfriend so I wouldn't have to roll the dice anymore. So I wouldn't have to take the chance that a handsome, smart, awesome guy I've been getting to know might hold his arm across my neck and say, "Not yet," every time I yell at him to get off me.

There are so many stories like that I could tell you, but so could we all. Each one of us has a lifetime of stories. A lifetime of being chipped away at, and then if we speak up, being told not to be so serious or that we "can't take a joke." If we speak up, then we have to sit and listen as our own experiences are explained back to us, handed over like corrected proofs. So we stay quiet. And then we're told we're complicit, it's our fault really.

The best thing we can do now is listen. Listen to the actual lived experience of women when they do try to say something about it.

Listen. Just fucking shut up and *listen*.

ORPHAN CHRISTMAS

The girl with the blue dreadlocks is intent on telling me she totally gets me. I don't know what she gets because I haven't even said a word. She's sitting beside me on a long bench, our backs up against a wall in a little dive bar in Kensington Market where everyone's wearing black and covered in tattoos and drinking a *lot* and the music is punk and loud and I don't really know anyone at all.

It's Christmas Day 2012.

What I haven't said at all to The Girl with the Blue Dreadlocks is that this is possibly the most surreal experience of my life. That to be *here*, on *Christmas*, is about as far from who I thought I was or where I thought I would ever be. For the past eleven years I've spent Christmas Day with my husband and his family, the last five of those with our daughter. That she's not with me now is something Blue Dreads cannot possibly understand.

That I'm not with my own little girl on Christmas Day makes about as much sense as me being here in this bar on Christmas Day.

But as if she *does* understand all these things I'm not saying to her, Blue Dreads puts her hand on my arm and just holds it there. She smiles at me with a quiet kindness. I look at her face and for a second I think she looks just like Birdie, if Birdie were a twenty-year-old girl with blue hair and a nose ring.

I turn my back to the overwhelming room and look outside. The snow is falling so hard that footsteps disappear in minutes. It's like a deep blanket and I briefly wonder what it would feel like to just go out and lie in it.

I contemplate how the fuck my life could change so much in one year. Blue Dreads still has her hand on my arm and she's saying something but who knows what. The music is so loud and I'm lying in a snow drift anyway.

CHAPTER THIRTEEN

VESPERS

FOOD

Birdie is telling me a story, chatty-chatty-chatty excitable. Something they made at school, artwork? I'm only half-listening as I scramble to make dinner out of whatever's in the fridge. She's five, and in Senior Kindergarten at a new school in this new neighbourhood in our new life.

And then she's holding it in front of me, a drawing of two buildings. Under it, in her signature mix of upper- and lowercase handwriting, it says:

I HAve two Homes. Thay ARe across the stret from EACHotheR. I like that we leve ACRoss the street FROM EACHotheR.

The homework was "Draw and write about your home." My homework is to not cry, to not burn this crap dinner I'm trying to cook, to not fall apart, to not fall down the well. My homework is to smile and say to her, "That's so great, Birdie!" To kiss her and give her a squeeze. To take a photo of her drawing and post it on Instagram with *#modernfamily* and *#coparenting* and *#totallyworthit* because in making it public it becomes more true. But in the darkness at the very core of me, where I'm holding everything together to make her this pasta and not cry, I really want to write *#shewassupposedtohaveonehome* and *#weshouldhavebeenworthit*.

We should have been worth it. *#thanksalotyoufuckingasshole*.

Instead, I make the pasta. I hold in the tears and the anger and the blinding, corrosive feeling of failure and I just make the pasta. I make it. I just make it.

This hang-up about food, this struggle to make dinner … in my new life, anything to do with food, I just can't get right. I can never figure out the amount of groceries to buy or how much food to make. Vegetables are always going bad in the fridge. I either run out of milk for Birdie or end up throwing out half the carton. And then there's eating alone. Food doesn't taste good when it's just me. I can't enjoy it. But after hearing enough friends go on and on about how they *love* to go to cafés and restaurants on their own, I make a plan to have brunch. By myself. In a restaurant.

On a Sunday morning I go to the diner at the bottom of the big hotel that's right between The Ex-husband's condo and mine. I say "Table for one" and feel like barfing. I sit at the tiny table and pull out a book but I can't read and I can barely eat. I can't taste anything but sharp shards of envy, as I watch groups of people laugh together over their meals. It is the longest hour of my life, maybe.

I never bothered to try again. There's just no point. Eating is social to me, food is for sharing. That was how I grew up, with life centred around what we were going to eat and how we were going to cook it and making it and eating it and talking about it while eating it. So eating alone is hard, okay? And it's a real problem I still struggle with.

Eating a meal with people you love is the most important part of Italian life. It's basically a sacrament! Everything important happens at the table. It's where you talk about your crappy day at school or work. Where you laugh at each other's stories — or just at each other — all while eating the lasagna you made together. It's where you talk politics and end up getting into an argument. Where one person cries and someone else defends them while putting the espresso on, and another person says sorry.

The table is where you make up. Where you pledge to do better while you eat rum cake for dessert. It's where you hear news of a new baby in the family, and where you hear about someone's death. It's where you bring your first love to meet your family, and scare the shit out of them because the meal lasts hours and hours, we never leave the table. We eat and talk and laugh and shout for *hours*. It's the best. How can you expect me to eat alone after forty years of eating like *that*?

DANCING

We loved dancing together. I fell in love with him on the dance floor, you know. Back in 1999, when The Ex-husband was just The Scientist. Each week we'd all go to The Dance Cave, which is exactly what it sounds like. My boyfriend at the time, The Musician, was the one that introduced me to the place, and I ended up spending most of my twenties there. When I watched The Scientist dance, I felt electrified. He danced, I danced. I would watch him and he would watch me.

Later, when we were a couple, we danced together all the time, and when we did it was pure joy I'd see on his face. He did crazy, hilarious dance moves and I'd be soooo embarrassed but also I could not stop laughing. I loved his crazy dancing. We had these moves we'd do together, these routines we'd bust out whenever we happened to be at an Italian wedding. Which, with a family as big as mine, was always.

My cousins adored him, they loved that this big tall WASPy guy had no shame and would tear up the dance floor. Sometimes, when we'd lock eyes and get into one of our silly routines, the dance floor would part and everyone would make a little circle around us. I would be so uncomfortable with everyone looking at us, but he was so into it, it was infectious.

My favourite part of these wedding receptions was when the old Italian waltzes would come on, all warbly accordions, and the old people would come out on the floor and partner-dance so beautifully. The Husband would always grab my mom, or one of my aunts, and pull them onto the dance floor with him. He didn't have a clue how to tarantella, but damned if he didn't try. He'd whip the older women around the floor and they would have huge smiles on their faces, even though he was terrible at it.

I'd watch him and my heart would swell a thousand sizes, especially listening to my cousins shout, "He's the *best*, you married the *best!*" I thought so, too. I really did. So is it any wonder their hearts broke when they heard what he did? Like all of our friends and family, they felt betrayed, too. It was like the day you realized the mall Santa was just a drunk old guy wearing a fake beard. No one in my family could *believe* he wasn't that guy on the dance floor, that guy who made my face light up.

But hang on, I was talking about dancing.

Everywhere we lived together, we danced. In the tiny basement apartment we shared the year before we got married, he'd grab my arm and slow dance me to whatever song we were listening to as we cooked dinner, his head grazing the low ceiling. In the first condo we bought together after we married, we got a new stereo and there we danced to OutKast and Justin Timberlake CDs in the big open-concept loft, like we were the only two people at a club. Each Christmas when we decorated the tree, we'd listen to the Boney M Christmas Album and Elvis' Christmas and even to those cheesy old recordings we would have at least one dance. Several times a year in the condo, we'd have these huge parties with forty or fifty people from his world and mine all mingling — work colleagues, people from my soccer team, old school friends, cousins, and siblings — all dancing to mix CDs I'd make. At 4:00 a.m., once everyone was gone, we'd clean up the bottles and the glasses, just the two of us, and then, dancing slowly in the kitchen, we'd talk about the night, our bodies pressed close, tired.

In the house we bought when I was pregnant, there were suddenly so many different rooms to dance in. If I think hard enough, we probably did have at least one dance in every room of that house. But the place we danced most was the kitchen. When Birdie was born she became part of our "dance parties," her face beaming as we twirled her across the floor, or as she watched us slow dance. Once we danced to "Rock Lobster," falling on the ground each time they sang "down, down, down ..." just like when we were teenagers. God, I loved that night — her laughter, his smile at me as we lay on the kitchen floor. I can still see his face. I can see his expression exactly as it was. That was love. Even if it's hard to imagine now.

Somewhere about a year into our separation, he complained to me that none of the women he was meeting liked dancing. He wished someone would dance with him, the way we once did, and he wondered if I had any suggestions for where he should go.

Like, are you fucking kidding me?

REVIVAL

February 2013. One year exactly from when The Bomb first dropped. I'm out with three of my favourite girlfriends and trying really hard not to feel The Lonely, that monster that sits in the pit of my gut whether I'm alone or not. The Lonely is such a bastard. It never lets its claws out of me.

We're out dancing in a bar called Revival, drinking tequila like water. I see a super-hot guy standing with a group of people and something about him makes me want to get closer to him. I'm walking toward Super Hot Guy, trying to catch his eye, when a different man steps in front of me. He says "Hey" with a nod of his head, so casually, so effortlessly, like he's been waiting there for me the whole night.

This guy is cool and cute and dressed really, really great. There's an immediate click between us, and I forget all about the original guy I was walking toward. We just start dancing and talking. At first we try to guess each other's ages, and though he's convinced I'm younger than him I know he will be wrong, I know I will be older, I'm always older. It turns out I'm right, but he is on this side of thirty, so that's something.

Then I make a game of trying to guess his astrological sign. I guess right on the first try (Taurus), and he laughs, saying, "All right smarty, guess the exact day then," and just because I think the universe is always up to something, I say The Ex-husband's birthday. And again, I'm right. They have the exact same birthday. *Yeah.*

We dance some more and then he says, "So when's our first date?" Like he likes me for real, not just for a hook-up. So I do what I've never done up until now — *all these firsts* — I tell him I have a kid. "How about Monday night?" I say, "Because my daughter will be with her dad that night." I hold my breath, sure this will scare him off, or he'll lie and say it's cool but then totally ghost me. Instead he says, "Great, Monday!" and then, "How old is your daughter? I have a son!" And he takes out his phone and shows me photos of a beautiful baby boy. His son is an infant still, and this puts me on guard, obviously. So I ask if he's married, and what's the deal with asking me on a date when he has a nine-month-old?

He tells me his son's mother is one of his best friends, a woman he sleeps with casually but they've never dated or ever even been a couple, and they are not, and have never been, in love. He says when she got pregnant she wanted to keep the baby because she was nearing forty and nowhere near finding a boyfriend to make that happen. He says he always wanted to be a dad, and maybe not this way or before he was thirty-five, but since this was the way, this was the way. He stopped working at a small music studio and got a job at a major bank to support them.

"That's what I'm doing now," he says. "I'm not married, I'm not in a relationship. I'm a dad and she is my son's mother."

I believe him. And I really like him. He seems so effortless and genuine and just ... a *guy*, a down-to-earth regular sweet guy. We continue to dance and laugh until 2:00 a.m. when my girlfriends and I all leave. He texts me ten minutes later to say he can't wait till Monday, when we will be less drunk and can really get to know each other. And that's what we do.

Three weeks later. Revival is standing in my kitchen, cooking. I just stand there dumbly, staring at his shoulders, his neck, the way the muscles in his arms tense as he grabs a knife, or reaches for a pan. *I can't believe there's a man in my kitchen, and he's cooking me dinner.*

This man is a sweet, real man. He's also the first man I've actually dated in the true sense of the word. For our second date we went to see a movie, and he had his arm around me the whole time. As the opening credits rolled, he leaned in close and whispered, "If this movie sucks then you better be ready for my hands to be all over you." I giggled like a teenager. It felt so good to be in a movie theatre with the arm of a cool, good-looking man around me and the laughing and the popcorn and the regular-people things. It felt so good after such a long stretch of getting drunk, meeting men, getting drunker, then having drunk sex. This felt different. It felt normal.

And now here he is, in my kitchen, cooking up jerk salmon with spinach. I hate salmon. But not tonight. The only other man who's cooked anything in this kitchen is my father, so tonight I am on a Cloud 9 of epic proportions. I will eat salmon on this cloud, obviously!

Also, I am wearing "the dress." The dress is the dress that for whatever reason renders them all dumb. It's my best dress for man-killing. He looks over at me, his hands dirty from food prep, his brow slightly beaded with sweat. "Damn, how am I supposed to cook with you looking like *that*?"

It's so unreal this way he has about him, this thing where he tells me every chance he gets that I am fucking awesome to behold. Remember, my self-esteem has been depleted to a big fat zero thanks to The Ex-husband, and I'm only slowly building it back. So in this kitchen, one year after The Bomb, with my self-esteem hovering at only 30 percent, yes, I am wearing "the dress" to get exactly this reaction. And yes, I'm wearing high heels in my own apartment. So what. It's distracting the hell out of him.

I feed him bits of crackers and cheese as he works. He kisses my fingers with each bite. We just met but this feels like heaven to me, two people in a kitchen making dinner. I snap a photo of him as he cooks. I feel like this might never happen again, this thing where a sweet, good-looking man cooks for me in my kitchen, so I need photographic evidence. It's just his back in the photo, you can't see his face, just the gorgeous place I like to rest my head, there between his neck and his shoulder blade, just his waist, his arms, all the places I love in this world because they are a man's body. A man's body doing regular things like reaching for the pepper grinder, or trying to figure out how to work the timer on my oven.

Once he figures out the timer, he puts the salmon in and turns, grabs me up into his arms, and says, "I don't even care if we eat that anymore." I swoon, literally, and then we do it right there in the kitchen, and it is so beyond all the other guys put together. It will stay that way, actually. More than a year later, we will find ourselves still talking about it, that's how large and mythical it is. "I always think about that time in the kitchen," he says in my bed one night, and I say, "So do I."

But back to February, and the salmon in the oven. After the magic goes down, we put all our clothes back on, smoke half a joint on the balcony, and sit down to dinner. "You have such nice things!" he says about the table setting, and I say, "Of course, I was married, remember?" and we laugh. My things *are* nice — crystal wine glasses, silverware, classic white china edged in platinum — all wedding gifts, all the "good stuff," as The Husband and I used to call it, as opposed to our "everyday" cutlery and plates. Now in my new life, I use the good stuff every day. Why the fuck not. One year exactly from the end of my marriage that I didn't know was ending, I'm sitting in my own home with this sweet man eating a dinner he made me, on the wedding china.

The next day I brag to two of my friends, Big Laugh and The Bright One, about how that was the greatest night I have experienced since The Bomb. We're having lunch at work, and I can't talk about anything else. I describe the dinner, and then the sex with waaaay too much detail, but they are good sports. They were at Revival (the club) the night I met Revival (the man) and they approve, but they're wary of how quickly I'm getting carried away.

They are right to be.

ADVICE FROM AN EX-HUSBAND

I have a little black book. Well actually, it's red, a little red note-book that I began writing everything in after The Bomb. I have hundreds of notebooks, I write everywhere, all the time, every-thing, but I also write lists. Lots of lists. So the list called "black book" inside my little red book should be no surprise to anyone. It's a list of all the men I've slept with since The Husband and I broke up. Like I said, before that, I could count the number of men on one hand, and now … well I'm not going to say, but it's definitely more than that. Significantly.

The list is in order of appearance. It has their first and last names and the date(s) we slept together. There's a star rating system — some have no stars (lousy, or just whatever), there are a few with one or two stars, and the best of the best have four stars (Way to go, Cute/Crazy Guy! Nice job, PG24!). There's also a symbol system only I can decipher that indicates whether we went all the way or just fooled around. I *know*, so high school of me … that is, if I had slept around in high school or even university, which I certainly did not.

Now you think I'm creepy, maybe even crazy. But I'm a record keeper, and always have been. I've written in a journal since I was eight. I used to keep detailed lists where I ranked my favourite songs, my favourite members of Duran Duran, the boys in my class from cutest to ugliest, then from nicest to meanest. There were lists ranking the concerts I'd been to, my favourite bands, my best friends, the teachers I hated. Even at a young age, I liked order, inventory. I guess it's my way of making sense of this crazy world. If that makes me crazy, so be it.

In addition to my "black book" list, the red book also has a list that's just about The Ex-husband. It details every single time we've slept together since we moved into separate apartments. There's the date, followed by the location, followed by a short description of the action and our state of mind.

June 20 — my place — after tense phone call, he comes over. No alcohol.

Sept 18 — my place — he stays for hours and hours after, lying around and talking in my bed. He kisses the top of my head and says "I love you" when he leaves.

Jan 26 — his place — middle of the day for a whole two hours while Birdie is at a birthday party.

There are a lot of entries. In fact, according to this list, for the first six months after we moved into separate places, we were sleeping together three times a week. That's more than some married couples, I know. But somewhere in the second year of separation, things started to change.

March 11 — his place — me despondent, go over in moment of weakness. Feels like nothing. Big, awful fight afterward. He is terrible to me.

After that night, I swore it would never happen again. I felt oddly at peace with it. Every time I saw him after that, he seemed more remote. More of a stranger. The longer I went without feeling his familiar body next to mine, the easier it was to defamiliarize myself with his heart, too. Over time, all that was left was a residual hurt. A precise but dull pain. A dent that was never fixed properly and just rusted over, corrosive and exposed to anyone else I tried to love.

"You shouldn't be too good in bed, you know," The Ex-husband says on that terrible night, the one I swore would be the last. We're in his apartment, lying in his bed, post-sex, Birdie asleep in her room.

"Guys won't like that," he continues. "You really shouldn't be this good the first time you're with them." And there it is. Dating advice from my ex-husband. *Is this how it is then? Honestly, is this what I want?* I feel like throwing up. There's suddenly no reason at all I should be lying there naked beside him. I don't want advice about sex from my own husband! *Ex*-husband! Especially ridiculous advice. I get up and put my clothes on and practically sprint across the street to my own bed.

But oh, I would be lying if I said it didn't scorch my heart from the inside out. If I said that stupid sentence hasn't haunted me since. *Is it true? Am I supposed to just lie there or something? Not say what I like, what I want? Will that make a man like me more?* The fact that I've seriously asked myself these questions means he still has an idiotic power over me. So that's why this time has to be the last time.

VANISHING

Revival is sitting across from me. I haven't seen him in over a month. Not since the epic night of the salmon and the sex and the swirly excitement of a man cooking in my kitchen. It was a slow fade. He'd text, but could never make plans and his reasons were vague. But now, he wants to explain why he vanished after that amazing night.

So here we are, staring across the table from one another in a noisy bar. He has a Manhattan and I have a Sidecar. We drink them pretty quickly. Revival says he thinks about me all the time and still wants to see me, but too much is going on in his life.

I nod. He says he bought a house for his son and his son's mother to live in and that's why he disappeared for the past month.

I blink. "Are *you* moving in, too?" And he says he doesn't know, he doesn't know. All he knows is he wants to see his son more, he needs to see him more, he doesn't know what else to do. There's a sinking feeling in me, but something else, too … relief? In the month since our last amazing night together, I had time to consider what this thing with Revival was, or wasn't. His disappearing act hurt my feelings at first, but not as much as you'd expect. Not as much as *I'd* expect.

Revival was my first real dating experience since The Bomb. My first brush with "normal" courtship — movies and dinners and an incredible sexual chemistry. But beyond that, there actually wasn't much else. We didn't have all that much to talk about. He wasn't the total package. And so as he explains his complicated situation to me in this bar, I realize I don't need him to be my boyfriend. I just want to see him from time to time, just have him come to my bed and make me feel the way he does. That's it. I tell him so. And that becomes our MO after that.

He comes and goes, I never know when, and I never ask questions. We stop the real dating, no more movies or dinners, our meetings always at my place where I answer the door barely clothed and we only bother with a few minutes of small talk before falling into hours of incredible sex all over my apartment. In this way, he is my favourite. My favourite lover. That's a thing now, in this life I still don't recognize and never could have imagined or wanted. I was once a wife who was loved. Now I have a favourite lover.

I ask no questions about Revival's situation. The situation with the son and the son's mother and the house and the does-he-or-doesn't-he-live-there. I don't ask him about anything. He doesn't ask me. I see other guys. More ones-and-dones because no one is right. Because I'm not right.

Winter turns into spring. I start to feel more conflicted about Revival's situation. Morally it feels indefensible — what if his son's mother is more than he is letting on? What if they really *are* a couple? That would make me the mistress, a thing that aside from just being plain ironic, also makes me hate myself, makes me a hypocrite. I decide to stop seeing him, no matter how comfortable he is, no matter how easy and amazing it is when he's in my bed.

I make a final push to stop the incessant drinking and hooking up with men. I'm actually tired of it — the small talk, the awkward first meeting and the more often than not awkward first fumbling in the dark. I'm tired of having sex with people I don't know, and in many cases don't even like that much. Now, I want to find a real boyfriend. So I try to go on real dates with men my own age, dates where no sex is involved. But finding a real someone isn't as easy as landing a superficial hook-up. There's a lot more rejection and disappointment this way, and it's trying. The small talk can be excruciating, the way they don't laugh at my jokes, or the way I don't get theirs. The times I think the date was awesome but then I never hear from them again. The times they are fun and sweet and nice and into me but of course I am not the least bit attracted to them. All spring, I go on what feels like a hundred first dates, and never a second date. They are all just wrong.

Here's what I've learned about dating — it feels like an unending audition. And you never fucking get the part, nope, you're always just *this close*. But I want to get the part. I want someone to wrap their arms around me when I've had a tough day. I want to have someone trace my face with their finger, to look me in the eyes and tell me they think I'm a beautiful, walking bonfire. I want to walk down the street holding hands with someone. I want to drive my car with the windows down while he picks our favourite songs off my iPod. (Yes, I still have an iPod.)

I want someone whose neck I can kiss after I pick a fluff off his sweater. I want to iron his shirts and give him a hundred orgasms. I want to look up from a book I'm reading and find his eyes looking at me, eyes that smile even before his mouth does, and when it does, that smile is the thing I live for. If I exist, he must exist too. Cross your fingers for me.

CHAPTER FOURTEEN

THE LONELY

What Lonely Feels Like

Loneliness is every cliché imaginable.

It's me, adrift on an ocean, unmoored, nothing to be anchored to, no land for miles.

It's me, standing at the bottom of a well,
a canyon,
a crater,
nothing but vultures circling overhead, waiting for me to just give up and die already.

It's me, waiting. But I don't even know what I'm waiting for.

It's me, except my humour, warmth, and self-esteem have been siphoned out, replaced by a wispy, petulant yearning that everyone can spot from a distance and smell up close.

Loneliness seeps out of my pores.
It floats around me like a cloud no matter how I try to be normal,
to be nonchalant, to be a person that's okay with being alone.

Lonely is a parasite that invaded my body and now I'm host to it.
I serve it hors d'oeuvres and champagne.

Lonely is here with me in the bar, getting round after round so I
can forget why I'm here in the first place.

It drunk-texts people who really wish I would stop doing that.

It flags down a cab for me and … whoever this guy is beside me.

Lonely wakes me up in the morning and says hello first thing,
so I know it's still there with me.

It squeezes my hand when I drop Birdie off at school knowing I
won't see her again for

six

whole

days.

Lonely gets my sunglasses out for me so the other parents won't
see me crying again as I exit the school.

Lonely is the most consistent thing in my life now, the only constant. It's always there for me when I don't need it.

Loneliness is my new boyfriend, I guess.

We walk arm in arm through the city streets.

SOLO TIME

One of my good friends is the exact opposite. She's always saying, "I *love* my solo time!" She just loves being in her apartment,
absent of anyone.

I don't get it. "What do you *do* there?" I ask her, and she says,
"I make tea, I take baths, I watch movies, I bake cupcakes ..." I
call her an old lady but envy winds its way through me. I want
so badly to feel happy on my own with baking and baths, but I
can't. Why bake cupcakes if Birdie isn't there? Why have a bath if
not with a lover? I've never even watched a movie on my own.
Ever. In all my life. What's the point if there's no one to share
these things with?

"You'll love it one day, too," says Solo Time. She's right. I
won't feel this way forever. There will come a time, years from
now, when I do learn to love being alone in my apartment.
Sometimes. But right now, in this part of my story, all I can do
is plan every moment of my life, fill every blank square in my
calendar with something. Someone.

Solo Time tells me to just do what I need to do. She doesn't
judge me, or tell me to change. She makes me tea and listens to
my cringey dating stories and responds with her own stories of
blissful Saturday nights enjoying her own company. She's very
upbeat. It's part of her charm, this enthusiastic pep. Independent
and assured, Solo Time is both young and old at once, perfectly
happy with the life she's built for herself. She doesn't cry, ever,
and jokes that she "has no emotions" but it isn't true. She sees
how hard this is for me.

She tells me how brave she thinks I am for choosing joint
custody. "So brave. Because you lose her half the time."

Leaving me alone. Really alone. While two-thirds of my little
family live across the street. Far away, so close, as I navigate my
own solo time.

DIVORCE OFFICE

We're standing outside a door that says, I shit you not, *Divorce Office*. It's June 2013. And as you may have guessed, we're here to sign away the end of our marriage. But the Divorce Office is locked.

The Ex-husband has made me drive us here to the northern edge of Toronto to sign the papers with some dial-a-lawyer he's found on the internet. He didn't bother to call ahead to tell her we were coming, so Dial-a-Lawyer is not here. We stand in a beige hallway staring at the door while he frantically phones and emails her.

Beside the words *Divorce Office* there is a graphic of two silhouettes — a man and a woman with their backs to one another. We find this insanely funny, and try to take a photo of ourselves with our backs to one another. I text a friend, *Can you believe it? Divorce Office!* and he replies, *If that was in a screenplay, it would have been sent back with the note, "Too on the nose. Think of something less obvious."*

I repeat this to The Ex-husband and we laugh. But the levity doesn't last. We start talking about the end of our marriage and it isn't long before I'm saying, "How could you do this?" like a broken record. I go outside and stare at the wasteland of the industrial park we're in. *Why am I even here? At the Divorce Office! How is any of this real?*

Dial-a-Lawyer *finally* shows up. We sign the affidavit and a cheque for two hundred dollars. The Ex-husband is so breezy, making jokes. He checks his phone at least three times. *Is he seriously texting some woman while we're signing our divorce?*

We get back into my car and I burst into tears. He sits in the passenger seat and waits silently for me to stop. Then I drive us back downtown, so we can both go to work. Outside of the massive old school he teaches at, we sit. I stare at the building where they both worked, and wonder if they ever had sex in there some-where, in some long-forgotten hallway, or in one of the offices on the fourth floor. This is how I think. This is how I get.

"Okay, please get out of my car now," I say and he replies, "No. You're upset. I wasn't there for you before when you needed me, and I'm going to be here for you now. I'm not going to desert you anymore, I want to help you." My grip on the steering wheel would win me a strongman competition. I say, "Honestly? What would help is if you just got out of my car."

He sits there. More silence. And then he makes a little joke and I laugh. We hug. "You're so stupid but cute." My hand in his hair. Then he says, "Oh, I meant to ask you — do you want to have any more kids?" Just like that, as if he's asking me if I want to go get some pizza.

"Uh ... I don't think so. But even if I did, what's it to you?"

"Well, I meant do you want to have any more kids with *me*?" My head — literally —explodes. Yours did, too, just now, didn't it? Do I want to have another baby. With *him*.

"Are you fucking SERIOUS?" Because, really, is he fucking serious? "WHY WOULD I DO THAT? WE JUST SIGNED OUR DIVORCE AN HOUR AGO."

He is really fucking serious. He says, "It's just that I'm think-ing of getting a vasectomy. But before I do, I just want to be sure with you, because you're the only person I would want to have a baby with, so if you did ..."

He wants to kill me. He won't stop until he kills me. He can't help himself. It's like he can't help himself. I cry and cry. "That's all I am to you, a baby-making machine?"

"No! No!" he says and I can see the desperation on his face. *This day will kill me. This man will kill me.* I suddenly feel profoundly sad for whatever poor woman comes after me. I say, "Why would you get a vasectomy anyway? You're only forty! What if you fall in love again and that woman has never had a baby and she wants a baby and can't have a baby because you're a stupid idiot who got a vasectomy when he was *single* and *only forty!*"

"Why do you care about a fictional woman?" and he tries to touch my face but I flick his hand away.

"Because I'm *nice!* Because first of all I feel sorry for her for having fallen in love with you, but second of all I feel sorry she won't be able to have a baby because you're an idiot!"

"She's not even real!" It looks like he's kind of enjoying this. But I've completely lost my mind. "GET OUT OF MY CAR!"

"Not till you're okay," he says, and I laugh. I laugh and laugh and continue to grip the steering wheel with the strength of ten men.

"I am not okay, I will not be okay. I *was* okay and you destroyed me and now I am not okay!"

He sits there. I sit there. I want to close my eyes and sleep and not wake up until summer. I want to know what I have done to deserve this. We stare at the teenagers jaywalking back and forth from the school to the pizza place.

My breathing and heart rate start to return to normal and he finally assesses that I'm fine enough for him to get out of the car. From the street he flashes me a peace sign. I flash him one back. But when he turns around, I flip him the bird. *Fuck you. A baby.*

And then I realize: *This is it. The divorce! This is it. Every decision is mine from now on. He's made all of the biggest decisions in my life for thirteen years, including this divorce, but it's signed, so this is it.* I feel lighter. I drive straight home instead of going to work. I crawl into bed and sleep for four hours straight, and when I wake up, I feel a strange calm.

I'm okay. He didn't destroy me. I'm okay. He didn't destroy me.

I'm okay. He didn't destroy me. He didn't destroy me. I'm okay. He didn't destroy me.

I'm okay.

I'm okay.

TOO CANADIAN

It's a hot one this year, the summer of 2013, my second summer alone. Exactly one year ago, I was a shelled-out mess who ran to Italy to be with my childhood friend. To sit with her in the mountains and at the seaside and among Roman ruins, to cry about the man I loved and how he deceived me, to feel the kind of comfort and support that only your oldest friend in the world can give. To be anchored to something, if even for a short while.

Now, that same friend is here in Toronto on vacation. She's in my car with me and even though it's been a year, The Ex-husband is still all we're talking about. She's shaking her head at my fairness, at the way we separated without acrimony, without courts, without me finding his mistress and punching that *putana* in the face. She finds this very un-Italian of me, and disappointedly shakes her head, "You're so nice. So *Canadian*."

I laugh and tell her plenty of Canadian women take revenge on their cheating husbands, or find some way to shame the mistress, or, at the very least, punch the *putana* in the face. I just don't want to do that. I just want us to be on good terms so we can raise Birdie. She sighs. "Well, at least you damned him to hell, right?"

At first I think she's joking. I mean, *what?* But she's dead serious. Obviously I should have at least damned him to hell, asked God to punish him if I wasn't going to. We're in my car as she says this, and I stare out at the lake from the expressway we're on, the sun blinding, the traffic crawling. *Holy shit, I've never damned him to hell. I've never even wished a bad thing on him. What's wrong with me?*

Her voice cuts through the static in my head, like an echo of my own self-doubt. "What's *wrong* with you? He had an affair! Like any good Italian woman you should have at least damned him to hell. I sure would have."

Affair. I hate that word. It sounds so romantic, like something that just happened one night in Paris or something. It's so whimsical, like a magical feeling that just swept two people up and caused them to act beyond their control. It also bugs me because it sounds like a singular event. And what he did was far from singular. I even said this to him once, right after The Bomb, as we were packing and dividing everything in two.

"Please, *please*, stop calling it 'an affair,' like it was this charming mistake you made once! It was over and over and over again!"

In the car with my Italian friend, I think about wishing him ill. But I just don't. I hate him, I do, but not *him*, the person. I hate what he did. I hate that I was an afterthought. But I know he has his own demons. And honestly, all I want is for him to be happy with his life, for this all not to have been for nothing. I want him to find a way to be a better man than he is, than he's been. I guess I *am* too Canadian. I guess I don't know how to damn him to hell. Instead it becomes a prayer.

A SURE THING

Revival is back. I've given in after several months of ignoring his texts. I can't help it, I need that thing he has, that way about him that's just right, even when the rest of the situation is wrong.

It's 1:00 a.m. and I'm in a bathroom stall at the back of a bar, texting Revival. *I swore I wouldn't contact you again, but I want to see you.* He instantly replies, *Hey baby, how you doing?* like I haven't been ignoring him for months. I tell him I'm out dancing with friends, and give him the intersection. He says he'll be there in twenty minutes.

Revival pulls up in a fancy-looking SUV. "Damn, will you look at you in that dress!" he says as I climb in. Hot fire rushes through me. I just spent all night dancing in that dress, to excellent and sexy music, but not one guy danced with me or talked to me or even *looked* at me as far as I could tell. As we pull away, Revival puts his hand on my hand. "Baby, I have *missed* you."

At my place he kisses and kisses me, says, "I've missed you. Damn, I've missed you," over and over again. I can't hear it enough. I let it fill all of the empty space inside me, those spare rooms. Revival is looking at me. Right into my eyes. His skin is so soft and warm. I brush the sweat from his forehead, kiss his eyelids, his gorgeous mouth. I nestle my head in his chest. "You have to come back again soon."

I know he won't.

He doesn't.

It's a few weeks later. He's supposed to be here at six thirty. But at six-twenty, I get that familiar sink in my stomach at the sound of the text notification. I think, *Maybe he isn't cancelling, maybe he's downstairs and the intercom isn't working.* But that, of course, is wishful thinking. Something's come up with his son, he's at his sister's, he doesn't know what time he'll be able to get out of there …

I'm sitting on the edge of my bed in lingerie. I came home from work in a hurry to freshen up, got myself all ready. I head to the fridge and stand in the open door, staring blankly. *God, I'd better go shopping tomorrow before Birdie gets here.* There's nothing for a kid to eat. There's nothing for anyone to eat. I forage a bit, then scarf down two pieces of salami, just plain like that at the kitchen counter, still in this goddamn getup like a fool.

I make myself a gin and tonic and can't be bothered to cut a wedge of lime. I consider a smoke but the rain is too heavy outside. Plus I'd have to put some actual clothes on. I'm too lazy to even do that, now that tonight's sure thing has left me hanging. You know it isn't good when your sure thing isn't so sure.

I watch the rain. I think about how I was once part of love, and now I am apart from it, standing on the sidelines in wasted sexy underwear.

HOW SHE SEES IT

When I was pregnant, The Husband and I had only one hope: that our crazy personalities would cancel each other out and we'd have a calm and gentle daughter. That didn't happen. All of the qualities we share — determined, impetuous, quick tempered, headstrong — they didn't cancel out at all. Instead we had a child who was all those things times a thousand. We called her the "über-us." She was, and sometimes still is, a force to be reckoned with.

In the second summer after The Bomb, her sharp, inquisitive mind becomes focused on the breakup. One day, The Ex-husband drops her at my place. As the door closes behind him, Birdie, six years old at the time, turns and yells at me, "I don't think it's fair that Dad gets to make the decision about where we live!"

"What are you talking about?" I say. "*I* bought this apartment, I chose it."

"Yeah, but he is the one that didn't want to live with us in the house anymore! So he's the one who decided we should live in separate apartments! And you didn't even fight for it!" She's got his face as she says this, how his jaw would get tight just before a giant wall would go up between us.

"Birdie, you don't know if I did or didn't fight for it …" I'm trying to be calm, trying not to burst into tears, trying not to phone him and fly into a rage over why he decided to tell her it was his fault, when all along I had been pretending, achingly, that it was both our decision so that she wouldn't hate him for it. But here she is now, hating *me*. Here she is, six years old, telling me I didn't fight hard enough to save my marriage. According to The Ex-husband, she doesn't have these kinds of conversations with him. As if he hasn't already gotten a free ride, he's been spared this, too.

I pull her close to me, her blue eyes blazing into my brown ones, and I just let the tears fall. "You can't make someone live with you if they don't want to anymore, Birdie." She hugs me, as tight as her little body can, and I feel like the worst mother in the world. She shouldn't be comforting *me*. Not again.

A few nights earlier, as I was reading her a bedtime story, I got so overwhelmed by a memory of him, my eyes filled with tears. She snapped to attention. "It's okay to cry, Mom. But don't cry. Look!" She jumped off the bed and made a series of crazy faces while hopping on one foot. I laughed. *Oh my little bird.* Then she said seriously, "I know it's about Dad," and my heart broke in a thousand new ways.

"Maybe he'll come back to you, Mom." *I can't believe she just said that.*

"I don't think so, Birdie. He's definitely not."

"But what if he did?" *God, how do I answer that?*

How do I tell her that even if, in some magical storybook way he decided he wanted to be together again, I couldn't do it. How could I say to her that sometimes loving someone just isn't enough?

"He won't come back, Birdie. But listen, we've got each other and this great place, and he's right across the street, so that's cool. And you've got both of us in your life. It isn't perfect, but it's all right, we'll get used to it. We still have love all around us, all the time."

"Yeah Mom, we have love. For sure we do."

The memory I had was this: Every time I would say I was cold, no matter where we were or what we were doing, he'd immediately say, "Want my shirt?" and begin to take it off. It was such a stupid joke we had with each other. It's hardly even a joke. But I laughed every single time. He would say it with his sincere, good-boy face on. The one where his eyes look like Bambi. He'd have his T-shirt half off even though we'd be in a restaurant or a movie theatre, and I'd be dying of embarrassment but also laughing. So stupid, but it was our thing.

So that's what made me cry in her bed. Because a dumb character in the book I was reading her said they felt cold.

THE MATCHMAKER

The Matchmaker loves me. "God, I love you!" she says. I love her, too. "*How* are you single?" she asks, and I shoot back, "How are *you* single?"

And here it is, the same question, the same conversation, it just keeps on happening, every time I meet new women, we say to each other, "How are *you* single?" and we mean it, it's not just false propping up. All of the women at my work, the friends of friends I've met — even The Matchmaker herself! — are all smart, funny, good-looking, grounded, with good jobs … blah blah blah, the list goes on.

"You're still young," I say to The Matchmaker, who's thirty-two. I say this to any single woman who isn't staring forty in its stupid face like I am. I say this to all of them, as if it's somehow easier for them, because they are slightly younger, and they don't have joint custody of a child and an ex-husband who lives across the street. At this point, I'm lost. Down a well of self-pity. When I'm down there, I don't even realize that everyone has their own stories, their own demons, their own struggles. And so I say, "You have time, you're still young, you have hope," because they don't have a giant Caesarean scar that runs across their abdomen. They don't have a daily needle to inject, because of a stupid anything-can-happen-or-not-happen disease. They don't have to hide the disease, or fret about the right time to mention the child or The Ex-husband. I agonize over the disclosure of these things. I forget sometimes, when I'm down the well, that other people have things to agonize over, too. *Jesus Christ, I'm not the only one.*

I don't tell any of the guys I meet about the MS. There just isn't any point. I already feel like I'm a scary baggage-filled old lady, why add to the pile? Dating and disease don't exactly go together, even a mildly-presenting, nothing-to-worry about disease like I have. Disclosing to the guys I date makes absolutely zero sense to me and so I never do. I don't tell The Matchmaker about the MS either. It never comes up. I answer all of her questions truthfully though, because what's the point otherwise? I want her to match me, since the internet and real life have brought me interesting and hot men, but no one to have a real relationship with. I tell her I would die and go to heaven if a man my age would want to date me for real, but so far that hasn't happened. She flatters me by saying that's because I look ten years younger.

"You wouldn't think so if you saw me first thing in the morning!" I say to deflect the compliment. I always deflect compliments. I haven't met The Man with the White Shirt yet, but it isn't very long after I do meet him that I tell him about the MS. I tell him about the everything, because that's how it is with him. He feels so real, so good. I also don't deflect his compliments, which are many, because with him I believe what he's saying to me, I believe what I see happening in those dark shiny eyes. I'm a hopeless romantic; I never learn.

Anyway. The Matchmaker asks me to show her photos of my ex-husband. "Wow, cute," she says, which is what everyone says (God, I hate them all). Then she wants to see photos of "my favourites." She means men I've been with since The Ex-husband.

Because I haven't met The Man with the White Shirt yet, I don't even know the real meaning of "favourite." I don't know yet what it's like to want to drop everything for someone you just saw across a room. I don't know yet what it's like to feel understood and connected on a deep, magical level.

So I scroll through the photos on my phone, because yeah, I have a folder full of photos of my "favourites." Sue me. There's Revival, of course. "Wow, niiice!" she says.

Then I show her Cute/Crazy Guy. "Whoa! So adorable!" which yeah, no kidding, but too bad about the crazy.

I save Hot Actor for last. She practically fans herself as she scrolls through his photos. "What … Oh. My. *Really*? Can I see him … oh, oh wow, really?" I feel that same mixture of pride and also what-the-fuck, since everyone always seems a little *too* surprised that I could have had a thing with him. "Oh, he's an actor. It was just a fun thing for a few months while he was in town."

"Ah-MAZING," she says.

Yeah, it is ah-mazing. What an amazingly fun experience this sexual liberation has been. I was once a bored wife, and now I am shamelessly showing a total stranger a folder full of hot guys on my phone. The perks of a skewered, broken heart. But I'm showing her these guys because I am paying her to find me a version of them that wants to have an actual relationship. "This will be so easy," she says, because she loves me, remember? We always love each other, the single ladies of Toronto. We're always so much better than any single guys we meet. It's the worst.

A few weeks later, The Matchmaker matches me with a man who is very, *very* handsome, like even more than Hot Actor! He is sharply dressed when we meet for drinks and a nice summer stroll. He makes me a bit nervous and I end up getting a little too drunk. We make out a bit at the end of the night, but nothing more. A few days later I text him about plans for the weekend and he texts back simply, *You are an amazing person, and I'd be crazy not to keep you in my atmosphere, but I don't want to date you.*

The words hit me hard. Really fucking hard. *I don't want to date you.* Later, I'll focus on "atmosphere" because seriously, what? My friends and I kill ourselves laughing about that statement, shouting, "Yo, you're great and all but I just want to keep you in my ATMOSPHERE!" But in the moment, seeing that text, I think, *Of course. Of course you don't want to date me. Why would anyone?*

I spiral quickly. It's disproportionate to the situation since I've only known him for one week, so who cares, really? But it's not about him. It's about the rejection, it's about the everything. It's about the parade of men who came after The Husband's bomb. The men who, yes, fill me with some kind of modern-gal conquistador's pride when I show off the folder of favourites, but none of whom wanted anything more than to sleep with me, or to keep me in their *atmospheres*, not actually date me.

I email The Matchmaker the next day to say it didn't work out with Handsome Dude. As days pass, I shake it off. I try to enjoy the summer. I invite Revival back into my bed, and then Tall Smart Musician, who has become my good friend and confidant, but sporadically we still do that thing, because that's what friends do in these modern times.

And then, just as summer's coming to an end, I see The Man with the White Shirt walk through a doorway and everything stops, just like that, in a single moment, when I see him smile for the first time. Everything slows right down, the earth tilts a little, and there's no sound or space or time. When he sees me, it's confirmed, although we haven't talked yet. And when we do talk? *Swoon.* We never want to stop looking at each other, we never want to stop talking, and we don't.

Only one week after I first see The Man with the White Shirt across that crowded café, I email The Matchmaker to tell her to take me off the roster because I've met the most amazing guy and I want to see where it goes.

CHAPTER FIFTEEN

HE EXISTS

THE ROSARY

It's August 2005. We're standing in Vatican City, the sunlight hitting the dome of St. Peter's on such a perfect angle it's like Michelangelo himself painted it for us that morning.

The Husband is patient with my odd fascination with Catholic objects. He stands around as I pick up tiny statues of Mary, try on bracelets with pictures of saints, and root through bowls filled with those tiny medallions old Italian ladies pin to their bras. I love all of that stuff, it reminds me of my aunts and grandmothers, the women of my childhood who wore nothing but black clothing and beige nylons, whose bodies felt like they were made of endless folds of the softest flesh. In their pockets were hard candies, prayer cards from funeral masses, and of course, rosaries.

Now, as an adult, although I'm not a practising Catholic, I still love all this stuff, and rosaries the most. So here we are at the centre of Catholicism, St. Peter's. I've already bought a few rosaries, including one for my mother-in-law, even though she isn't Catholic. But this particular rosary I've just picked up is the most beautiful I've ever seen with its tiny metallic rose beads. So I buy it.

The Husband and I climb the inside of St. Peter's dome, to the very top until we're out of breath, faces red. You can touch the gilded walls and be that close to beauty and still feel a strange hollow inside of you, it's the weirdest thing, or a metaphor maybe, I don't know.

The night The Bomb drops, seven years later, the world falls out from under my feet and I have almost nothing to keep me from falling out with it. I'm moving into the guest room because I can't even *be* in our bedroom anymore, can't even be there. I'm hyperventilating, crippled by the near-constant images in my head of my husband having sex with that woman only two nights earlier, maybe our whole marriage long, forever.

I scramble in the junk drawer of the dresser until I find the rosary, with its beautiful little roses. I'm so relieved. Trying not to let the panic take over me, I start to do the rosary. I haven't said a prayer aloud in probably fifteen years, maybe more. I gave up on it all a long, long time ago. Tonight it comes back.

I start on the first bead with *Our Father*, then do a *Hail Mary*, and repeat, again and again and again, round and round the rosary. When I'm done the rosary, I feel almost like a normal living, breathing person. Almost. I put it over my head, and it falls, down against my collarbones, my skin, the cross hanging. And there it stays. For one whole year. I'm not even kidding. I wear it every single day, every night, 24/7. I even wear it while having sex, with The Ex-husband, with The First Guy, and Cute/Crazy Guy, and Hot Actor, and anyone else who is with me the first year. Any photos you see of me at that time, you can see it poking out from under my sweaters or T-shirts or summer dresses or blazers, always under my clothes so that the beads are close to my heart, on my skin. The cross always tucked into my bra.

One day, months in, I'm hanging out with a bunch of co-workers at a bar. A woman I've known a long time notices the rosary and asks me about it. I tell her: I can't stop wearing it, I can't stop doing the prayers, even though I'm not sure I believe in what I am saying. She nods and tells me when she and her wife divorced a few years earlier, she started to do the prayers, too, on her old childhood rosary. Even though she considered herself an atheist, even though the prayers felt hollow. *She gets it.* She understands how a relic from the past can make the confusion of the present bearable. And so we have a moment, the two of us. The kind of moment where you realize a little bond has been created. We are two people tied by this one experience.

I wish I could say doing the rosary got me closer to God, but that didn't happen until the next year, and even then it was more desperation than faith. I had one of those nights where I was crying my eyes out and couldn't sleep. I was in a vortex of self-pity. So I reached for the rosary with the tiny etched roses. I took it and ran my fingers along the chains that link the beads. I said the prayers over and over again, and then, just in case, I mean, why not? I asked God to send me something good for once, to send me someone to bring me a little joy.

Look, I know I don't even believe in you, so I totally get that this isn't cool, but really, Lord, I'm just so tired of no one loving me, of sleeping alone, so can you send me someone who at least wants to hang out with me and have sex with me? If you do, I will totally start believing in you. I will do this rosary every night.

This is a completely pathetic admission, I know, but I said I would tell you everything, even these unbearably shameful moments, like asking a God I didn't even believe in to give me a boyfriend.

If he exists, you exist. Let me see what you've got.

THE MAN WITH THE WHITE SHIRT

I'm washing a white shirt in my sink. It's a man's shirt, and, yes, all the pioneering feminists are rolling in their graves right now, but I don't care. The man who was in this shirt is sleeping in my bed looking like the most beautiful form of beautiful I've ever seen.

It's 8:30 a.m. Labour Day, and I can't sleep, so I'm washing the mud off his shirt, mud that got there when he rode his bike here in the rain last night. In just twelve days, this gorgeous man has turned my life into one buzzing, electrified hum. Everything feels sunnier, I'm walking on a cloud, I'm over the moon, I am every cliché you have ever heard. I exist, he exists. *Holy shit, this is happening.*

I make some espresso, I fry up some bacon, I whip up a batch of pancakes from scratch and flip them perfectly, one by one. I set the table, I cut up fruit and arrange it artfully on a plate. I'm playing some reggae low on the stereo so I don't wake him, and I sing along like the happiest woman in the world. I'm like Snow White in the forest, with all the birds and animals drawn to me. I'm glowing so much it must be blinding.

Who is this person? Look closely, I assure you this is me, the me you've come to know, just with butterflies.

I'm scrambling eggs when he comes out of my room looking like God's gift to man, but wait, there's more to him than that, I promise. Here he is saying, "It smells so good in here!" then, "Oh wow, look how beautiful that plate of fruit looks!" Oh. My. *God.* He noticed my artful arrangement! *Ohmygod.* He smiles so warmly, like with his eyes, and puts his hand on my face. I'm evaporating now, into the ether, look at me gooooo. With his hand like that he says, "Look at you, oh my God. You're always so beautiful, day and night." I suddenly remember that I was so intent on washing his shirt and cooking him breakfast that I forgot to fix myself up. I'm in a nightgown, and my short curly hair is probably sticking up! *Shit, I have no makeup on!* But here he is looking at me like I'm dreamy, and telling me so.

We spend the entire day like this, dreamily looking at each other, talking and talking, sitting out on my balcony, or lying around in my bed, laughing. At one point I say, "Man, this day is so nice!" and he says, "I know, it's like Christmastime nice!" which seems in the moment like just about the best thing anyone has ever said out loud. It's probably a line. He probably says and does all these same things with all the girls, but I've already checked into La-La-Land so it all feels as real and special as I think it is.

He exists, he exists, he exists.

He tunes my guitar and plays me a song. As he sings and plays I feel like I've actually, truly, died and gone to heaven. I can't stop staring at his neck, his jawline. I take photos on my phone like a teenage girl in the bed of her first love. Then he plays me a song he's written, although he's shy at first. The song is good, his voice low and sweet, and I am floating on Cloud 9. Have you been there recently? It's been so long, *so* long for me, I've forgotten it feels this awesome.

"Now you," he says and passes me the guitar. *Oh God, I can't play and sing for him!* But I do. I play Smokey Robinson's "You Really Got a Hold on Me" and he beams at me the whole time. Now, if this were a movie, the fact that I sing that particular song would be some kind of super-lame foreshadowing. I mean, *really*, of all the songs in the universe! The lyrics of that song will basically become the very essence of me when it comes to him. But I don't know this yet. Instead, I'm on a cloud singing about how madly I love him and what a hold he has on me despite how badly he treats me. Of course I can't know the irony of this moment, not like I will see it later. But back to the Snow White, pancakes, butterflies, and Christmastime nice. The Man with the White Shirt in my bed like a god, me floating, and I'm just so happy to *feel* again. This man makes me *feel things again*.

As I play the last chord his eyes light up like two struck matches. The ends of his mouth turn up ever so slightly. He takes the guitar from my hands, puts it aside and wraps his arms around me. He smells so good, *holy shit*. We lie there together, shaky and emotional. I don't know what has just happened, and I'm terrified I've scared him off. But instead, he says how happy he is we met. He says he can't wait to introduce me to his friends. He says his mother will love me. Jesus, we've only known each other for twelve days.

Twelve alcohol-free days, I should note. Just a few days before I met him, I'd started a detox, making it the longest stretch without drinking since The Bomb. So when The Man with the White Shirt met me, he met *me*. And he liked me. *Me*.

He runs his hand along my shoulder, and I feel like the whole bed will catch fire.

IT AIN'T ME

The Husband always wanted me to sing "It Ain't Me, Babe," by Bob Dylan. I'd be strumming my guitar and that was always his request. He could never remember the name and would always ask me to play the "sad, sad song." I found this endearing, adorable. But it also used to worry me a bit, his obsession with a song that pretty much says *he's just not that into you*. The song that I'd always imagined was Dylan's kiss-off to Joan Baez. Here they were, this perfect couple but then he was just like, *nah*.

I'd imagine poor Joan listening to the lyrics, realizing that Bob didn't love her quite as much as she thought he did. And here's a not-so-fun fact: just as I called The Husband "My Rogue," Joan called Bob her "Little Vagabond," which is basically like calling him The One Who Won't Stay. Anyway, there's a line in "It Ain't Me, Babe" that always physically hurt when I sang it, the one where he tells her he has no feelings left for her and by the way, he's already moved on to someone else.

Can you imagine it? She's standing at his door, there to convince him that their love is worth fighting for, and he tells her he's nothing but stone, motionless, not worth it, and look he can prove it! See? There's someone else already here with me, someone else who isn't you, because I'm not the one for you, I'm not the one.

Why did this particular line haunt me so much back then? Back there, in the thick of our happiness. Did part of me have a hunch that one day he would turn to stone? Or was it just that my deepest subconscious fear was to be left outside of a doorway, heart shredded, as I'm told to fade back into the night? I couldn't bear the thought. But even though I dreaded getting to that line, sitting there like a pit of despair in the third verse, I would always sing it for him. I'd spend a minute trying to remember the chords and then launch into the world's saddest song. As I'd sing, he'd continue doing whatever he was doing, cooking dinner or marking papers, and I wasn't even sure he was really listening. But when the song ended he would always say something like, "You sing that so well," or "Thanks for singing me the sad, sad song."

When Birdie was born he'd say to her, "Doesn't your mom have a beautiful voice?" even though she was just a baby sitting there, no clue what he was asking her.

You should Google the lyrics of that Bob Dylan song. Go ahead, I'll wait. You need to read how deeply sad it is, how apt it is, how *significant* it is, that for twelve years he asked me to sing him a song that basically describes the way he would one day feel about me. Or maybe always did. A song that says *I do care about you, but I will never love you the way you love me. I just don't. I just can't. I'm not the one for you. It ain't me, babe.*

I get it, Rogue, I fucking get it already.

IT AIN'T HIM, EITHER

It's probably clear by now we weren't soulmates, if you believe in that kind of thing, which I actually don't. I believe in all kinds of crazy cosmic shit, but not that.

The truth is I never thought of us as soulmates, or even that we had to *be* such a magical thing in order for our marriage to work. I saw us as a team, a strong united force. I thought we were meant for each other if only because we said we were, because we said we would love and take care of one another for the rest of our lives.

After The Bomb, The Ex-husband said many times, "I was flip-flopping all the time. To stay or go. I loved you, but you were driving me crazy."

I can't fault him for this. This is life. We fall in and out of love, we're confused, we change our minds, we feel trapped, we're tempted. I get it. But the flip-flopping caused more damage than if he would have just left, before he had an affair, before he turned to stone.

I didn't need him to be my soulmate. I just needed him to have been man enough to walk away.

TILT-A-WHIRL

The Man with the White Shirt spins my head around so much I know I'm not thinking straight, but I don't care. I want to be as spun as cotton candy. I want to feel like I'm on the ride where the carny shouts, "Do you wanna go FASTER?" Why yes, yes I do! I want to feel this rush of adrenalin, all sugary and about to throw up.

White Shirt shows up at my work just to see me one afternoon, the very first week we met, because he says he can't wait the four more days till our next date. He holds my hand on the street. He kisses me on every corner, every time the light turns red and we have to wait to cross. No matter who tells a story, one of us says, "Oh my God, that's exactly like *me*," and the other answers, "Well obviously, because I'm you!"

I've never experienced such a thing in all my life, this totally getting someone who totally gets you. It's like we're each other's mirror, twin. And we get so instantly wrapped up in it, this spun-like-gold thing that's happening.

One night we're dancing in a club, so close, and the way he holds me, it's like I'm meant to fit there, folded into him. No one's on the dance floor but us. "I can't stop smiling!" he says, and I say, "Me either!" and here it is for me finally — romance. Romance! Imagine how lucky it is to find someone who reminds you that life is full of exclamation marks! It's the fucking best.

When I saw him the first time, it was like the air came out of me, but in a good way. That night, as I said, I was sober, and when I first saw him walk in, wearing, yes, a white shirt and a bunch of other perfectly put together things, I just thought *wow*. But it wasn't his clothes that caught my eye, it was his *everything*, the way he walked around, the way his face lit up while talking to people — the total package.

It was a Thursday evening in this café-bar in Kensington Market, a goodbye party for a sparkler of a girl I know through a mutual friend. It was a cabaret thing, where her friends performed songs and burlesque, and I expected to just go for an hour or so and then duck out because it's not really my thing. But, oh, The Man with the White Shirt. I watched him the whole time, his every reaction and changing facial expressions, his eyes when they fleetingly locked on mine. I *knew* I had to talk to him. After the show, while we all stood around chatting, I couldn't concentrate on anything my friends were saying. I just kept watching him.

Finally, I walked right over to him and a woman he was talking to, and asked to bum a cigarette. He said he had menthols and I said, "Oookaaay, thanks Grandma," and bummed one off the woman instead. Later, he tells me that everything about me lit him on fire immediately. My dress, my confidence, the Grandma insult, all of it. He and the woman were clearly close. She smiled knowingly and said, "I'll just leave you two" and with that, the rest of the world left us, too.

By the time I got home, there was a text from him saying he was so glad to have met me and he couldn't wait to continue our conversation. So we continued to text till 2:00 a.m. After that, I typed a memo into my phone with every single detail I could remember about him — his full name, his birthdate, the country he was born in, the places he's lived, everything we talked about, my overall impressions of him.

Angolan and Portuguese
Scorpio like me
Dreadlocks
Great dresser like amazing
Beautiful face
Even beautifuler smile
So unpretentious kind and funny … Is this guy really this perfect?

This memo is still in my phone, stamped with the 2:00 a.m. date of August 23, 2013. We had our first date later that night.

The next morning at breakfast in a diner nearby, I took a photo of him and he snapped one of me. That photo is still the one that pops up on his phone when I call or text. I printed out the one I took, wrote the date on the back, folded it and put it in my wallet where it would live for five years. It's hard to let go of magic sometimes, what can I say?

Anyway, after that whirlwind of the first 48 hours together, we continue to text and talk and see each other as much as possible. We do real dating things. He's fun and bright and just brims with positivity. He's gorgeous and dorky and exuberant.

He talks a lot, and he listens so well, and he always, always says the exact right thing but it never feels like a line, even though maybe it is.

There *are* downsides, which the spun-like-sugar me is ignoring. He's a bit of a bohemian, which is to say, a musician, and his friends all seem to be burlesque dancers that he's slept with, or still is sleeping with. He doesn't have a career, doesn't own anything. He lives like my friends and I lived when we were twenty-two, his apartment small and untidy, crammed with instruments and recording equipment, and in the kind of building and neighbourhood that make me feel positively bourgeois. But all spun like I am, all butterflies and unicorns and cotton candy, I ignore all this. I just want to be with someone kind. Someone who looks at me like they can't believe I'm in front of them. So I focus on his gorgeousness, his charm, the way we can talk for hours and still have more to say. It's bliss, pure bliss, this romance thing, this we-saw-each-other-from-across-the-room-and-wow! thing.

I like this hazy glow of magic that surrounds us. This golden mist. Those eyes, goddamn it, those eyes. I don't want to pull back the curtain just yet.

INDEPENDENT WOMAN

I get a letter in the mail. It's stamped: Supreme Court of Justice. *Shit, am I being called for jury duty??* Jury duty happens to be my biggest fear, after being abandoned or having to be alone for the rest of my life. Yes, that's right, that's the hierarchy of things I'm afraid of:

1. Being alone forever and I'm not even forty, God.
2. Being abandoned. (Check.)
3. Being called for jury duty.

Lucky for me, it isn't jury duty. It's a notice of divorce. Not the divorce itself, but a *warning*, a friendly reminder that yes, the divorce is coming. On October 27, 2013, it will finally be official and legal.

I burst into tears and call my friend, The Practical One, but she isn't home. *Who else, who else?* Now, there are a lot of people I could call next, but I call The Man with the White Shirt. Don't roll your eyes at me. Don't say I'm crazy to call a guy I just started seeing to cry about my divorce. I mean, maybe I am a little, in the sense that my new crazy is just being me, and not hiding my emotions or trying to play it cool. This guy feels like the real deal.

I'm not crying when he answers, but he knows something's wrong. I say, "I just got the 'Congratulations, you're divorced!' letter."

"Oh honey, I'm sorry. But also, that's awesome!" he says, and I break into a huge smile. "It must be really hard for you to see it just printed on a page like that," he says, all best-guy ever, all unicorn-like. I tell him honestly, I feel numb, punched in the gut, achingly sad, incredibly free, angry *and* happy.

As I'm talking, he texts me a link that makes me want to drive straight over to his house and tackle him, bury my head in his shoulder, and wake up three days later. It's an old music video by Destiny's Child, the song "Independent Women." What a hilarious thing to send me! Instead of letting me feel sorry for myself, The Man with the White Shirt sends me a badass lady anthem.

It makes me laugh. It makes this heavy moment *light*. And with that, the divorce becomes just the divorce, the next logical step. Just a piece of paper that says in two weeks' time, I will be an independent woman.

The night The Husband asked me to marry him, back in 2001. Remember? 9/11, the Italian restaurant, the diamond ring. That night, before I agreed to take a chance, I said to him, "Look, I really, really don't want to get married just to get divorced."

"I know. It won't be like that," he said, but I wanted to be sure. So many people in my family have gotten divorced. They all said vows, *believed them*, and then broke them. A marriage contract meant nothing to me.

"I'm only going to ask you one thing," I said to him that night. "If we get married, do you promise you will fight? Even when things get hard, or confusing, will you fight to make it work, fight to stay together and do everything it takes not to get divorced? I want us to fight for what we're saying today: that we love each other and want to take care of each other for the rest of our lives."

And he said, "I will always fight for you, Parise. That's who I am."

But it wasn't true. As I suspected, our vows held no currency. They just got us a piece of paper that said we were married. Just like *this* piece of paper that says we aren't.

THE UNICORN

"The Unicorn." That's the nickname my friend Solo Time gives to The Man with the White Shirt. You know, him. Dreamy, dreamy him.

"I didn't know unicorns were real!" she shouts from the back seat of my car the night she first meets him. We erupt into fits of giggles as he climbs into the passenger seat beside me, saying, "What are you two laughing about?" with such an impish fire behind his eyes.

"Oh, *nothing*," I say smiling, and for the millionth time since we met, he says, "I love your smile."

"Shut up, because I love yours."

He squeezes my hand. We've known each other for one month.

Okay go ahead, I don't care, go on, you can make gagging sounds here, because you know what? I'm on Cloud 9. He likes me and he tells me so. Out loud. It's like a fucking dream come true. For that exact reason, "Dreamcatcher" is the nickname my friend The Bright One gives him. My friend The Painter just calls him "The Man" because a man doesn't have to play games or hide his feelings.

And yet, I will admit to you, I keep waiting for the other shoe to drop. I sometimes think it's all too good to be true. What if seeming like he isn't a player is what actually makes him a player? The trusting part of me has been short-circuited by The Ex-husband, and now I feel like I've lost my sense of instinct, my ability to read cues. What if he seems like a unicorn, but is really just a pony, or ... whatever this metaphor is trying to say, you know what I mean?

There's an undercurrent of worry, of knowing the bubble is going to burst at some point and probably soon. But I can't let this darkness get the better of me at these early stages. I actually really like this guy, and I don't want to mess it up. One day after I express my insecurity about us he says, "Are you afraid of me just, I don't know, running screaming or something?" And I tell him yes, I'm afraid I'm too intense, too damaged, have too much baggage, I cry too much —

He stops me. He holds me very close and looks right at me, hard. "I like *you*," he says. "A lot. Even the sad parts. I like *you*. All of you. And I just want to keep getting to know you. All of you. Okay?"

I nod and my heart feels like it's going to bust right out of my chest and bleed all over us. He kisses and kisses me. I'm grateful, but I know better. I know in reality I'm *cautiously* on Cloud 9. I know that unicorns aren't real.

Cautious or not, the cloud I'm floating on prevents me from seeing anyone else. I just don't want to. From the moment I meet

The Man with the White Shirt, I don't sleep with anyone but him, not even Revival. It's not a conscious choice, it's just what happens; I am that enthralled, that focused. It feels like magic.

WHAT MAGIC FEELS LIKE

The Man with the White Shirt sits on the edge of my bathtub while I fix my hair in the mirror. He has my guitar and he's singing to me as I get ready. It's like I invented this man, like I conjured him or something, he's so exactly what I need and want in my life right now.

And then he starts singing a song I just love. "The Messenger" by Daniel Lanois. I sit down on the floor, there in front of him, my kindred spirit, brought to me from an unknown cloud. His eyes locked to mine, he finishes the song then puts the guitar aside. We lie down on the cool tiles and kiss, and I'm sure there's never been anyone who gets me like he does. We understand each other on a level that I've never experienced. I'm sure that we need each other, that we've been given this magical gift for a reason.

"You have such a summertime way of smiling," he says to me. And my heart grows fifty sizes.

CHAPTER SIXTEEN

SO IT GOES

ART

Here in the autumn of 2013, I start to have something of an artis-
tic renaissance. Singing, playing guitar, drawing. A lot. Somewhere
in the short time since I met The Man with the White Shirt, I've
started drawing trees — tall and bare, branches reaching out and
over crazy little buildings. Cityscapes of strange futures, where
trees are ten times bigger than skyscrapers.

The drawings aren't all that great or anything, but I love
doing them. I lose myself for hours. Listening to music, feeling
the smooth run of marker on paper. Letting whatever thoughts
I have come in and out of my mind. Enjoying, for the first time,
small moments alone.

It's been happening lately, a return to self. A return to a part
of me that was dormant for so long, especially when I was in a
busy house with a small baby. There was hardly any room for art

back then. But here, with 50 percent of my time free, despite how awful and scary and hard it's been to be away from Birdie, to be a woman without her little family, here is where the old me starts to seep its way in.

Here is where I draw crazy trees. Where I sing songs with friends or with White Shirt or just with myself, playing guitar so much I develop calluses on my fingers, like the ones that were always there back in my twenties.

Here is the first faint glimmer of a silver lining.

THE RED HILLS

The single happiest day of my life since The Bomb happens a month and a half after I meet The Man with the White Shirt. Although it's the end of September, it's as hot as a summer day. We're both wearing T-shirts and jeans and big vintage sunglasses and white sneakers. Even the way we look together feels magical to me. I pick him and his dog up and we go for a drive. I don't tell him where we're going, just that it's a special place I haven't been to since I was a teenager. I'm not entirely sure it exists still, or even how to get there, but that's all part of the fun.

We leave the city behind and head out to the country, northwest of Toronto, driving along winding roads with the windows down. He picks songs off my iPod, and it's like all my dreams are realized. The way the trees sway against the blue sky, the warm air on our skin, our smiles as we discover how much of the same music we love. I'm not kidding when I say that still today, no other day has come even close to being as wonderful and fun and special and fulfilling as the one where White Shirt is smiling that million-watt smile at me as I drive us to the Red Hills.

The Red Hills are exactly what they sound like, red earth — terracotta — that just appears in one part of southern Ontario in a crazy, bumpy, beautiful way, on the side of a winding country road. As teenagers, we'd drive out to the hills for "bush parties." These parties were really just drunken kids running up and down the hills, making out and getting lost. I never actually saw it in the daytime. Here we are though, twenty years later, parking the car on the side of the road. I take his hand, and he takes the dog's leash, and we walk to the crest of the hill. That's when he finally sees it, and the look on his face is just pure wonder. It's a beautiful thing to behold, his face I mean, but yes of course, also this natural wonder that is the Red Hills.

We walk around and talk and explore and get two young girls to take a photo of us. Then we take some selfies. These are still my most favourite photos of us. He still has one of them framed on his desk at home, where he makes music and lives his life, with or without me.

After we explore the hills, we get back in the car and I drive us to a little town I know that's high up some winding roads. It's during this car ride that I tell him I have MS. He says he noticed I take a lot of pills and wonders why, but instead of lying I just tell him the truth. I just tell him, and for a moment I hold my breath. I'm certain I will lose him immediately. But he's so kind. He doesn't make a big deal about it at all, not then or any time after. It was like the greatest weight is lifted off me that day, telling him that.

When we get to the little town, we walk along holding hands in the bright hot sun. We get coffees and ice cream and sit on a bench. And that's when he asks when he will be able to meet Birdie. I swoon a little. It also scares the shit out of me. And then he goes even further, saying that if it would help he would be happy to meet her father first. I'm floored. I don't know what to say, other than how that wouldn't be necessary. I say that it would have to be pretty serious for me to introduce someone to her, and that I wasn't ready for him to meet her just yet. But inside I'm freaking out. *This is a real thing, he is like, my actual boyfriend! Praying the rosary worked, holy shit.*

The perfect day continues with vintage shopping where we like all the same things and I buy us both so many of those things — plates and glasses and shoes. As we drive back to the city, he falls asleep in the passenger seat beside me. I hold his hand in mine and try to push the thoughts out that this is all too good to be true. I try to hold on to this feeling, this simple, beautiful day.

TOO GOOD TO BE TRUE

We're sitting on a park bench holding hands, his eyes so sad. It turns out that despite our deep connection, despite my summertime way of smiling and how crazy he acts for me, how different he says he feels about me, The Man with the White Shirt is still sleeping with other women. He always will. "That's something I can't change," he says, as if he's talking about a scar or an extra finger, not something he has free will over, something he can choose or not choose to do.

I don't get it. It's been almost three months since we first met and we've been inseparable since the beginning. I mean, we talk on the phone almost every night, don't we? More than once now he's asked about when he can meet my daughter. We hold hands in public, walking along like couples do. And yet, here is the shoe dropping. He *is* too good to be true.

My mind races. *Walk. Walk now. If you stay, you'll only get more attached, it will only get harder.* But then I think, *God, I want to keep seeing him though. He's the closest thing I've had to a boyfriend, and I like this feeling, I like the way he makes me feel.* His face says he doesn't want to lose me, and my mind whips back again, *The cake. The cake. I am always the fucking cake. Don't be the cake again!*

"You act so boyfriend-y though!" is what I manage to say to him, like I'm Drew Barrymore in a fucking rom-com.

"I don't know what that means," he says. "I don't really believe in categories."

I roll my eyes and say, "*Of course you don't*," because truly in that moment, I'm exasperated by the whole bohemian thing he has going on. What seemed adorable and idiosyncratic about him up until this point now feels put-on and exhausting. I have no clue what to do. *The relationship is still new; it's not anything serious, right? So maybe I just keep seeing him and see what happens?* But the news that he "doesn't believe in categories" sits with me, hard, like a heavy stone, somewhere just under my heart. My heart, which during this conversation, has slowly started to put up a small wall around itself, a nice protective layer.

It's the *Don't-be-the-cake-again* wall. The *Jesus-Christ-doesn't-anyone-believe-in-monogamy-anymore?* wall. The *Oh-well-back-to-square-one* wall.

Stupid wall.

"Do you hold hands with these other women?" I ask.

"No!" he says, like I'm crazy.

"Do you talk to them on the phone every night? Do you feel about them the way you feel about me? Do you just say these things to me because they're what you say to everyone?" He answers an emphatic no to each of my questions.

He says, "There's nobody like you. I don't feel this way or act this way with anyone but you. I haven't in a long time." So what's the problem? Why can't he just let them go?

"I also have casual relationships," I say, "but I can let them all go at any moment, I don't care!" I think about Revival, and realize I let him go months ago without even thinking about it.

"It isn't like that," he says, trying to explain his theory of life and love to me. "I just think people should be able to sleep with whoever they want, if they want to." My heart sinks. I get it, but I also don't *get* it get it. I mean, sure, monogamy is a construct, blah blah blah, but I'm not asking him to marry me, just be exclusive with me while we're dating. I just thought he was my boyfriend. *Mine.* Possessive, how positively mainstream of me.

In a few days I'm going to turn thirty-nine. I can't believe I'm even having this conversation with a man my own age. With a man who has basically been perfect in every way until now. A man that has been more of a boyfriend to me than some people's actual boyfriends are. It's so fucking confusing.

I don't make a decision. I can't. All I keep thinking about is my birthday party coming up in a few days. The one where I invited all of my oldest and dearest friends so they could meet my new boyfriend. *Ugh.* We stand on a street corner near Birdie's school and say goodbye, his face so sad I can't even comprehend it.

I say, "See you in a few days." And he says, so quietly, "Okay."

We stand there for a long time, just looking directly into each other's eyes. I turn around and head into the school, my heart like a deflated balloon after the world's best party. The next day, to ease the sadness, the immense jealousy and confusion I feel, I fall back on the familiar, comfortable, and unbelievably satisfying Revival, who's happy to make his return after a three-month hiatus.

"Been a while since I've seen you," he says as he walks in my door with that swagger, that casual smirk. "Yup," I answer, and that's all we say on the matter, falling into each other's arms like no time has passed, like no other lives are lived, like there's only this moment, this time and place that has no tie to anything or anyone before or after it.

So this is what everyone wants? This is what's so great? Moments?

It isn't long before I send The Matchmaker an email with the subject header: *I am back on the market.* She replies, *Bummer, my friend. Back in the saddle!* And I say my favourite thing to say when there's nothing else to say, stolen words from a favourite author — "So it goes." Because really, so it goes.

LOSS, REVISITED

And so *this* is why I'm a little mean to The Man with the White Shirt, here in this fancy bar with the tarot card reader, as we celebrate my thirty-ninth birthday. He knows it, but he's being sweet and generous anyway. Well, what's he going to do? Be impatient with the cake? It's his *cake*, come on! Instead he smiles for photos, he holds my drink, he laughs with my friends, he looks perfect in his jeans. I continue to be petulant. Then I take my one-millionth fancy cocktail and stumble down a hallway to see the tarot card reader.

Here she is, the giant chair, the giant wine glass. Here she is turning the cards over, *Loss, Fear, Futility*, which may as well be *Your husband cheated on you* and *Now you think no one can love you*. Then she says the stuff about how all the bullshit I've been through over the past few years is really a test, a test for me to learn how I say yes to things, and how I say no. Not if. *How.*

I wake up the next morning in his bed, my head bashed in by French liqueurs, my veins filled with lead. Massively hungover. It's my thirty-ninth birthday. I shouldn't even be here, I should leave, but instead I'm dead from having torn my body apart because my heart and mind couldn't handle things.

The Man with the White Shirt gets up and makes me an espresso. I just lie there and look at my phone. There are birthday greetings in every possible format — emails, texts, Facebook messages, Instagram comments. I feel loved. But it's not enough. I want a man to love me. I want *this* man to love me. Just me.

I lie there some more, staring at the cracks in his ceiling, thinking how that's a metaphor for the fissures inside me, then realizing it's a crap metaphor actually. I lie there and I think about how last year, on the morning of my thirty-eighth birthday, I woke up in the bed of The Ex-husband. How I snuck away before 7:00 a.m. back to my apartment across the street so my own daughter wouldn't find me in bed with her own father. *Well, at least I'm done with all that.* White Shirt's cat climbs up on the bed and stares directly into my eyes. I stare back in case she has any advice for me, which she doesn't. So we stay like that, her purring, me staring at a crap metaphor above us.

White Shirt makes eggs. He's No Shirt right now, which I wish you could see because *wow*, but that's beside the point. He serves me the eggs in his bed, cut fruit and avocado fanned out beautifully on the plate. He massages my tired shoulders. He brings me Extra Strength Advil and water in a mug with his name written across it. We laugh and talk and kiss and fool around and talk some more. The hangover starts to lift, and yet I continue to just lie there in his cozy apartment of confusion. I don't know what I'm doing or who I've become but I realize I can't move. I'm just exhausted — physically, emotionally, spiritually. I'm at a crossroads with myself, again.

"This isn't for me," I say to him, over and over. It isn't for me, I'm right. I don't want to share him, to be shared. I don't want to feel this magic we say we both feel, and then feel the empty despair on nights when I know he's out with some other woman. Although I'm not ready to let him go just yet, I know this will last another week, tops, before I break things off. I'm already feeling farther away, the cement all set in the wall around my heart. His face is sad. He holds me tight.

How did I get here? What happened to my life, to love? I wonder this all the time now.

THIS IS THE LAST TIME

I have a confession to make. Oh, you're going to be angry with me, worried even. But it's fine, I'm *fine*. Here it is (deep breath). Later that night, still on my thirty-ninth birthday, I sleep with The Ex-husband.

"Man, what are we *doing*?" I say to The Ex-husband as we tear each other's clothes off.

"It's your birthday!" he says. "Whaddaya mean?"

"I'm still angry at you." I'm on top of him as I say this.

"You *should* be. I'm a jerk!" His hands on my skin.

"We aren't going back to being friends after this. It'll be right back to not talking about anything other than Business." Business is the word we use to refer to our daughter.

"Okay," he says, but do I detect a little sadness? Our bodies move together, effortlessly, as they have for fourteen years now.

I say, "Okay, hurry up now, my boyfriend's waiting for me, remember?"

"Right! Your pretty boyfriend!" he says.

It's true, White Shirt *is* expecting me to sleep over at his place that night. Whether or not he's my boyfriend, well, let's just say that inspired by him, I'm exploring a disbelief in categories at the moment.

Here we are in the bathroom together afterward, showering, bumping into each other, pinching, joking, comfortable, just like we're still married. Instead, the divorce will actually be official in two days' time.

I want to say that something profound came out of this, that I get in my car and realize something deep about myself. But I don't. I just put on my clothes and kiss The Ex-husband goodbye. As I go to leave, he flashes me a peace sign and I flash him one back.

"See you around, jerk," I say, and he smiles with his eyes and his face and his everything, all parts of him shooting directly into me, like a quiver full of arrows launched all at once. I smile, too, and shut his apartment door behind me.

Actually, just before the peace signs and the invisible arrows, I said, "I really hope when I turn forty next year I won't see you at *all*."

He pouts, then says, "Ah, of course you will! Why not?"

But really, Lord in heaven, I sincerely hope that I will make it through my entire fortieth birthday without sleeping with my cake-eating, lucky bastard of an ex-husband, without seeing his face, or hearing his voice. Electrical current be damned. This has to be the last time.

PERFECT DAY

Two days after my thirty-ninth birthday. It's a Sunday afternoon. My kitchen counter is littered with empty bottles and dirty dishes. I had a party last night, where White Shirt played co-host, cutting lime wedges, greeting guests, arranging a tray of vegetables, inventing a rum punch with me, all kisses and laughs and "God, you're so incredible," his hand on my waist. I enjoyed it all, but in the back of my mind there was a ticker tape that kept scrolling round and round: *If I'm so incredible, why do you need to be with other women too?*

The party was fun, filled with some of my oldest friends, and some new. White Shirt played the piano, and then my guitar, and we all sang songs until 2:00 a.m. Once everyone was gone, I stood there tipsy, eating crackers as he put Saran Wrap on leftover food. He said something to me but I didn't hear him because I was remembering cleaning up with The Husband after the parties we used to throw. It was one of our favourite things — washing the dishes, putting the food away, talking about the night, and then slow dancing, always dancing. In the morning we'd wake up and the place would be spotless, because we enjoyed the end of the party as much as the party itself.

When he put the last wrapped food in the fridge, White Shirt said, "We don't have to clean the rest of this now. Let's go to bed." And we did, inhaling each other for a couple of hours, not falling asleep until sometime after 5:00 a.m., when the sky was starting to turn that eerie navy blue.

Now it's afternoon and he's long gone. The dishes and empty bottles are still strewn around but I don't care. I haven't cleaned a thing yet and it doesn't matter. And then I get a text from The Ex-husband saying, *What are the chances Lou Reed died on the last day of our marriage?*

Right. The divorce. It's actually official today. Poor Lou, like some kind of punk rock bookend to the story of us. His song "Perfect Day" was our wedding song. So what *are* the chances? I mean, really universe, when you get married Lou Reed sings a song? And when you get divorced he dies?

Like everyone else in the world does when a musician dies, I immediately put on his music, starting with the first Velvet Underground album. Then I listen to all of the solo Lou Reed songs I have. When it gets to "Perfect Day" I freeze. I haven't been able to listen to this song in two years. I cannot listen to it. I've walked out of rooms when it's come on. I've frantically launched myself at stereos to quickly click it to the next song. But today I steel myself and let it roll. It's such a beautiful song.

As it plays, I catch my face in the mirror. *My hair is so much curlier now than when we got married, my face is so different.* Whoever I was when I was a bride, it isn't the same person I am now, not inside, not out. Whoever he was, that groom dancing to this song with me, he isn't that person now either.

For a second I struggle to remember the feeling of dancing to this song as our friends and family watched. It all comes back to me when it gets to the part in the song that always made us hug each other a little bit tighter when we danced to it — in our first apartment, in the kitchen of our house when I was pregnant, and certainly on our wedding day when The Husband sang it to me, so sweetly and low, half-whispered.

As our marriage was falling apart, he told me, "When I asked you to marry me, I believed in it. The day we got married, I believed in us. I didn't think I would do this. I really didn't." He thought he was someone else. Someone good.

I walk away from the mirror and sit on the couch in a bit of a daze, my whole being transported back to 2002, to promise, to the belief that we would hold each other up, keep each other hanging on.

RIP Lou, and RIP our marriage. Everything turns into something else, and that's all right.

SOMETHING ELSE

Find me here, in a washroom stall, in a bar, taking out my phone to look at a picture of The Man with the White Shirt. This. *Again*. I'm on a third date with a really cool guy. He's great, but like everyone I meet, he can't compare. And so, even though I'm on this date with Totally Acceptable Guy, my fingers ignore my brain. I text,

I don't know how to stop.

And White Shirt texts back immediately,

You're asking the one who doesn't know how to start.

Two years later. It's no different. The two of us, back and forth. Beating a path between our houses. *Years* of not being my boyfriend, of being the best not-boyfriend. Of me dating Totally Acceptable Guy versions 1 through 8. Of him "not dating at all" and "not getting involved with anyone," which I can only take to mean having excellent casual sex with women who are supercool about it.

We say we will stop. We say we will try.

We say we tried, but now we should stop.

We say, I love you. *I love you, too.*

We say, You aren't right for me! *YOU aren't right for ME!*

We say, I can't let go. *Me either.*

We say, *We should take some space, we can do it this time.*

Yes, I believe in you. *I believe in you, too.*

We say, I can't imagine not having you in my life but we have to do this.

I need this. *Me, too.*

We say, *Of course you can come over, of course.*

Our love is a serpent eating its own tail. So tell me, what should I do? Because I still don't know how to say goodbye, how to be alone. Because I'm forty-one now and I still don't know how to stop. Because he's forty, and he still doesn't know how to start.

PART ❤ THREE

I want a love that doesn't need to
wring its hands so much.
A love that puts all its money down on one horse.

CHAPTER SEVENTEEN

BLOW AWAY

THE BAD ONE

The first time I break up with The Man with the White Shirt is on his thirty-eighth birthday, Hallowe'en 2013. The very same week as my own birthday and the tarot card reader and Lou Reed dying and the divorce coming through. What a week!

I tell The Man with the White Shirt it's over. I'm upset that he's spending the next night with another woman, Rockabilly Redhead. "I gave you tonight!" he says, "I chose to spend my *actual* birthday with you, and see her tomorrow!" like he's awarded me the highest honour. I'm repulsed by him for a moment. This ranking. This sharing of himself — what a great guy. "This doesn't work for me!" I shout. "This is over between us!"

I wait until 1:00 a.m. to do all this shouting, after we've had sex. *Happy Birthday!*

The next night, the vampire version of me crawls out of her apartment and onto the streets. I am hungry for blood. The blood of anyone will do, I don't even care. I want to forget White Shirt ever existed. I want to forget that he's spending the day after his birthday with his second-favourite not-girlfriend. I want to forget The Ex-husband, who texted some woman he was trying to hook up with tonight, but sent it to me by accident. *Honest to God.*

So I drink all the alcohol I can. All the booze I wasn't drinking those few happy months before I realized Rockabilly Redhead existed. I dance and cry and dance more. I down tequilas. I take home a stupid boy I just met and don't even like that much.

I'm almost blackout drunk as he climbs on top of me. And then, instead of being numb to it all, I burst into hysterical tears. I ask him to stop. I ask him to leave.

I say, "I'm sorry, I changed my mind."

I say, "I'm so fucked up, I'm sorry. I shouldn't have done this. I'm too sad. Please leave. I changed my mind. I'm too sad, I'm too sad."

He does stop. But he refuses to leave. He yells at me for being a tease. He yells at me for being fucked up. He yells at me for changing my mind. He yells and yells. I'm shaking so hard. All I want is for him to not be here. All I want is for this to not be my life. And so I give him fifty dollars. I don't know why, for cab fare and damages? He takes it, calls me a fucking cunt, and leaves. He finally leaves.

I am so scared. Because he knows where I live. Because I was so busy drowning myself I almost forgot the things worth breathing for. Because I don't know how this happened. *How did I lose the life of love and safety I always had?*

I text The Man with the White Shirt. I want to call him, but also I don't, in case he's in the middle of having sex with Rockabilly Redhead. I don't want *her* night to be ruined, too. So I text a crazed message about what just happened to me, but he doesn't answer it. Not until the next *afternoon* when he calls with excuses for why he didn't see my text until the morning, and didn't have a chance to call until now because he was too busy with "other stuff."

I cry and cry to him, about that stupid boy who wouldn't leave and how scared I was and how sad, but he can't understand me. Not through my hysterical tears and the spotty cell reception. And even if he could hear my words, he could never understand what they *mean*. He could never understand what this is like for me.

I spend the next three weeks in a trance. Hating myself for being so stupid. Again.

Wondering how I would survive my own spiral of booze and bad choices. Missing the comfort of White Shirt, the excitement of him, the fun. I work very hard to not text him or call him or email him. I broke up with him because he wasn't right for me, and I try to honour my decision. He tries to honour it, too. But as you well know, we are very, very bad at it.

We last twenty days before we meet in a restaurant close to my house. He's already there at a table when I walk in, and he stands when he sees me. He pulls out my chair, and waits. When I see him there, like that, it feels like the most confusing punch I've ever felt. It feels like knives in my gut. Like icicles. Like fireworks. It feels … great. Terrible and great, all at the same time. The best terrible ever.

When he hugs me, I inhale as much of his scent as possible and my whole body relaxes. He says he's so happy to see me. He says he missed me so much. He says he spent the last three weeks listening to every bit of audio there is of me: my radio documentaries and essays, the show I produce each week, recordings of me singing. *Oh man, coming here was a huge mistake.* If I was smarter or stronger, I wouldn't be sitting here drugged by his scent and his voice and his eyes and his in-depth reviews of my work. But I'm not smart or strong and now I *am* here and his face is a beacon. I just want to stay in its light. He's a magnet. He has actually, literally magnetized me. *Shit.* I should have walked away for good when I broke up with him on his birthday.

After dinner, he kisses me on the street outside the restaurant, and I know we're ruined. Now we'll be tied together, from this point on, going round the same loop. Now we're in our very own indie film and I'm Julie Delpy and he's Ethan Hawke but browner, and we're just gonna walk around the city having a conversation for the next ten years.

BITS AND PIECES

"You're amazing — you're so on top of things, your life is so in order," says Revival, usually a man of few words, but not tonight for some reason.

"Are you kidding? I'm a *mess*."

"Man, you're not a mess *at all*. You've got it all happening for yourself! You manage it all!"

"But I'm so tired," I say, and he gives me a squeeze. He pulls me onto his chest and I nestle my face there against his smooth, smooth skin.

"I wish you could just sleep over," I say for the first time ever, and I mean it.

"I wish I could, too," he says. "I wish a lot of things."

I'm overwhelmed by his sudden candour, the way he's speaking about me admiringly, as if he's speaking about someone else, not me, not the woman who just lets him come and go, the woman who asks no questions. And so we lie there, 3:00 a.m., wrapped up in each other, two strangers in a way but also weirdly connected. This is what it is. This is me, taking the little bits and pieces that the men in my life offer.

Revival asks me how it's going with The Man with the White Shirt, and I sigh and roll my eyes and complain like a heartsick teenager as I tell him. "Why do you want a boyfriend so badly?" Revival asks, and then before I can even answer, "It's not all that, you know. It's a pain in the ass to be in a couple, don't you remember?"

Of course I remember. I remember it's a pain in the ass, but I also remember that it's wonderful. How it feels to fall asleep beside the person you love each night, to have someone know you, really know you. "It's worth the pain-in-the-ass parts to me," I say, ever The Saddest Optimist. He smiles. I watch him put his clothes on. We kiss. And away he goes.

When I lock the door, the first thing I think of is The Man with the White Shirt. His face, his smile, his smell. *Him.* Lying beside me all those nights, how we'd talk and talk until we fell asleep. How opening my eyes in the morning and seeing him there filled me with a kind of joy I miss and crave so deeply.

How each moment with him felt like a gift, something special for me, but never really mine to keep. A placeholder. A million-dollar necklace to wear to the Oscars that you have to give back the next day so some other woman can have it for a night.

Something that sparkles, casting a perfect glow on you, before it turns and shines on someone else.

BLINDNESS

So, I'm a monogamous person in a non-monogamous relationship. I live for the next time I can be with him again, the man that makes me feel whole, even while the situation splits me in two. Ugh. *How did I get here?*

It actually begins at the beginning, where if we're really honest with ourselves, we *both* could have seen this coming. Like, from Day 1, the day of our very first date.

The Man with the White Shirt and I, standing on Dundas West, outside of the bar we were just in, where he had a beer, I had a ginger ale and we had great conversation. Out on the street, we linger to see what will happen next.

I think we are probably going to kiss, but instead he says, "I need to tell you something." And I say seriously, "Me, too. I have a kid. And an ex-husband." I hold my breath. We've just had an amazing night and he is so hot and I want to take him home with me, and usually I don't tell guys about Birdie and The Ex-husband but I want to tell this man for some reason.

"Wow, cool," he says, and asks how old she is and how long it's been, the usual questions. I ask what he has to tell me.

"I see other women," he says, and I say, "Yeah, obviously," because we just met. Of course we see other people!

At the time, I didn't understand what he really meant. But also, he didn't really tell me. If he said, more clearly, that he was polyamorous, or that he didn't believe in monogamy, maybe I would have cut my losses right then and there. If he said, "Being in a monogamous relationship isn't right for me," it's possible that despite how hot he was and how special he seemed, I would have decided not to get involved.

But he didn't say that. And I heard what I wanted to hear. I heard him saying he's non-monogamous until he meets the "right one." Just like me.

We kiss in a doorway. Our first kiss. And *this* is the moment where we both choose blindness, however subconsciously. In this doorway, I tell myself he will probably just be okay in bed. Or maybe it will be amazing, but that will be it, it won't amount to anything more. I tell myself that even though we don't know each other that well yet, it's possible that because we saw each other across a room and had that fireworks moment just the night before, that thing they call Love at First Sight, maybe he will turn out to be my second great love.

You can think a lot of contradictory things during one kiss.

We decide to go back to my place. And there's this moment where we are trying to shove his bike into the back of my tiny car, arguing like we've been a couple forever, *Put it here! No, move it this way!* ... an unusual foreplay that, for me, adds to the magic. Because it's comfortable and intimate, the way we negotiate the bike's placement, forcing it to fit in my tiny hatchback so we can close the trunk.

Already, we were trying to make things fit that didn't. Or at least, didn't fit *easily*. I don't know how I didn't see that until now.

MAYBE

After a particularly hard week of torment and tears over The Man with the White Shirt, I arrive at work one morning to find a Tupperware container on my desk with a tiny note attached to it. It's an entire brisket, from my friend Pint Size, and her note restores all the power back to my heart for a bit. It says:

I don't know the answers to your questions about love,
but I know that this meat will make you feel better.

Later, we meet in the kitchenette for tea. I try to hug her and say thanks for the brisket and her kindness but she is very no-nonsense and won't stand for my mushy stuff.

"Listen, it has got to be a *Fuck Yes!* or it isn't worth it," she says to me, like a tiny scolding schoolteacher. I roll my eyes and say, "Yeah, I knowww …" and sometimes I can't believe I'm forty and these are the conversations I'm having.

"Have I told you my Jenga Principle of Dating?" says Pint Size. "It's simple: If you both aren't taking a block from the bottom and putting it on top, then forget about it!"

I laugh because I always feel like I'm in a sitcom when she talks, and I sigh, because she's always right. Because up until now love had always been a resounding *Fuck Yes!* in all my relationships, but with The Man with the White Shirt it was nothing but *Maybe??* So many maybes. And I'm willing to cry into my brisket for the maybe, because I believe we are different, that he's special, and we are special, that one day he's going to see that and change his mind and go all-in with me.

So for now our relationship is just the two of us driving round and round in a parking lot where he can never find a spot that's good enough, and I'm just shouting "Squeeze in there!" and "What about there?" because any spot is fine as long as we just fit ourselves into it.

ROAD TO NOWHERE

It's a Sunday. Sometime in the second summer after The Bomb. I'm dropping Birdie off at her father's and he makes me an espresso. It's in one of my grandmother's old cups — dark brown ceramic, a bolt of my childhood served up by my ex-husband.

Here in his apartment, we sit at my old Formica table, having a coffee in my *nonna*'s cups as we fold and separate Birdie's laundry. She's playing in her room. We're just talking about regular stuff, nothing to do with anything in particular, when he suddenly grabs me and kisses me hard. Long. With so much passion. He's never done that before. I mean, since the breakup we've only ever kissed while having sex, so I'm taken a little off guard. We just do that for a while until I casually stop him. We finish the folding and I leave soon after.

Does it melt some part of me? I'm not going to lie and say it doesn't. But so what. Between The Ex-husband and The Man with the White Shirt, I've had it with these sporadic bursts of love and affection. The reeling in and casting out. This isn't the love I want. I want to be loved the way I love, with conviction and risk in equal parts, wholly invested and hopeful and honest. The way it seemed for us *both* when we first met, back when he was still just The Scientist to me. Back when he was the most fearless person I'd ever met — besides myself. We were well suited then, it seemed, because life was a thing we both approached with the same spirit — a mix of adventure and independence and fortitude and enthusiasm.

226

There was this time once, at the end of 1999 and the begin-ning of us. We were twenty-five. The Scientist had a rented car and one of us suggested *Let's run away somewhere for a night*, so we drove north of the city with absolutely no plan and no belongings and telling no one. *Look at us, on the run!* we laughed, escaping the city and our lives and feeling more free in running than we did standing still. We just drove and drove, only stopping when we were about to run out of gas. At an old motel perched on an exit off the highway, we got a room for the night.

We didn't even know where we were and it didn't matter, but it's funny now, isn't it? The first trip we took together was to nowhere.

THEY MEET

I'm sitting on the edge of the playground, half-watching as Birdie plays. It's the usual scenario — me sitting alone, surrounded by happy couples chatting and laughing with other happy couples while their multiple children run around screaming. But today, I'm not as bothered as I usually am by these loving, intact families.

Today I'm sitting here with butterflies swirling around my head. Not literal ones, but the lovey-dovey gooey complicated butterflies that come with having fallen for The Man with the White Shirt. Complicated, *complicated* butterflies.

White Shirt is texting me. He's on his bike and going to drop by the park, he says. I think hard on this. I don't want Birdie to meet any man in my life unless that man and I mean serious business. Serious in the traditional sense. He's gotta be my boy-friend. And White Shirt, as we know, is *not* my boyfriend. He's The Not-Boyfriend.

Birdie is six years old at this point, and isn't very physically affectionate. She refuses to be hugged or touched by almost any-one but her dad and me. Even then, she manages to worm her way out of our arms in a matter of seconds. It's like she has no use for most people. She's met a lot of my friends, both men and women, and although she's friendly and polite, she doesn't usually pay all that much attention to them. So I figure there's no harm in The Man with the White Shirt coming by the park to sit with me a bit. She won't even notice.

When he arrives at the playground, it's like extra sunlight was ordered in. And a wind machine. And sparkly mist. I can smell every single flower in the park. He gets off his bike and smiles, and I have to remember to breathe. *Fuck.* He hugs me and I'm super stiff. I don't know how to reconcile the volcanic eruption in my body with the wholesome family-ness of the playground. As we sit down, Birdie, who never pays attention to me or *anyone* in the playground, suddenly comes running over.

"Hi," she says to The Man with the White Shirt. She doesn't acknowledge me at all. "Do you want to see Sir Mew?" Sir Mew is a tiny eraser in the shape of a white cat.

"Yeah I do!" he says, and before I know it, they're playing with eraser cats and laughing and talking like it's no big deal. It's a big deal to me. My two worlds are colliding, and I'm freaking out. I really thought he was just going to drop by for a bit, but instead he's deep in storyline creation with Birdie and this is all so ... unexpected. Here she is, draped over him, touching him, even. *Why hasn't she gone back to her friends on the playground? What is going* on?

White Shirt suggests we get some frozen yogourt and Birdie is thrilled. I agree but it's like I do it from a great distance. This wasn't supposed to happen. She isn't supposed to love him so immediately, like I did. He isn't real. His love is only partial. It has limits. I need to protect her but it's all happening so fast. *This can't be good.*

We walk through the park, the three of us. My child who touches no one reaches for his hand and he takes it. And just like that, walking along the path, we look like a family. Just like that, it's so easy for my heart to be swindled.

Frozen yogourt with sprinkles. And cookie dough. And ... jujubes? He obviously loves kids, but has never been a parent. She's laughing with that husky Janis Joplin voice of hers, and it makes everyone in the shop smile. My obstinate child is suddenly delightful. In public! It's hard not to make it about him. It's hard to not be swept away by the fact that his presence has calmed my little tempest of a daughter. The exact way he made me feel when I first met him. *Calm.*

On the street we say goodbye, but Birdie won't have any of it. She jumps on The Man with the White Shirt. Like, takes a running jump onto his back screaming, "Nooooo, don't go! *Take me with you!*" He laughs and hugs her and doesn't seem uncomfortable at all. "We'll hang out again!" he promises her as I try to pry her off his body. She is unbelievably strong and will not let go of him. Her mother's daughter, through and through.

White Shirt is beaming. He's had so much fun. But my insides are a mess as I cycle through the contradictory facts: *He can't be in a monogamous relationship. He doesn't know if he'll ever be able to be in a committed relationship.*

"I LOVE YOUUUUU!" Birdie shouts as we cross the street. And *this* is how they meet, The Man with the White Shirt and my Birdie.

Their relationship becomes so deep, so quickly. It grows easily into its own thing over the next several years. He teaches her to play the drums. They walk his dog together. They build elaborate LEGO structures. She hugs him like hugging is what she does. He picks her up from school. Or watches her on summer days while I'm working. They call it "Camp White Shirt."

For years there will be one or two nights a month where I get home from work to find him cooking dinner while Birdie happily plays nearby. I always look forward to these nights. The anticipation of the life going on inside. The warmth of light and food and other human bodies that floods me the second I walk in the door. The *warmth*. The three of us at the table, joking and eating like a family. The way they cut each other off trying to tell me a funny story. How she writes our dessert orders on a little notepad, then returns with three pudding cups and three espresso spoons neatly laid out on a tray.

In these moments, I *glow*. Watching them, listening. Feeling whole again. But his phone keeps beeping. Soon he'll be gone. Out … somewhere, with … someone. And Birdie and I will be back to a family of two. The warm light slightly dimmed.

The Man with the White Shirt comes in and out like this for years and years. I let him. I encourage it. I want it, even if it's occasional. We are not a couple to her. We don't kiss in front of her, he doesn't sleep over. In her eyes, he's my best friend and I'm his. Which is true. Except I have never been so attracted to a best friend in all my life. I'm not sure I've ever wanted anyone more, in a way that I imagine addicts want drugs. It defies all reason. But she doesn't need to know that. She will only know us as friends, unless a miracle happens and we ever become a real couple in a real relationship. This is a thing I never stop hoping for. A thing I wait for, even while I move forward. I can do that, you know, move and wait at the same time.

Birdie told The Man with the White Shirt she loved him the very first day they met. Just look at them together. That's why I know that one day he will change his mind and be ready to commit, not just to me but to *us*. From the moment they met, she loved him. It was a sign.

It was a sign. Wasn't it?

SIGNS

Yeah, about signs. You might be rolling your eyes at me. The way I find magic in every coincidence. The way I think the universe is always telling me something. It's like everyone wants to make sure I understand life is flat and boring, that coincidences are just that, coincidences, they don't have *meaning*.

The truth is, to me these signs are just little Easter eggs, there for us to unearth in this game we live in. Sometimes the Easter eggs give us power or extra life when we find them. Sometimes they make things worse. But most of the time they're just fun to find. It feels *fun* to find them. It feels special because not everyone finds them and experiences them. *That* is what these signs are to me, these coincidences I imbue with extra meaning and magic. The meaning and magic is that we unearthed them. What's so wrong about that?

The night I first met The Man with the White Shirt, he gave me his phone number and I couldn't believe it. The last four digits were the numeric pin code I've used for practically my whole life! And then I saw his bike. There, on the crossbar in a 1970s script, was one word. A word from my childhood, the title of my favourite Paul Weller song, and my most common password at the time. *Wildwood*. There on White Shirt's bike for me. I mean, yeah, it seems silly now that I'm saying it, *passwords*! But I like this stuff. It feels special to me. *He* feels special because of these things.

So, you don't have to humour me about all this hippie shit, okay? I just need to know you understand me. Signs or no signs, to me there is only him and everyone else is fifty stories below that. He's in the penthouse. He's the entire top floor.

CHAPTER EIGHTEEN

THERE, THERE

FIREWORKS

Every time I see The Man with the White Shirt, it's just like the poets said, it's fireworks. Actual goddamn fireworks. Inside me, above his head, all around us, everywhere, *boom boom boom.* And he's talking about whatever, talking about what I don't know because I just see his lips move and it's all *boom boom boom* and my whole body just melts beside him, every ligament is taut and every neuron is firing and every hair stands on end and every bit of my skin wants to touch every bit of his, *boom boom boom.*

Listen to me, I whisper as he sleeps, *you are loved like a fireworks display. Your very presence is fireworks.*

I love you like that.

WIDE AWAKE AND DREAMING

Spring 2015. I go out a lot, trying to forget, trying to find. Trying not to drink too much. Trying to keep it together. Tonight I had a good night out dancing with a friend of mine. We walked home because it wasn't that cold and I wasn't that drunk and it wasn't raining that hard yet. And it's past 2:00 a.m. but still, I call him anyway. I call The Man with the White Shirt.

I promised my friend I wouldn't. But I walk maybe fifteen steps away from her, long enough for her to go into her apartment building, as long as I can last before I pull up his name on my phone, there with a photo of his smiling, Jesus Christ gorgeous face and I call him even though I swore I wouldn't. I call The Man with the White Shirt at 2:00 a.m. and he doesn't answer. If I call a second time, he will. It's a promise he made after The Bad Night, the night with the crazy guy I had to pay to leave, the night he didn't answer my distress text because he was busy with Rockabilly Redhead.

After that night, The Man with the White Shirt promised he would always answer my calls. He told me if for some reason he didn't, and something was really wrong, I should call a second time and he would answer no matter what. And he does. He has kept this promise, his one and only commitment to me. It's the only consistent thing he does, no matter how inconvenient it is, no matter who he's with, no matter how late it is or how drunk and belligerent I am. He answers. He always answers.

But tonight it seems ridiculous and not an emergency at all for me to call him a second time. So I try a new thing for me: restraint. I try instead to imagine he is just sleeping. Alone. Sleeping alone in his bed on a Friday night. As I walk, I say to myself, *He's sleeping, he's sleeping alone, he's dreaming of me.* But I know how unlikely that is. He's lying beside someone who isn't me. While all I want is to be holding his hand, trying to remember song lyrics and Simpsons dialogue as we walk home. Crawling into his bed, or mine, and the way he always unlaces my boots for me.

And then the mornings. The mornings are my favourite part. The sound of his snoring, me staring at the ceiling, the espresso whistling and bubbling over on the stove. Those breakfasts he makes from what seems like no ingredients. His hands on my body, the daylight streaming in ... sigh.

Now I have to unlace my own boots. And stare at my own ceiling. I'm wide awake. I'm wide awake and dreaming of him.

I SHOULD SLEEP BUT I DON'T SLEEP

I should sleep but I don't sleep. I pace around my apartment like I'm looking for something I've lost. I can't find it so I wander some more, in and out of rooms, back and forth across the floor like I'm gathering forensics of my own mysterious existence. I look at old photos. I zoom in on faces, look right into eyes, trace pixelated jawlines with my fingertips. I read and re-read old emails and journal entries. I live the past like it's a boulder I've swallowed.

I should sleep but I don't sleep. I'm just sitting here thinking about everything I've lost — love, time, a sense of belonging. The woman I once was, the woman I thought I would be. Now I'm a stranger in my own home, a drifter in my own life. A tourist in this city I was born in. Lost and left to wander it, a sad girl in rags.

I should sleep but I don't sleep. I stand on the balcony and stare out into the night. I have so much to say and no one to say it to. So much to give, but in giving it I have been told it is too much. *Too much.* Always too much. Or else not enough.

I should sleep but I don't sleep. I look in the mirror for longer than I should and I think, *I'm pretty, I'm smart, I'm interesting.* Why is that too much? How is that not enough? Why am I alone? This is how I get. It's all I think about. *Alone alone alone, I am alone.* It's on a loop and it's all I can do to not be driven crazy by it. This longing for a thing that will never return. A disease I've been infected with and will have for the rest of my life. The fact that I have an actual disease I don't think about very much is ironic, I guess. But MS doesn't hang out with me the way the longing does, it doesn't run through my veins the way The Lonely does. Every day I shoot a needle into my body, an expensive drug to modify the disease I actually have, but all the while I'm just wishing there was some drug to modify the loneliness that's taken over me. No one will ever love me completely again. Maybe no one ever has … why isn't there a drug I can take to modify that?

I should sleep but I don't sleep. Not until I've exhausted myself with self-pity. Not until I convince myself that in sleep at least, I will not feel the way I feel right now. I should sleep so I lie down and try, finally, in this too-big-for-one bed. Eyes staring up at the ceiling, I straddle the past and the imagined future, neither of which resemble this current reality. Eventually it will just happen, sleep, it has to, I know it. I will hold hands with The Lonely and drift off to the sound of my own beating heart, irregular as the rumble of trains outside my window.

TIME

It surprises me now how much time can pass where I have no contact with The Ex-husband, where I don't even *think* about him. It can be weeks, sometimes. It's amazing, isn't it? That you can spend twelve years with someone, and several years after that, where they are always on your mind, in your heart, a funny story about them on the tip of your tongue, and then suddenly one day without realizing it, you stop thinking about them as much. Finally.

That's how I feel now, I feel like *finally* his power over me is diminished. Like I am moving on. But it's always short-lived. We have to connect, because of co-parenting or to talk about some vestige of the separation agreement that still needs to be ironed out. We have to talk, and that means we also flirt or fight or both. And then the moving on, for me, grinds to a halt.

There are other ways, too. Like that time at a party, when a woman I know callously started talking about how she's sleeping with a married man and *BOOM!* I was shell-shocked all over again. Or the time he showed up on a dating app and a ton of women I know screen-capped it and texted it to me along with, *Is this your HUSBAND?!?!* To which I replied, *Ex-husband. Also that photo is from like, 15 years ago. As IF!* And we all had a big ol' laugh at his expense and also at how awkward modern life is. But inside of me, the awful, twisty pang returned.

It's an actual pang, not of nostalgia for our good happy marriage, but of regret that I married him in the first place because it brought me here, to this moment, where I have to relive a precise pain over and over again. A pain that upends me when it is triggered so easily by a word or phrase or a laugh or a goddamn screencap of my own husband's dating profile.

I want to be able to laugh it off, I mean, really laugh it off, like laugh him right out of my life, but I'm stuck with him forever because of Birdie. Without a child, I wouldn't have to talk to him at all, ever. There would be a distance, and it would be easier to get over the heartbreak and hurt. I know it wouldn't change some things. I'm sure I'd still want to *scream* when people talk casually about infidelity like it's some fun adventure they've been on. I know I wouldn't avoid the screen-capped profile pics. But maybe, just maybe, I would have a real chance at healing if he wasn't around so much. If he wasn't there with his smirk and those shiny eyes and his words that hit me like so many slivers of flying, broken glass.

Time is healing the wound, just like they said it would. But it will always be there. The Scientist, The Husband, The Ex-husband … he's always with me, and in that way I will never be free.

BROOKLYN

A friend of mine is getting married. She lives in New York City now, and I'm going with Forever 21, The Lawyer, and a bunch of other friends. It's Spring 2015.

The Man with the White Shirt kisses me on the morning I'm flying out. "Have fun. I'll see you in three days when you get off the plane!" he says. He is the best not-boyfriend in the whole world.

My friend The Bride, has been telling me for a year that her almost-husband's best friend is "Toootallyyyy your type. You guys would *love* each other!" He's going to be the best man at the wedding. But I'm not going there thinking about hooking up with him, or anyone, on this trip. My heart is tethered to the best not-boyfriend in the whole world. I can't think of anyone but The Man with the White Shirt.

It's a short flight to New York from the Toronto Island airport. The wedding is only a few hours after we land. We walk from the hotel down to the pier to have cocktails overlooking the Hudson River, Lady Liberty not far with her slightly disapproving look. The room is crowded and as I'm heading to the bar some dude knocks into me, spills his drink all over the top of my fancy fucking dress and doesn't even notice. A super-cute guy jumps to my defence quickly with some cocktail napkins, trying to blot out the spill but then realizing he is basically touching my boobs while doing it, he jumps back and shouts, "Ohmygod *sorry!*" We laugh. We talk. We get to know each other. I learn he's the cousin of The Best Man, the guy with whom I'm supposed to be a perfect match.

"Where is he?" I ask. "Apparently I *have* to meet him."

"He's late, so lucky for me," says The Cousin with a smile. I smile back. *Oh well, too bad for Best Man.*

The ceremony is beautiful. The atmosphere is beautiful. The Best Man gives an amazing speech and he seems really cool, but I haven't met him yet. I've spent the whole night with The Cousin, drinking and laughing and drinking and more drinking. He is much, much younger than me and we have nothing in common but he's adorable and brash and this is fun.

Eventually, The Best Man comes over and we meet. He is not brash. He is not crazy party drinking guy like his cousin. He's thoughtful when he speaks and looks at me in a calm, arresting way even when he isn't saying anything. I am *captivated*. The Best Man works in radio just like me. He's an artist who also is into sports, just like me. He's soft-spoken and seems like a real man in comparison to The Cousin. A really real man compared to The Man with the White Shirt, even though Best Man is five years younger. All I want to do is talk to *him* now. What's he all about? But he cuts through the crowd, leaving me and the now-very-drunk Cousin to resume our silly party. We dance close on the dance floor but we haven't kissed or anything. Instead I keep looking over his shoulder to find The Best Man, to see what he's doing. And that's when The Cousin casually mentions his fiancée back home in New Jersey.

"Your *what*?" I say, pulling away from his body quickly.

"We aren't married yet!" he says, trying to pull me into him again.

No no no no no. Nuh-uh. Nope. I walk away. Fast. And that's when I realize the place is half empty. The chairs are being stacked. That song was the last song, the wedding is over. I look for my purse and jacket, and then The Best Man is there in front of me.

"We're all going to a bar now," he says, and takes my arm in his. We walk along Avenue of the Americas, talking to each other, arm in arm, while the now-very-drunk-and-dejected Cousin trails along behind us with some other people. We walk past the hotel most of us are staying at, then down a few side streets until we get to a little Irish pub. The bride and groom and all the Canadians are already inside.

I stopped drinking hours ago. I want to be present for this conversation with The Best Man. He's so soft-spoken and mild-mannered and unassuming and totally, unbelievably interesting to me. Also, full of surprises. I'm in the middle of telling some story when he suddenly just puts his big arm around me and pulls me into him for a kiss. A capital-G-Great kiss.

"Wow," I say teasingly, "that was bold!" He just shrugs like *no big deal*, and I am electrified. I pull him into me now, and kiss him hard, right there in the middle of this crowded pub in Lower Manhattan, even though I'm usually the least PDA person in the world.

At 2:00 a.m. he walks me back to the hotel. We are carrying enormous vases of flowers back for The Bride, but even still, we stop every few feet to make out against a wall or in a doorway. It is the sexiest walk I have ever taken in all my life. I feel like I'm in a movie. *I'm in New York City, everyone! Where dream men appear and kiss you perfectly in half-lit laneways!*

For the last bit of making out we're in a little crevice in the side of the wall of the hotel. People walk by, but I have never cared less. I'm wearing my fanciest fucking dress and there are vases of gorgeous flowers at my feet and this man can kiss and he can smile and have I mentioned the absolute gloriousness of his arms? They are huge and strong and his body feels like the best thing I have ever felt maybe, or at least it does right now, here pressed up against a wall in Manhattan.

We kiss a million times in the lobby. We say, *See you tomorrow, Yes, for sure, I have your number, I have yours. Tomorrow, tomorrow, tomorrow.* I go up to the hotel room I'm sharing with Forever 21 and two other friends. They woot and wooo at me about The Best Man. I blush and demur and fall onto the bed in the most blissful state and check my phone. Best Man has already texted, *Can't wait till tomorrow!* and I text back, *Me either!*

And then I see it. Another text, sent only an hour earlier when I was involved in the world's longest street kiss. It's from

The Man with the White Shirt. He wonders if I got there safely since he hadn't heard from me. He says he heard a song on the radio and it made him think of me. He says he hopes I'm having fun. My heart sinks for a second. *Goddamn it, if you were just my actual boyfriend you would be here with me. I wouldn't be making out with Brooklyn Dream Boy, I'd be with* you *in our own hotel room! You wouldn't have to hear songs on the radio that make you think of me, you would actually* be *with me!* I turn off my phone and try to fall asleep.

The next day I walk the High Line with my pals. We have the world's best Mexican brunch. We go to a Mets game. The whole time, The Best Man and I text each other until finally, *finally*, later that night, all the Canadians and the bride and groom and The Best Man get together in a bar on the Lower East Side.

The Best Man is wearing a leather jacket with jeans and a black T-shirt. He's got some kind of a cool hat on and cool bracelets and his overall style seems effortless and timeless. I like it all so much, holy shit. We sit together at the bar and talk, our legs pressed together, our hands touching. After a while we look around and realize everyone we know is gone. I say, "So you want to take me back to Brooklyn?" and he says, "Obviously."

For the first time in my life I go to Brooklyn, New York, where we fall together easily onto his bed, and he is quiet and I am loud, and his body is to die for and he says mine is and the whole thing is pretty fucking Great, capital G. At around 5:00 a.m. when the light of morning is starting to crack the sky, we fall asleep. We wake up starving at ten. "Let's go for brunch," he says. "I'll take you to my favourite spot."

Meanwhile, the Canadians are all texting me like crazy. *Where are you? Was it fun? Are you coming back?* And I answer with rows of exclamation marks.

I'm in Brooklyn!!!! I type, like I've been to Narnia or the moon.

I assume once brunch is over we will say goodbye, so to make conversation I ask him what he's doing the rest of the day.

Without hesitation, but also as if it's obvious, he says, "I'm going to spend it with you, right up until you have to go to the airport." And I swoon. Like for real swoon, like a swoon I haven't felt for anyone since I met The Man with the White Shirt. *Oh my God* — White Shirt. It's been hours, more? since I've thought about him. Did I ever even answer his text? Do I care?

He keeps insisting he isn't my boyfriend, so I can do whatever I like, right? I can do anything, including having this unexpected thirty-six-hour romance with The Best Man. White Shirt wouldn't mind anyway. He wouldn't even care. He'd say, *As long as it makes you happy.* And I wouldn't like the way it would feel to hear him say it. I promptly push him out of my mind.

The rest of the day with The Best Man continues like a New York City rom-com montage. We ride the subway from Brooklyn to Manhattan. He takes me to Little Italy, where we wander the crowded streets hand-in-hand and snap selfies of the two of us nestled against one another. We walk through SoHo, then Chinatown. We just walk and walk, his arm always around me or leading me somewhere new. It all feels so *romantic.*

We make our way slowly back to my hotel so I can pack my bags. All the Canadians are staying until tomorrow, but I'm leaving today to get back to Birdie. He lies on one bed while I pack my little carry-on luggage on the other. Then I lie down beside him, my head on his chest. We text The Bride one of our selfies with the caption, *You were right!*

Told ya so! she answers.

"Why don't you exist in Toronto?" I ask him, because I really mean it.

"Why don't *you* exist in New York?" he asks back, which is impossible to believe is true. How can a smart, super-cute, interesting, fit, talented, shit-together thirty-five-year-old man *not* find a girlfriend in this giant city?

He shrugs. "Dating is the worst."

And I say, "Oh believe me, I know."

We both sigh. When it's time for me to go he carries my luggage to the subway station and then all the way down the steep stairs. He walks me as far as he can, right up to the turnstile, and kisses me goodbye several times. He waves once I'm through, and I wave back.

Only a few hours later, I'm back in Toronto, standing outside the downtown island airport. The Man with the White Shirt pulls up in my car and hops out. He reaches for my little carry-on luggage and when he touches it, I flinch. He hugs me hard and kisses me sweetly, then puts the luggage on the back seat beside his lovely old dog, who is also happy to see me, but I feel like I'm having an out-of-body experience. *How can this all be the same day?* I woke up in Brooklyn. I woke up in a dream man's bed in Brooklyn. And now I'm here with White Shirt and his dog and our city and our complicated non-relationship and what, everything is supposed to be normal even when it isn't? Even when it's never been?

At my place, White Shirt cooks us food and we watch a TV show in bed and then, for the first time ever, I do not want to have sex with him. I want instead to just fall asleep with my New York City romance preserved in a snow globe that doesn't include The Man with the White Shirt in its tableau. I want to keep our Brooklyn morning and the hand-holding walks through Manhattan and the whole all of it. I want to keep it unpolluted by the complication that White Shirt brings to everything in my life.

So I tell him I'm exhausted, even though that's never once stopped me before, and if he finds that strange he doesn't betray it. Instead of having sex we just fall asleep together, my mind swirling with how much life can fit into one unexpected day.

Best Man and I text a little after that, but not much. He doesn't want to have a long-distance relationship and neither do I. It could never work anyway, I have a kid and an ex-husband

and a career so I can never leave Toronto, and he has *his* career and besides, he doesn't even have a passport, he's so super-American. But we stay in touch. We like each other's Instagram photos a lot. Every few weeks one of us will send a short email and the other will respond, but there is no trace of the romance. We write like two kids who met and became best friends at camp but don't know what to say now that they're back in their regular lives.

CIRCLES

Summer 2015. White Shirt suddenly turns the awesomeness dial up to 95 percent, showing up with flowers and calling me all the time and making plans, and we spend three or four days a week together. It feels like something is different, like we're *trying*, but it's hard to say for sure. It's just a lot of the same circles, the feeling he might change his mind, the disappointment when he doesn't. The things he says to me that give me hope. False hope.

Feelings can be misleading, according to my new psychologist. And that's what I have to remember every time White Shirt tells me he loves me. Or buys me perfect little gifts. Or helps me with Birdie and home repairs. The things that make it feel like he's my boyfriend, my partner. The things he says and does that only a person in love would say or do.

I'm really not sure if this is how love is supposed to feel. This circle we keep tracing. It's the world's biggest loop, and we are in it and we both know it. But *why* we are in it, well, that's another thing altogether. And it's misleading, yes, to think that the very act of going round and round means we're headed somewhere.

"Just let life be!" a semi-crazy guy shouts at me. It's midnight and I'm standing outside on the street while White Shirt is in a convenience store. I smile politely, because semi-crazy guy looks the worse for wear but also harmless. He has a kind face.

"No, really," he says to me, coming closer and shouting less. "Your man is strong." He gestures toward White Shirt in the store. "Just let Mother Nature take its course! Let it *go*, you know?"

"I do know," I say to him, because duh.

"So you do," he says, satisfied. And then, "If you can let it all go and let nature take its course, it's all going to be okay for you two!" He says this last part with a flourish, like he's pretty fucking happy to have shared his insider knowledge about love with me. "What's going on?" White Shirt says playfully to us as he comes out of the store. "Just respecting Mother Nature, you know," I say all casual-like, and semi-crazy guy laughs and winks at me, because we've got this shared secret now.

"So long!" he calls out and shuffles off down the street. White Shirt loops his arm in mine and takes me home with him. I try to let it go. I try to just let life be. Let nature take its course. I wait, and hope, in case semi-crazy guy is actually right.

WANDERLUST

And so, now, I spend a lot of time thinking about wanderlust. The roaming spirit. The desire to move from one place — or person — to the next. To never sit still, settle down.

"Why do you always love these baby birds?" my friend The Bright One asks. "When you're a tree with your roots dug in? You know those birds are just going to keep flying away, then come back to sit on your branches a bit before flying off again when a warmer breeze comes by."

I laugh at her poetry but she shakes her head at me. She knows my deal. She knows I like to have my roots so deep you can't dig them out. Roots so big they start to squeeze out sewage systems, burst through pipes.

And yet I fall for men made of wanderlust. Men that live so far into the unknown future they can't enjoy what's right in front of them. Men with roaming, roving hearts. Meanwhile, my own expansive heart just keeps on expanding until it's the size of the world. So big I can keep them with me, wherever they go.

CHAPTER NINETEEN

IN REVERSE

THE OPPOSITE OF DESTROYING

If I could lose the memory of the bitter cold, that night of The Bomb, the way the trees scratched the sky, The Husband's eyes wild and the air like a sheet of ice hung between us, oh I would.

If I could. I would take that memory and crumple it up like a piece of paper with a bad poem on it. I'd toss it into the little plastic wastebasket of a hotel I'll never go back to.

If I could, I'd take it into the woods and set it on fire, then bury the ashes in a hand-dug latrine. I'd cover it with a thousand rocks, the bigger the better, then add some fallen tree trunks for good measure.

If I could, I'd take the memory of that horrible night and feed it to a bunch of carpenter ants, who'd devour it slowly but completely. The Queen would get the best part of course, the snow and the cemetery gates and how different he suddenly looked. *Fearful.*

I would take that memory, so precise in its pain, so profound in its damage, and I'd put it in a capsule, heavy and secure, and throw it into the sea. I'd watch it sail out in an arc of momentary beauty before it suddenly pitched hard downward, falling toward the water, sharp as a dart.

It would sink to the bottom and land there, deep in the muddy darkness, where the absence of everything folds around it until it's nothing to me anymore. So far down I can't hear it. I can't feel it. I've destroyed it, and I'm free.

If I could have, I would have. Instead, I didn't destroy the memory of that horrible night at all. I wrote it down. I whispered it into a microphone.

I gave it life so it wouldn't only be mine to forget.

DAY TO DAY

I'm rushing to Birdie's after-school daycare, again. The Single-Parent Dash. I run in at exactly 6:01 p.m., but I'm met by the disapproving looks of the women who work there. Birdie is, as always, the last child waiting to be picked up. I'm sweating, exhausted, guilty. So guilty — for having to leave work "early," for deigning to work at all, based on the daycare ladies' faces. Guilty when Birdie says, "I'm starving! What's for dinner?" I have no idea what's for dinner or even if there's anything in the fridge.

We walk home together, from her school, past The Ex-husband's apartment building, across the major city intersection and through the little park to my building. She chats the whole way about warrior cats, and I half-listen, going over my favourite fantasy instead, the one where I'm a man in the 1950s: *After my long day at work, I come home to a clean apartment, the smell of a delicious meal in the air, a martini waiting. After dinner while my wife washes the dishes, I relax and read the newspaper as my child plays happily but quietly on the floor.*

I would give anything to be a man, and especially a white, middle-class man in the fifties. Those guys had it *made*. Instead I'm a white lady in 2015. A single lady. A single mom. I will not get to sit down and relax until ten o'clock tonight.

At seven I'm cooking pasta, when Birdie calls out from the bathroom. "Uh … Mom? Mom! You need to come in here nowwww!" The toilet is overflowing. *A lot*. I grab a plunger and start madly to work, plunging, sweating, plunging, so much sweating. *How does this work?* It isn't working. I flush, plunge, sweat. Brown, stinky water goes all over the floor and my shoes, which of course I haven't taken off yet since I went straight to the kitchen to make dinner the second we walked in. My shoes covered in disgusting sludge, hot tears starting, and then Birdie from the kitchen, "The pot is overflowing!"

I run, tracking brown toilet water with me and the pasta water is a geyser all over the stove. I grab it … and burn my hand. My toilet-water hand. "FUUUUCK!" I shout, and Birdie doesn't flinch, she just says quietly, "Mom?" and I shout, "I CAN'T DO ANY OF THIS! IT'S TOO MUCH!"

She's looking at me with her big blue eyes, not with fear but with a compassion that calms me. I say, "It's too much," again, but this time in a resigned whisper because it is, sometimes. Sometimes, being a single mom is too much.

I know, I'm not a real single mom. *They* do this 24/7. *I'm* a part-time mom. A "co-parent." So it's definitely different. But I still suck at it sometimes. There are still these moments. There are still no Mother's Day gifts or Christmas gifts, and no gifts of sleeping in and breakfast in bed. No one to stop the pasta water from overflowing while I stop the toilet water from overflowing.

"Check this out, Mom!" Birdie says, and makes a series of hilarious faces at me. I'm crying and feeling sorry for myself while the real gift, this kid of mine, is saying, "Mom, this *is* a lot of stuff happening at once!"

I laugh. I hug her and agree, it *is* a lot of stuff. Together we put towels down on the bathroom floor. I show her how to pee in the bathtub. Then I just shut the bathroom door and put on a new pot of pasta.

PICK A DIRECTION

On what I believe will be the last time The Man with the White Shirt is ever in my bed, I say to myself *He's just a guy. He's just a guy. He's just a guy.* We have fought (again) and cried (again) and reached the conclusion (again) that this has to end, it has to, *God,* this has to be the end. We want to stay friends. We can't imagine our lives without each other. He wants to see Birdie, he loves her, he loves *me*, and God do I love him, but we don't know how any of that works. All we know is we can't keep running in circles. We need to pick a direction.

There's no more denying it — we want different things. He doesn't want a monogamous, committed relationship. I want exactly that. You can't get past this, I finally, somehow, *finally* realize. He's a Jet and I'm a Shark. One of us is Palestine and the other is Israel. Or oil and water … anything that *can* come together, and *wants* to come together, and feels *good* together, but always, always, ends up apart. Wanting to make it work isn't enough.

And so, after the fighting and crying, the talking and dismantling, we inevitably fall together. Sex is our truce, our ceasefire. We sign a peace accord on each other's skin. But it's also where the heartbreak climbs. It starts to take over, nullifying the truce and sending me back to the front lines. I forget all about Jets and Sharks or oil and water and think, *OhmygodIloveyouwhycan'twemakethiswork!* I think, *Ican'tnothavethisIhavetohavethiswhatwillIdowithoutyou?*

And then, for some reason, I hold my breath. Just for a bit. Our eyes are locked and then, just as he cries out, I let all the air out and think, *He's just a guy.*

He's just a guy.

He'sjustaguy. He'sjustaguy. He'sjustaguy. He is.

Just.

A.

Guy.

I remove the specialness of it. The we-are-meant-to-be. I throw the rich madness of us out, and in that moment we're just two people who have had a couple of orgasms.

But when it's time for him to go, I can't take it. There's still the discarded wife inside of me that can't take *any* goodbyes, let alone one with a ring of finality to it. Every goodbye from The Man with the White Shirt is like The Husband all over again. Every time, every goodbye, *alone alone alone.*

"Just leave once I fall asleep," I say and he sighs, lies down in his clothes, me naked beside him. Four hours later I wake up to go to work and he's still lying there in his jeans and jacket. We look at each other, bathed in the blue light of early winter morning. *He's just a guy. He's just a guy. He's just a guy.*

I cry, and it isn't so much about White Shirt leaving as it is about me being left behind. It's me as a young teenager, pretending not to care that my parents were breaking up. It's me in the emergency room alone, not knowing what was wrong with my eyes. It's me the night my husband didn't come home for the first time in twelve years. It's me left behind. Always left, never leaving.

And so when the door clicks shut behind White Shirt, I cry all of *that.* I cry so hard I'm sure they can hear me right through the concrete walls and out onto the street four storeys below. I feel like I've collapsed, like I've folded in on myself. He suddenly bursts back in, fast, and pulls me into him hard, his arms tight around me. He wipes away my tears and I say, "Go, go." And he does, for real this time, he goes.

I unfold myself. I feed the cat. I stop crying and put makeup on and fix my hair. I'm relieved that he's gone, and surprised by that feeling. I stare long and hard at myself in the mirror. I'm forty-one years old and I've cried every day for the past two weeks. I've cried for four years. I've had everything and then nothing but, look! I'm still here, I'm still strong. I stare longer in the mirror. I think, *I look pretty good considering my age and the lack of sleep and the non-stop heartbreak.*

Goddamn it, I'm tired of going round in circles with him. I'm tired of the way we keep doing this same dance, just with variations on a theme. We've gotten so good at it, we can do all the steps with our eyes closed. And I've craved the dance, because at least it's something. To him, it's not enough. It shouldn't be enough for me either — I know I want a love that's consistent, less intermittent.

For him it's the opposite. He needs my love like people need a vacation— just every once in a while. Just enough to get the sun on his face and salt in his hair before heading back home, well-rested. I'm like a really nice postcard stuck on his refrigerator door. A memory of a place he went once that he has great stories about. It's just not anywhere he'd want to actually *stay* for very long.

But Here's the Thing

Love is strange and wonderful and you cannot choose it. You can choose to not see it or feel it when it's there with you, but you can't choose it out of existence.

Love floods you like a high beam on a dark country road.

Love is a defender that sometimes gets in your way.

Love shoots you up in the sky like a corner-store firework, cheap but exciting.

Love sticks to you like gum on the bottom of your shoe or parsley in your teeth.

Love is a flood that cannot be stopped no matter how many sandbags you put out.

You can't prepare. You can only act. Action is the antidote to anxiety. Certainty is a myth.

So you may as well let that light flow right into you, right through you, and experience it now, even if it's only temporary.

Even if it's just in knowing that there's no real way of knowing.

Love is at ease with itself, man. It doesn't look before it leaps, it just leaps.

It

just

does.

CAREFUL

The Ex-husband stands in my doorway. He seems so big in the small space, here between two doors, my apartment behind one and his freedom behind the other. Birdie's on the floor between us, playing with the cat. She's nine now, long and lean like him but with a big bold heart like mine.

I say something to him in our own language, that way we communicate with phrases and expressions and smirks only we can understand. It excludes the rest of the world, including Birdie, who tilts her head quizzically, like we really *are* speaking a different language.

The Ex-husband smiles at me, boyishly, almost shy, and I can't get over how much I suddenly want to kiss him. How much I just want to put my hand on the side of his face. I will not do these things. Not anymore. Not here, between two doors. Not anywhere. Our bodies have made no contact for more than a year.

For some reason we linger on this August day. We have nothing to discuss, so there's no reason for him to still be standing here, but he is still standing here, and I don't make any move to suggest he shouldn't be. So we linger, making the smallest of talk, having the smallest of laughs, silently acknowledging the energy that still exists between us.

He should probably go. *Yes.* And so he hugs Birdie goodbye, saying, "See you in eight days," as cheerily as he can muster, even though it's so hard, for both of us, to ever be apart from her for very long. "Bye Dad!" she says and takes off to her room. His face as she disappears. My heart falls a little with it.

We stand there alone together, awkwardly. Our arms slightly touch and we hug, a thing we don't do anymore. My hand flies up to his face on autopilot. I feel his skin against mine for the first time in a very, very long time. We look at each other fast, with the same shiny eyes and flushed cheeks we had when we first touched, way back then when we were twenty-five.

"Be careful," I say to him, I don't even know why, but he smiles as if he understands, saying, "Okay, I will." And slower than the tide, we pull our bodies apart.

I love you. Is what I mean, but don't say.

I don't say, *Your love split my heart open like an axe, but all that did was make more room inside it.*

This Love is Not Simple

Between his third and fourth snore, I whisper, "I love you."

I always wait the same amount of time, there between the third and fourth snore, as if it matters if he hears me or not. As if it matters, since he knows it. Everyone knows it. And yet I work hard to contain it, contain *I love you*, saving it only for the times when wine or weed help it to just slide right out of my mouth. Those times when it rushes out of me too fast for me to catch it, my defences down as I look at him looking at me and then all bets are off and out it comes, "I love you I love you I love you," like a burst pipe on a summer street, beautiful and tragic, all short-term happiness but so much waste.

So usually I wait for The Man with the White Shirt to nod off. I know that by the third loud rumble he is surely asleep, and there I can safely say, "I love you I love you I love you." I can just whisper it into his ear and not feel like a heartbreak soul singer from the sixties, lovin' a man no matter that he can't love her back the way she needs. But that's who I am. I am a heartbreak soul singer from the sixties. I'll take whatever he gives me, but sing sassily about it.

I lose my feminist card between the third and fourth snore.

I lose the game, my edge, I lose the future. I lose it all when I just lie there unlocking the contents of my heart as he so contentedly sleeps. And me, so content just to look at his face I may as well be fanning a palm frond over him, I am that clichéd a woman at this point but

this love,

it isn't simple.

MAPS

There are so many things people don't understand. "Why do you cry so much?" they ask. "Why are you still so sad about it two years later? Three years … four?" as though having a family one day and not having it the next, *poof!* in an instant, is a thing that one stops being sad about. That I once had a partner who loved me and supported me and wound his legs around mine each night. Someone to talk to in our own secret language. Someone to argue with. Someone to raise a child with. Someone to take out the garbage and fix the leaky faucet. Someone to make plans with. To unfold an old road map on the table with and say, "Where should we go?"

Why do I cry so much, *yeesh*. Now what I have is a faucet that's been dripping for years. I fall asleep alone to the sound of water droplets gently click-click-clicking onto whatever plate I haven't bothered to wash yet.

Why am I still so sad about it four years later, *c'mon*. For twelve years I was part of a beautiful, messy, important thing. I was in it. It was in me. Then, *poof!* I had to make my own thing, also beautiful, messy, and important. But different. Really fucking different. And it's obscured by this new love, now old itself. A complicated and unnecessarily protracted love affair that only gives me occasional tastes of what I once had and what I want to have again —

> legs touching mine in the night, and
> secret languages and arguments and maps and
> someone to fix the goddamn faucet already, or at least add a little gold to the cracks in my heart.

DATING

I still do date, sometimes. Because although The Man with the White Shirt is the one I love and want to be with, I also want a love that doesn't need to wring its hands so much. A love that puts all its money down on one horse. I want monogamy. And commitment. The two things he can't give me.

The only way for me to find it, then, is to meet other people. To go on dates with them. To have sex with them, in order to really know if they could be the one. Or at least the one for now. I'm not searching for "forever," you know. I'm searching for right now. I mean, forever is great if it happens. But forever is the real problem, if you ask me. Forever is why people in monogamous relationships struggle. I should know, I was married once.

Forever is a scary thing to consider; it's crazy that we vow to do it at all. We should vow to be kind to one another, to respect each other, to not forget desire and laughter when we're on the hamster wheel. For as long as we're together, let's commit ourselves to these good, attainable things. Forever is a lifetime. Living up to it is the real wrench in relationships, not the need to fuck other people. Look, I get that polyamory works for a lot of people, but for me, it doesn't. And yet, I have to do it anyway. As long as I'm dating, my love life is non-monogamous. I am non-monogamous, even though I don't want to be. It's that or celibacy. These are my choices.

Dating is hard. It can feel like an endless rejection loop. The ones you like don't like you, the ones that like you, you don't like. It's like high school. All the fucking time. What's so fun about that? Everyone is playing. Playing it cool or playing themselves up to be more than they are. Playing that they're breezy when they aren't, playing that they're smarter than they are (or dumber, if you're a woman, since we need to play *down* how smart we are a lot of the time). We all have to play the game of texting now, exhausting and confusing, especially when you're juggling more than one person. There's the juggling. Remembering who said what and which person you saw that movie with and which one is the one who … ugh.

It goes on and on. But I have to do it, if I want to find a committed relationship. So when I meet interesting people, I ask them out. I schedule them between single-parenting and loving The Man with the White Shirt. There have been a few times I dated guys that wanted to be in a relationship with me, and I wanted to give them a chance, even when I knew right away I wasn't feeling it. I hoped I would feel it in time. I wanted to believe I could. But something was missing, even though I liked them so much. In those situations, *I* was the one who didn't want monogamy. I wanted to keep seeing them *and* The Man with the White Shirt. And maybe even one other person. Who knows where I found the energy or time!

I don't know why I didn't feel passion and excitement for these guys. These wonderful, smart men that wanted to give me what I say I want. Is it that I'm most attracted to the ones that make me feel crazy with desire, the ones whose passion is at a ten? The ones who say they love me but can't be in a relationship? Am I not able to feel love when it isn't torture?

THE WELL

The Man with the White Shirt is fixing a window blind. The one in Birdie's room that has fallen down three times now, the third time hitting me in the face, splitting my lip.

I can do so many things, you know? Why not this? I can carry my own mortgage and own a car. I can single-parent, book vacations, captain a soccer team, and have a successful career, but every single thing I hang, including this window blind, falls. Shelves, curtain rods, paintings, everything, they all fall. I mean, so what, but in the moment of the fallen blind and the split lip, I feel hopeless, helpless, so alone and exhausted. I text White Shirt.

He's here now, gorgeous, my not-boyfriend of two and a half years, standing on Birdie's bed, holding a power drill and fixing the blind while I sit beside his legs doing nothing but feeling sorry for myself. Sorry and sad that I once had a husband and now I don't. That my husband would have hung the blind properly the first time and instead, waah waah me, I live alone and hang things badly. I imagine The Ex-husband somewhere at this moment having the best day ever in his best life ever now that I'm no longer in it.

"I feel like I'm falling down the well again," I say in a small voice. Because I do feel like that lately, lost in that loop where I go back to the beginning of this chapter of my life, back to The Bomb, over and over again, replaying events of the past instead of living in the present. White Shirt stops what he's doing and sits beside me. He takes my hand, firm, and looks right into my eyes.

"I will never let you fall down the well," he says.

It has a startling effect on me. Like, not to be melodramatic, but it actually startles me. It's as though he's thrown a bucket of ice water on me to wake me from this self-pitying daze. I sob into his lap. I'm so grateful he's here. That he's my friend. That his is a wonderful, complicated kind of love.

It's not the love I wanted from him, it didn't turn out the way I wanted at all, but it did turn into this, this very real caring I'm receiving from this man. This man, with the white shirt, who's always searching for himself and for another happiness, but will still come over in a flash to fix a broken blind or read comics with Birdie or stop me from falling down the well.

And then I cry more because after all these years I'm still crying, still feeling sorry for myself, forgetting how blessed I am to have a huge social support network. I've got my own self-support, too, if I would ever take two seconds to remember that. Yeah, *me*, I also will not let myself fall down the well. I have Birdie to think of, and a life to build. And I can do that on my own, even if I'm not so good with power tools.

Later that night, even though The Man with the White Shirt is out somewhere having Saturday night, he sends me a text. *I've always got your back,* it says.

And he does.

CHAPTER TWENTY

TRYING

TO THE SEA

Summer 2016. I'm off to Italy again. This time on my own, a totally different experience than last time, in The Year of The Bomb, when I went with Birdie and my niece. This time, it's all about going out for expensive drinks and dinners, night after night, with my friend The Expat Journalist, who's been living in Rome for the past few years. She's Italian Canadian like me. Unlike me, she's young and thin and living a happily single life in the country of our blood. Each day she rides off to work on her cute Italian bicycle, dressed stylishly and never seeming to sweat.

"Fuck you, you never sweat!" I shout at her.

"Fuck you, I do SO!" she shouts back.

"WHATEVER. Okay have a good day at work, see you at dinner, love youuuuu!"

"Love YOUUUUU!"

This is how we talk to each other. This is why I love her and have missed her back home where we used to work together and she was the only person that seemed normal. Normal because yelling. Because swearing. Because Italian.

Anyway, here we are in actual Italy and she goes to work each day and I am alone in the city, a city I love, a city I don't mind being alone in at all. All I do is wander. I walk and walk for hours, watching people, talking to people, and getting lost. I get lost a lot, because I like to think I know where I'm going in Rome, and sometimes I do, but a lot of times I don't. And I refuse to pull out my phone to look at a map. Or even to look at the paper map I have stuffed into my purse. I don't want to look like a *turista*.

So I get lost. A *lot*. But it doesn't matter because I have no plans, no one to worry about. I can do whatever I want at whatever speed. A thing you probably don't know about me is that *this* is when I'm truly happiest alone — wandering city streets, soaking up the smells and sounds and colour all around me. I'm truly happiest alone when I'm getting lost.

It's really fucking hot, though, right now, even for Italy in July. There's some kind of record-breaking heat wave happening all across Europe, and it's like fifty degrees with the humidex. I love the heat, but even for me it gets to be a bit much. My dress is soaked through, and I need to find a breeze. There are no breezes on the tiny, crowded streets of the *centro storico*. So I head to the river, stopping at a little stand to buy a rice ball that's as big as a baseball and a peach that's even bigger.

At the river, I climb halfway down a steep set of concrete steps, then sit on a flat section overlooking the water. There's no one around, except for a man in a business suit at the bottom of the steps who's picking up rocks and throwing them into the water. He's not even trying to skip the rocks or anything. He just pitches them hard, one by one. It's strangely cathartic and lulling to watch. I wonder if he's okay, even though I feel sure he is.

Sometimes you just need to hurl rocks into the Tiber. I'm sure he's not the first. So I just eat my gigantic *arancini* and watch him.

Eventually, he stops. He wipes his hands on a handkerchief then stands perfectly still for a second, staring at a boat going by. When he comes up the steps I realize how handsome he is and how fancy his suit is. As he passes me, he tips his head and says, "*Salve!*" in greeting, as though I haven't just watched him have a controlled midday meltdown.

"*Fa caldo oggi!*" he continues, fanning himself with his hand for extra emphasis.

"*Si, si! Ma troppo!*" I say, hoping I sound Italian enough.

"Yes, ah, eees verrry hot," he answers in broken English. "*Verrry hottt*, ah?"

We laugh in transatlantic agreement and away he goes.

I continue to sit and look at the river. Yes, I'm on vacation in Rome and I could be looking at a Michelangelo or shopping at Fendi or whatever it is regular people do on vacation here, but I'm sitting cross-legged on a concrete slab feeling the breeze. For the first time in a long time, I feel content. Fortunate. Satisfied. I feel absolutely okay with not having someone to share this moment with.

I feel okay.

This is the very beginning of a very different me. A slow return to the me I used to be a long, long time ago. Back when I travelled on my own without any hesitation. Back when I used to be totally comfortable sitting in cafés alone for hours. Back when being alone wasn't a big deal at all. For the past four years it's been a huge deal, as you well know. The Lonely grabbed hold of me and held on. Tight. Only now, here, across the sea, do I start to wrestle free from its grip.

A month later, back across the sea, but on the Canadian side, Birdie and I are with my friend Solo Time in Nova Scotia. We stay at her parents' cottage for a week, perched on a windy cliff overlooking a harbour where the tide comes in twice a day. It's one of the most relaxing weeks of my life.

I lie on a lawn chair in the sun, playing guitar for hours while Birdie and Solo Time read. We nap each afternoon underneath billowing curtains. We search the shore for beach glass. We set the table for dinner and clean up afterward. We sit around bonfires and listen to tall tales. We fall asleep to the sound of waves crashing right outside our doorstep.

When the tide is out, the three of us walk out as far as we can along the muddy ocean floor. It's amazing to think that we're even doing this. Birdie is SO happy here and Solo Time, also an only child, is relaxed and content back home in Nova Scotia with her parents. I feel good to be a witness to other people's happiness. To be part of that happiness. To be at peace with the present. To recognize it.

Don't get me wrong. I think of The Man with the White Shirt every single day. I miss him and dream about him and have so many stories I want to tell him and there are so many gifts I want to buy for him. But, as in Italy, I'm okay being here in this beautiful place without him. I wish he was here, but I don't *long* for it. His absence doesn't get in the way of my enjoyment. Both sides of the Atlantic have mellowed me out this summer, and I feel good about how far I've come. I no longer have to fill the empty spaces inside me with empty experiences. I don't need to numb myself with alcohol and one-night stands anymore. I don't have to try so hard to make love happen so I can get over White Shirt. I don't have to try so hard to control what I can't control.

And most importantly, here in the summer of 2016, it finally doesn't feel like something is missing when Birdie and I are together. It feels whole again. Nothing is missing. All we need is for me to be present and grateful and hopeful and alive to the now. The tide goes out, but it always comes back in. You can swim over top of the exact spot you walked on earlier that day. That's just how it goes. In and out.

In.

Out.

It took me a while, but I get it now.

It's Late on a Saturday Night

I text him,
I miss your smile, your smell, blah blah blah.

And even though it is some ungodly hour and he is who
knows where, The Man with the White Shirt texts me back
immediately,
I miss your blah blah blah.

IT EXISTS

Birdie is skipping ahead on the sidewalk in front of us. Okay, not
skipping, but jumping along, full of cotton candy and the wild
night air. We're under the expressway, walking home from a night
at the CNE, the giant fair that sets up for only two weeks of the
year, signalling the end to another summer.

I love the CNE, especially at night. I take Birdie every year
at least once, and always on a weeknight. We walk through the
midway, thick with people and colourful lights, eating mini
powdered doughnuts, going on rides, wasting all my money
on Ring-toss and Skee-ball. And then, when most kids her age
are home and asleep for hours, Birdie and I walk back home
to our apartment.

The first few years after The Bomb, when she was still so
young, I'd carry her the entire way home. Away from the lights
and corn dogs and rowdy teenagers, and through the big arch-
way they call the Princes' Gates, gleaming white and ornate
against the night sky. From there we'd walk along the south

entrance of the army barracks, then under the expressway, Fort York to one side of us and a new fortress of condos to the other. When we reached the Bathurst Street bridge, we knew we were in the home stretch. That's where I'd always point out that this was the only place where she could see both her homes at once — The Ex-husband's building on the west side of the bridge and mine on the east. "Pretty cool, eh?" I'd say, and she'd say, "For sure, Mom."

As she got older, we'd make a show of who was more tired on that long walk back, who could drag their feet more, or who could drive the other crazier with peppy positivity, who could run the fastest. We'd stop and watch the trains rumble under the bridge. We'd take blurry selfies with the city lights and the CN Tower behind us. The walk home almost as good as our night at the fair.

This year is a bit different. This year, The Man with the White Shirt came with us to the CNE. He's walking beside me now as Birdie runs ahead of us.

He's taking my hand in his.

He's saying, "Happy Anniversary."

Holy shit.

It's August 22, 2016. Three years to the day that *kaboom, kapow!* we first saw each other across a crowded café-bar. *I* know this of course, because I know the dates of everything, but for White Shirt to know it and acknowledge it is big. *Big* big. I'm almost paralyzed by the bigness of it. *Happy Anniversary.* And we stop to kiss, but not for too long, because Birdie's up ahead and it's 11:00 p.m. and we're under the roaring highway in our beautiful city on this perfect August night. We sprint to catch her and she laughs. And even though she's almost as tall as me now, The Man with the White Shirt lifts her up onto one of his shoulders and carries her there, side-saddle. Looking at the two of them, I feel light.

When we get home, he puts her to bed and I eavesdrop on their conversation, staccato with laughter. We kiss long and hard at the door when it's time for him to go.

"I'll see you in a few days and we'll talk," he says, and I am afraid. Afraid of what this all means or doesn't mean. Three years ago when I saw him, everything changed in an instant, but it's been so rocky and painful and confusing since then. I want this anniversary to be happy, I do. I want to let the happiness in, but I don't know if it's real this time. "Everything's going to be okay," says The Man with the White Shirt, and I only sort of believe him.

Four days later, I'm at his apartment. He's acting so strange and I can't breathe. Or speak. I feel like everything is on the line even though nothing is. I don't know what he's going to say and I've never felt so frightened of what it might be. You can't blame me, can you? He's been unpredictable these past three years, so inconsistent with his push-pull. The way he always keeps his love for me on a retractable leash.

The Man with the White Shirt is *really* taking his time now, to say the things he says he needs to say to me. Everything in my body is tense, waiting for the firing gun. And then he says, "I want you to be my girl," like it's the fifties, and we're at the Chock'lit Shoppe and he's finally picking Betty or Veronica. Still, my insides flip over, my throat constricts.

"I want to be able to introduce you as my beautiful girl-friend," he continues.

"I want you to never have to call me The Not-Boyfriend again."

"I love you, and I only want to love you. I don't want to love anyone else."

I say nothing. I say nothing and this scares him because I'm never quiet. But I actually have no words. This isn't a maybe from The Man with the White Shirt. This is a *Fuck Yes!* I've waited three years for this moment, and I can hardly breathe. And then we kiss so sweetly it *is* like it's the fifties and we're in the Chock'lit Shoppe and he's chosen Veronica. *Obviously.*

I can't believe this is happening. Especially now. He's just gotten his dream job with an airline, and in a few days he's about to leave for flight school and will be gone for the next five weeks. *What a weird way to start.* I know he'll retract it, I just know it. In a few days, once he gets there and settled and is surrounded by all those young flight attendants, he'll realize he's made a mistake. He'll change his mind. He's always changing his mind. Why would this big declaration be any different?

I take him to the airport to see him off. I remind him he's going to do great. I give him a small rosary I bought in Vatican City when I was there at the start of summer on my solo adventure. I always travel with a rosary because flying scares me. I don't trust it, you know? It just seems very unlikely that airplanes are even possible. It's sorcery. With this job, White Shirt will be flying all the time, sometimes several times a day! This freaks me out, and I make him promise he will always have this little rosary on him when he flies. He promises. We're both crying as we say goodbye, hugging and kissing at the gate and totally That Couple in the airport.

For the first few weeks he's gone, every single day I expect him to call to tell me he's changed his mind, that he was swept up in the moment of getting his dream job and feeling emotional. I wake up every morning and think, *This will be the day.* So I say to my friends, "We'll see! Who knows what's going to happen. You know White Shirt," and I shrug and roll my eyes and pretend to be breezy about it. I remain unconvinced. *Cautious.* Cautiously on Cloud 9, yet again.

One of Us Cannot Be Wrong

Dear White Shirt,

I had a hard time sleeping. I woke up early thinking of heavy and light. How even the heavy can be light, but rarely the other way around. How even clichés are feelings, too.

I tried to pray last night but for once I didn't have anything specific to pray about, other than the persistence of fear. I felt unease. I felt so much unknowing. I kept impatiently thinking about patience. The more I thought about trust, the darker it all got. The more I thought about the things you said before you left, the lighter it all got.

I told you once that we were a fire that burns unattended. I'm really scared and unsure if I'm ready, but I am willing to start tending this fire with you now. Maybe that will make it go out, or maybe it will become the bonfire I always imagined it could be. Maybe I will get burned again, I don't know. I couldn't sleep at all last night because of all the I don't knows, you know?

I'm not sure I've been this uneasy in this whole three years. I'm not sure I've been happier. But I'm scared. I'm scared about everything you've said because I'm programmed to believe you are unpredictable and fickle. All my caution flags are up.

This got heavy. My intention was to send you light.

Will you change your mind? Neither of us can be sure.

xo,

mp

THE OUTLIER

He doesn't change his mind. Every single day he messages me or calls me or Skypes. He says, "I love you," over and over. He tells me how much he misses me, how much he needs me. After five weeks, he returns from flight school and it's the same. The Man with the White Shirt is finally, actually my boyfriend. We are doing this.

It exists.

I can't believe it. Neither can a lot of people. "It's like a miracle from The Baby Jesus himself!" says my friend The Bright One. We're eating take-out Thai food in my apartment with Solo Time and Big Laugh. "The Baby Jesus, riiiiight!" Big Laugh shouts and slaps the table with laughter. She can't believe it either.

"Oh, I *knew* it would happen!" says Solo Time, ever Team White Shirt, and Big Laugh changes her mind. "I thought so, too, I thought so, too! He loves you, I knew it."

But love isn't what's at question. That he loves me has never been the issue. It's whether he knows what to do with that love. It's whether he can manage that love within the parameters he's set up for himself. And this remains open. It remains to be seen. It keeps me cautious. It keeps my own love at bay. The Bright One kisses her teeth. "It is a damn *miracle*," she says, and I can see she's unconvinced that he's changed. Still it's easy to be swept up in it, The New Man with The White Shirt.

"You would have the cutest mixed-race babies!" says Big Laugh, who is here in a rare moment away from her own mixed-race babies. And then the four of us launch hard into a discussion about using the term *mixed-race* versus *multiracial* or *biracial*. And then how different it is to be biracial but to present white (or white-ish) like The Man with the White Shirt and his sister, versus Big Laugh's two children who also have a black mom and a white dad, but who present black. We talk about the recent

Black Lives Matter movement, what's happening in our careers, and which Chimamanda Ngozi Adichie book is our favourite. We all love her and can't agree on one book and end up talking about all of them. And *that* gets us back to race, and romance, and right back to that miracle from The Baby Jesus Himself, The Man with the White Shirt. God, I love my friends.

Now that the miracle is real, I have to explain to Birdie what it all means. "You guys are going to kiss now?? Ewww," is what she says, making a disgusted face, because she's nine, and anything kissy or lovey-dovey is super-gross to her. But all she *really* cares about is one thing. "Does this mean we get to see him more?!" Her eyes are bright with expectation and I tell her yes, we will see him more and sometimes he might even sleep over. "Awesome!" she says, "Because I *love* him. He's so *fun*."

In a closed women's Facebook group I'm in, someone posts about how awful the dating scene is, how all the men are boys and we're all doomed to be single forever. And I post back a few words about White Shirt's change of heart and how you just never know, sometimes when you least expect it, the boy becomes a man. The Matchmaker, who's become my friend and is also in this group, posts in reply, "Yes, of course, except for White Shirt, THE OUTLIER!!" And this new nickname sticks. The Outlier. It's perfect. I knew he was better than all the others. I knew he would choose love over wanderlust. I knew he was right for me despite all the wrongs, and that if I loved him hard enough, he'd want to try, for real.

For the next nine months anyway.

THE END (AGAIN)

For nine months, we are a couple. That Couple. The one that looks great together on Instagram. The one that has birthdays five days apart and at the same time blow out the candles on a giant crème brûlée in a hipster bar on a trivia night while the waitress snaps a photo. It's all so perfect, I could die.

But we're also trying to figure it all out. The *relationship*. It's so new to both of us, and we aren't that great at it at first. Even though we've been in love (and circles) for the past three years, now we are Doing This Thing and the pressure is on. We act like we just met or something. We're shy and awkward. We make so many assumptions about each other, almost all wrong. This Thing We're Doing is bigger than us, and we make a million mistakes at it. We are not at ease in This Thing. It's a shirt that doesn't fit us right.

If you looked behind the photo of us smiling at our birthday candles on the crème brûlée, you'd see that later that night we had a huge fight. It was about mansplaining, if you must know. He mansplained mansplaining to me and I thought my head would explode. And it did, so much so that I talked over him, interrupting and indignant, laying into him about the origins of the term and not hearing what he was actually trying to say — that he'd originally misunderstood the term. He was trying to explain how wrong he'd been about it, not trying to explain that he was right.

We had other arguments, too. About how much time we should spend together and when. About not hearing each other. Or not understanding. Relationship stuff. *No big deal, these things are normal,* I thought. *They're just growing pains.* We were just trying to get in shape so the shirt would fit better. We wanted it to fit. We wanted it to be right, even though for some reason, it didn't feel right. To either of us. It's hard to say what or why. The love and attraction and friendship and deep connection were there as always, so why were we so off? *Did putting a label on it really change it?*

Still, we continued as That Couple. On Christmas Eve we returned home from my cousin's at 1:00 a.m. and White Shirt carried Birdie to her bed. Together we put the little gifts in her stocking, and then secretly slid gifts into each other's. Since The Bomb, my stocking had been merely ornamental, hanging there empty for four Christmases since The Grinch came through back in 2012. Now here it was, filled with little shampoo bottles and chocolates again for the first time in forever. It was his first stocking in almost twenty years, he said. And he cried when he saw it, how I'd written his name in silver sparkles and fancy script.

We went on trips together, because now he had flight privileges and I did, too, as his *companion*. We went to Miami Beach and Mexico. We got stranded in Charlottetown for five days in a snowstorm. It all felt so romantic, even if sometimes it was a struggle. We were doing it, The Thing, finally. The Man with the White Shirt and I were trying. Together.

One spring night, my father and his lovely girlfriend hosted a dinner for White Shirt's parents. White Shirt, Birdie, and I were there, too.

I'd tried to dissuade him when he called to tell me about his plan for the dinner. "Dad, I don't know if it's a good idea."

"WHY NOT?" he shouted, because he always shout-talks when someone disagrees with him. "I had The Scientist's parents over for dinner to meet them that time!"

"Dad! 'That time' was when we were getting married! This is not the same thing at all! White Shirt has only just decided he wants to *try* to be in a relationship. We don't even know if he can do that! This is going to scare him away!"

"NO ONE IS GETTING SCARED AWAY! IT'S JUST DINNER!"

He was right, it was just dinner. But I still worried. I was already very close with White Shirt's parents. We texted and called each other and often made plans first and then just told White Shirt about them after. They treated Birdie like a granddaughter, cooking her favourite dishes and always bringing both of us gifts from the places they travelled. Since we started Doing

This Thing, they'd told me more than once how happy they were that their son now had a great job but also that he had me and Birdie in his life. They told me they loved me, all the time. We were even planning a trip together for the summer, where White Shirt, Birdie, and I would go to Portugal with them, and where his sister and her family would join us, too.

It was all I could talk about for months. *When we go to Portugal it's going to be so amazing! ... Your father says the sea is only 1.8 kilometres from their house! ... Will we have time to drive up to Porto, do you think? ... Ooh, when we're in Lisbon can we see all the funiculars? ... For the next trip your dad and I decided we'll all go to Angola!*

I couldn't wait to see where The Man with the White Shirt was born, to be with him in the place he grew up, to see where he had spent some of his teen years, to walk the streets with him, helping him to carry the load of memories, good and bad. The homeland of my love, the heavy and light of his heart. I started learning to speak Portuguese, practising with his father as we played cards. I could read it okay, but my pronunciation was terrible. I studied it alone while White Shirt was gone on long sets of flights, writing out the words and practising the difficult pronunciation out loud in my room. I wanted to surprise him when we got to Portugal, with how much I'd learned to say in his first language.

Anyway, my dad and his girlfriend got along wonderfully with White Shirt's parents, the four of them speaking in a mish-mash of languages — Italian, Spanish, Portuguese, English. There was wine and food and laughter and the promise of another dinner, this time hosted by White Shirt's parents. That dinner happened only a month later, the seven of us again, like a family, like a thing I'd only dreamed of having again one day.

A dream, really, to see my dad so thrilled about using every single glass from his *cristalleria*. To see White Shirt's mom and my dad's lovely girlfriend compare jewellery and recipes in high-pitched, heavily-accented voices. To look across the room and see The Man with the White Shirt and Birdie, deep in their own conversation and world. To sit there and feel loved and fed and *alive*.

A few weeks later, we're in my car and I say we should buy the plane tickets for the trip to Portugal soon. He makes a strange face. A grimace, maybe. A tightening. But I soldier on, chatting about how I can't wait to finally be there with him after all the times he's gone without me. Reminding him how he always came back from his trips to Portugal with the most perfect little gifts for me. And how he always told me how much he missed me while he was there, how everything made him think of me.

"Now finally I'll be there *with* you!" I say, but he's silent, not excited at all. I press him about it and with an exhale he tells me he finds it difficult to get excited about the trip because he's worried about us arguing while we're there.

"You're worried about a fight we *might* have *two months* from now?!" It seems absolutely ridiculous to me. But it isn't ridiculous to him. He is serious. He really is paralyzed by the thought of us maybe arguing on vacation two months from now. I can't understand it. First of all, who cares if we argue on vacation, it's no big deal, but secondly, we may not argue at all. We've been on plenty of vacations together already, and it isn't like we argued the whole time on any of them. *Where is this coming from?*

As we drive, we talk it through some more and I'm happy we're working stuff out. *Relationship stuff.* But when we get to his place, he says, "I can't do this. I can't do it. It isn't right." Just like that.

He says, "We argue too much. I love you so much, and I wanted this to work so badly. But I can't do it. It isn't right." And I am shocked. Again. It isn't right. It isn't right. It isn't *right*, he keeps saying. "But what is?" I say. "Is anything, really?"

"I don't know. I need time. I don't know!" he says, shaky and sad.

I go home to give him time. But I'm not very good at it.

A few days later I return to ask him if he's sure. *Sure.* And he says he is. We both cry and kiss and talk. And somewhere in all that, I just fall asleep, right there in his apartment in the middle of us talking. My entire body just shuts down. At 8:00 p.m.

I wake up at 8:00 a.m. to the sound of him getting ready for work as quietly as possible and everything feels normal for a second, until I remember it isn't normal at all. It's over. When he comes into the room I sit up and say, "I'll drive you to the airport," and he says, "Okay," in the quietest, saddest voice I've ever heard. He looks so handsome in his suit and I hate him for it, because everything will be easier for him going forward because he is a man and a handsome, charming one at that. Because men don't lose cachet or power as they age and I was aging myself out of love by the millisecond.

I drive him to the airport. Every song that comes on feels like a dagger, so I turn the radio off and we drive in a heavy silence. *Gardiner Expressway. Highway 427. Airport Road. Terminal 3.* Normally I love this route; ever since he got the airline job it has been nothing but pleasure for me to drive him to the airport, or better, to be there to pick him up. On this morning though, I'm taking the same route but without pleasure, just a boulder in my gut making all music unlistenable. This. Again.

I pull over at the usual spot on the departures level, somewhere between taxis and hotel shuttles and frazzled people spilling out of minivans. Our usual routine has always been this: I get out of the car with him and wait patiently as he removes his luggage from the trunk and arranges it just so, in his meticulous manner. Once perfect, he adjusts his suit jacket and airport tags, smiles at me and pulls me into his body, giving me the kind of hug that feels like a thousand hugs and the scent of summer. What, that's how it feels, okay?

This time, I stay in my seat. My hands on the wheel. I hear him taking the luggage out, then arranging it just so. In the rear-view mirror, I see him adjust his jacket and tags. And then his face, so sad, through the open passenger window, my name coming quietly out of his lips, an angry horn blast behind us and a string of swears shouted in another language. I turn to look at him.

"I love you," he says.

And I say, "Goodbye," and drive away.

I don't cry on Airport Road. Or Highway 427. Or even the Gardiner Expressway. I don't listen to music either. I just watch the road. And the cars. And the lake as it comes into view, sparkling in the sunlight as if nothing's happened. As if everything hasn't changed. I don't cry until I reach the elevator in my parking garage. As soon as the doors shut, I'm a firehose of sorrow. At street level, a guy gets in the elevator and looks afraid. "Are you okay?" he barely asks and I say, "No." He looks at the ground.

In my apartment I don't know what to do. I don't know how this was a thing and now it's not a thing. I don't know how I can be back at the beginning. *Why did he change his mind? How can he say he loves me but not want to be together?*

After an hour of crying I get a second wind. A new wind. I decide on the spot to swap my bedroom with Birdie's. Yes, you heard me right, the bedrooms. I work steadily for six hours straight. I dismantle all the furniture in her room and pull it all out into the main part of the apartment. Then I dismantle my furniture and drag *it* out. I take every piece of clothing out of each closet and swap them. I take down every photo, piece of art, and knick-knack. I make a huge mess and scrape my leg and hit my head and strain every muscle. There are so many holes in all the walls. I make new problems where old problems were. The place is a fucking disaster, but at least it's stopped me from crying. At least this was something I could control.

I can't control that night after night, I drunkenly call him, crying, shouting at him for being immature and callous. Or pleading with him to come back to me. To us. Where I cry about the family trip to Portugal that will never be and get angry about concert tickets I already bought for us, as if that matters. Where I mewl, "The summer, though! We were supposed to have the summer! What about the summer?!" like summer is a thing I've never had before, and never will again.

I'm so fucking dramatic. But it hurts, okay? He says he still loves me. But he doesn't know shit about love. The Ex-husband and I, that was love. We had nothing in common and we fought, but we fought fair and maturely, knowing that with love comes war sometimes and in that war, there were rules of engagement. We knew that every argument didn't mean we weren't *right*, every bump in the road didn't mean the end. We fought like anyone else does, because people fight.

White Shirt doesn't know what love is, because he's never really let himself find out. He always retreats. I just wanted to keep going, *forward march*, because against all odds, he came to me that August night as The Outlier.

Even though he dropped The Bomb on me and our marriage and family and turned into a huge asshole at the end, The Ex-husband and I were as real and true as it gets. He knew what he wanted. And he knew how to love. At the very least, he knew *how*, goddamn it.

CHAPTER TWENTY-ONE

HOME

The Thing About the Heart

Here's the thing about the heart, no matter how full it gets, how weary.

No matter how many pieces it's splintered into, *again*, the glue barely dried. No matter how resolutely it stands before a dead-end sign, or how stubbornly it wears that sign itself.

It doesn't matter how many makeshift walls the heart puts up around itself, or how it tries desperately to scramble up the walls of another's. The heart will do what it always does — surprise, confuse, delight, ache. It will continue to be the trickster, the lovelorn, the protector.

You can't stop the heart.

So lean into it and listen.

Its whispers are sunlight on blue, blue water, ready to dive into again and again.

RECOVERY

I guess I like the ocean in times of crisis. Since we aren't going to Portugal anymore, I've chosen to go as far away from it as my broken heart will allow. For the first time together, Birdie and I go to the Pacific Coast, to British Columbia and my older brother.

For twelve days we stare at the Pacific. We hike through mountain forests each morning and spend each afternoon at a different beach. It is hot and lovely here, but it's no Portugal. Still, it's good to be with my brother and his girlfriend, who feels like a sister to me, as well as her two daughters, my two nephews, and *their* girlfriends. They're all one big intermingled family here, in two homes, always texting each other and popping by and everyone hanging out together always, a raucous bunch of young adults and my loud brother and his awesome girlfriend and so much laughter.

It feels good to be around this much energy and life, to be a witness to the love and madness, so different than the quiet two-person life Birdie and I have back at our apartment in Toronto, so different from this small town on the west coast, where everyone seems to know everyone and deer walk down the street.

Birdie is having a great time and so am I, but I am also deeply, deeply sad. Not because British Columbia isn't Portugal, but because I was more in love with The Man with the White Shirt than I even realized. There was a future I'd imagined, and now it would stay that way, lingering as imagination only, never materializing. So I cry a lot. Or stare at the ocean a lot. I talk with my brother a lot. About our crazy family, about heartbreak, about children and relationships and soccer and coffee and what we're going to eat for the next three meals and how we're going to cook it. I'm actually relieved to be here, five thousand kilometres from home, here with my big brother, who is gruff sometimes but also really funny and kind and who laughs so hard his blue eyes disappear into tiny slits.

Those same blue eyes comfort me when we're both up early each morning, sitting in the kitchen talking. He hands me coffee in a Spider-Man mug I bought him when I was still a teenager. A deer runs through the backyard.

"The Man with the White Shirt loves Spider-Man," I say, and my brother rolls his eyes and changes the subject to something funny, which is his way of saying *I know, I know it's hard,* and he makes me perfect little pancakes that we eat while planning the next three meals.

While on this trip, Birdie and I talk a lot about what's happened between me and The Man with the White Shirt. What it *means.* She's very concerned. Well, she mostly has one concern: "Are you guys in an argument? Or can I still see him?" I tell her we're not in an argument, we love each other and he loves her, but being in a relationship with me just isn't right for him. I tell her I'm sad ("No kidding, Mom!") and that's why I've been crying so much ("I thought so"), but I assure her we are still friends and will always be friends.

"I'm sorry you're so sad, Mom," she says, "but I'm really glad I'll still be able to see him." I try to imagine what that will be like, how it will work. How now, I will have to further divide my time with her.

On the last day of our trip, early in the morning, my brother drives us to the ferry that will take us to the airport that will take us back home. He waits with us until the ferry arrives, gives Birdie and me a no-nonsense hug and a quick goodbye and turns to go. My heart sinks a little as I watch him leave. I wish we didn't live five thousand kilometres apart. I wish we lived close enough for me to walk over to his place and have a coffee in an old Spider-Man cup.

The salt air whips through our hair as we stand on the deck of the giant ocean ferry watching my brother's town slowly disappear from view. I drink coffee, and we eat the snacks he packed for us. We laugh and talk and it's easy to forget she's a child sometimes, now that she's ten and almost as tall as me and is cool and easy to travel with.

"Everything's going to be okay, Bird," I say and she says, "Uh, yeah, Mom, obviously. Everything's going to be *great!*"

GOING HOME

Everything *is* great. The kid is right. It's also really terrible sometimes. *News Flash! LIFE!* Life, it goes on. It just goes and goes. With or without The Man with the White Shirt, which is to say always with him in some way, because we can't stay apart. In truth, we are each other's best friend, the closest person we have on this earth, and that in itself is hard to let go of, let alone the magic and the magical sex and the magical magic. Agh.

This time around, I don't date hard. I don't date at all. I don't have the heart for it or the time. If something happens, it will happen, but I'm not going to *work* at it now, not like I used to. I'm not going to try and find someone to replace him, someone to help me get over him. I don't want to get over him this time. Or at least I don't want to have to work at getting over him.

So I focus on my actual work, my career, my writing. And I focus on Birdie. I hang out with my friends, especially women. We go to movies and clothing swaps and for coffee and text each other when we know something important is happening, or something hard. I cultivate these female friendships like I never have before. Birdie tags along a lot. She's one of the girls, even though she's decidedly un-girly. I love that about her. I love that she wears only jeans and baggy hoodies and doesn't know or care about brands or trends. She does her own nerdy thing. She looks more like her dad now than ever before. Same long straight hair he had when I first met him, same facial expressions. But she's got her mother's heart.

This is a new phase of my life, where I'm not concerned about being single again, not concerned about chasing men. Where I can't be bothered to waste my small amount of free time texting them endlessly even though they never want to make real plans to meet in real life. I'm over it. I'm ready to be chased. I'm ready to be adored. I'm ready to not have to guess. Or haggle. Or hustle for someone's time and attention. I'm ready to get comfy around someone who feels comfortable to be themselves around me and who thinks that's a good thing when that happens. I'm ready for someone who will love me *and* want to be with me. I'm done with part-time affection.

I'm finally thinking about love as not only a thing I give, but a thing that's also given to me. Consistently. I want to feel the way it felt with The Husband for most of our twelve years together. It feels amazing, to love and be loved, even when it's "not right." To fall asleep talking with your legs touching. To be comfortable with someone and still so attracted to them. To *share* your life.

I actually can't think of a more worthwhile feeling.

Okay not true. Another worthwhile feeling happens sometime that same year, after White Shirt breaks up with me, and it is this: I want to go home now. I like it. On the few nights I *do* have free each week, I want nothing more than to go home. I know, right? *Finally!*

It's like my apartment's been a train station since I moved here after The Bomb. I've always thought of it as temporary. I've never articulated this, but it's been here, waaaay down in the basement of my heart's mind, lurking, tricking me into thinking this wasn't permanent. I just assumed that I would only live here for a few years, then *of course* I'd meet someone, we'd fall in love, we'd move in together, and I'd have to sell this place. But that simple thing I thought would be a given may not actually ever happen. So this apartment isn't temporary. It's mine. I bought it with my own money and filled it with tiny, eclectic things. And I guess I'm ready to finally see it as it really is — my home, and Birdie's home. It's ours.

You would never know to look at it, that all these years I considered it a waystation. If you know me and have been here, I bet you found that all very surprising. But it's true. And once I realized that it really was *my* home, suddenly it was easier to come back to, without trepidation or needing sedation. I just started walking in the door and enjoying it, even when Birdie isn't here. I start to really look forward to having the time to make music or do sewing projects or write this story for you.

It took nearly six full years after The Bomb to be okay with being alone in my own home. To want to be alone here. To love it. Not all the time, but at least some of the time.

And so, I go home. I finally, *finally* go home. And it's good.

Still,

every time I see two people holding hands as they walk along the street, I wince.

SHAMBLE

In October 2017, I meet a boy in a coffee shop, the one that's in the bottom of my apartment building, actually. He runs it with his brother, a cute little place with his paintings hung beautifully on the walls. He's made me many a delicious Americano in the past, but I've never paid him any attention until now. For some reason today we strike up a real conversation.

For the next few weeks, every time I come home from work (because I come home now, hooray!), I find him sitting outside the coffee shop having a smoke. He always waves me down and I sit with him and talk for a bit, about love and music and philosophy. He's very sweet and young and kinda goofy. He's an Albertan farm boy who's relatively new to the city, and I like how un-Toronto he is. We become friends. We bond over broken hearts.

The Farm Boy talks non-stop about The Brazilian Girl, a woman his heart bleeds for, even though they only dated a short time and she did not feel the same. So he understands how my heart beats only for The Man with the White Shirt. He understands the addiction that is another person, how powerful the magic is, how much of a trickster it can be. It's ninety percent of what we talk about — The Brazilian Girl and The Man with the White Shirt. I even make a joke that they've probably slept with each other, and we laugh, then both wince at the same time. Even the thought is like tiny shards of flying glass right into each of our hearts.

The Farm Boy is an abstract painter; his paintings are so absolutely beautiful I can hardly believe this goofy stoner is the one that painted them. He is supremely talented. I watch his process, the way he pours the paint and resin, the colours he chooses, and how each of the finished canvases seems to be named after The Brazilian Girl or some other ex-girlfriend. I can look at them for hours, staring at the swirls of turquoise and magenta, the flecks of gold, the long straight lines that bisect the madness with an incongruous precision. I even help him with taping the lines of one painting, which he names "Shamble" (after himself this time, not an ex-girlfriend), and later I will buy that painting and hang it in my apartment, a long canvas of complicated beauty, not unlike The Farm Boy himself.

For the first few months after we meet, we text a lot, just buddies. I feel almost like an older sister to him sometimes. One night, we hang out at my apartment and just talk and talk for hours straight. There is no heat between us. He seems absolutely uninterested in me in a romantic or sexual way and I feel the same. So we smoke a lot of weed and talk about the ones we love who don't love us back the way we so desperately need them to.

At the beginning of December, I bring him to a big annual party my friend Pint Size always throws. It's a huge bash and I figure it will be good for him to meet new people. He's fun and sweet and a bit shy in the crowd of mostly older and more sophisticated big-city media types. Sometimes he puts his arm around me tentatively. When Pint Size says to him, "Well, aren't you the most adorable thing! Are the two of you *lovers*?" he lets out a loud nervous giggle and looks at me, then quickly at the floor. His reaction makes me consider him differently for a moment. The innocence of it all.

Then at 2:00 a.m. in the kitchen, while the party thins out in the living room, I laugh at something he says and out of nowhere, Farm Boy just leans in and gives me a fantastic kiss. A knock-you-off-your-feet kiss. A time-to-take-this-elsewhere kiss. I haven't been with anyone but White Shirt in well over a year, but in my bed, everything goes incredibly right with Farm Boy. Everything goes *great*. I sleep deeply and comfortably beside him all night. In the morning he cooks me the best eggs I've ever had.

At first, I find it all a bit swoony, just to be swept up out of nowhere like that. Just to be around a guy that isn't like all the rest of the Toronto guys. I call him Farm Boy and he blushes and calls me Darlin'. Even his texts: *Night Darlin'* or *Hey, Darlin' how's yer day goin'?* He always capitalizes Darlin'. It's charming and even a bit disarming, like maybe it's okay for me to try to date again.

Farm Boy helps distract me somewhat from my obsessiveness over White Shirt, and it's nice, for the first time since The Bomb, to be with someone I was friends with first. But in short enough time it's clear that although we enjoy each other's company, it's not in any kind of serious, long-term romantic way. We are way too different. He's twenty-seven and lives in near-squalor. I've just turned forty-three and live like a full-on adult. He's intelligent and talented and has plenty of ambition and ideas, but lacks focus or direction or know-how. He's a happy-go-lucky stoner who smokes *all* the time. It's one of the things I find really disagreeable, the so-much-smoking.

On the plus side, he texts and calls me frequently, and we hang out regularly and have a lot of fun together, but when I look at him I just don't get the *thing* inside me, the *feeling*, not like when I look at The Man with the White Shirt, whose smell and skin and body are the most intoxicating drugs to me. Not like when The Husband used to look at me, and it felt like he was setting fire to me from the inside out. But Farm Boy is cute and sweet, and really, *really* great in bed. *So* great. And he is the first and only guy I've enjoyed as much as White Shirt when it comes to sex. It's pretty cool, this being friends and not being obsessed with each other. This having amazing regular sex without all the heartache and drama. All in all, it's a pretty good thing, this thing that isn't a thing. This thing between The Farm Boy and me.

At midnight on New Year's Eve, he kisses me long and sweet, in my friend The Lawyer's living room, so close to the spot where just the year before, The Man with the White Shirt kissed me at midnight then said it was the best New Year's kiss he'd ever had, that it was his happiest New Year's Eve. And right after, Fleetwood Mac's "You Make Loving Fun" came on, and we laughed and sang it out loud in each other's arms and it had always been my least favourite song on that album, I thought it was so cheesy, until that moment when it became my favourite, because now it was a memory and a feeling. The feeling of being someone's happiest, best New Year's Eve kiss.

The Farm Boy kisses me good at midnight, close to the spot of that memory, then lights a cigarette and looks away. I know he's thinking of The Brazilian Girl just like I'm thinking of The Man with the White Shirt. I know and it's okay. This is our undeclared agreement.

In the new year we continue on, seeing each other once a week or so, not really dating, but spending time together. I don't like going to his place, which is cramped and messy and in a house with a million other people. So Farm Boy comes to my apartment, with its spaciousness and cleanliness, and we order in Thai food and watch movies and smoke weed on my balcony. I listen to him talk for hours until finally we go to bed.

We don't go out for dinner or go to the art gallery or have expensive cocktails or go dancing like I would do if I was actually dating someone. Instead, our relationship is about hanging out. I'm fine with it that way. As long as I can have regular good sex with one person, I'm halfway to happy.

It's something for right now, me at forty-three, tired of dating and being disappointed, tired of texting and being ghosted, and not at all interested in swiping some app where men my own age will ignore me or send me dick pics. So I choose this instead. For now I will hang out with this sweet twenty-seven-year-old, who calls to make sure I'm doing okay and cooks me amazing meals and gives me, *finally*, a body I want to sleep beside on a regular basis.

If he's had a lot to drink, he snores, and I kind of like it, because it makes me feel like The Man with the White Shirt is there beside me. I don't even put my ear plugs in like I normally would. I turn away, and pretend White Shirt is at my side. Even though Farm Boy feels and smells different, his snores are White Shirt's snores and I feel no guilt pretending. And I know he wouldn't mind anyway, because he's dreaming about his Brazilian girl and the magic only she can give him.

So we go on like this for a long, long time. We are friends and lovers and pretenders together. It works for us. It's just this, it isn't something else.

MONOGAMISH

After a time I'm seeing both of them, The Farm Boy and yes, *occasionally*, The Man with the White Shirt. Here I am with two lovers, two men who care deeply for me, but neither of whom is my boyfriend. And together, they don't add up to one, either. In this rare case, one plus one equals negative one to me. Negative one real partner.

It bugs me that this is my love life. That my only choice is polyamory or celibacy. So what can I do? Sex is one of the main reasons I want a monogamous relationship, honestly. I want to have safe, good sex, regularly and often, and the best way of getting that is in a committed relationship. For The Man with the White Shirt, and others like him, variety is important. Being able to pursue whomever you're interested in, whenever you want. Something about the energy you get from a new relationship. Which all sounds great, I'm not going to lie. And he and I have talked about it, a lot. But I'll tell you what I told him: the scales are tipped waaaay in his favour in this arrangement.

White Shirt and I are both in our forties now. And that means he is still young, and I am old. Even though we're the same age. White Shirt is a handsome and charming man. He is kind, sweet, and very non-threatening to women. I am as threatening as you get to men. I own my own home. I have a successful career. I'm often smarter and funnier than them.

And let's not forget the baggage. I have a child and an ex-husband and a gigantic hole in my heart caused by the gigantic trauma that was The Bomb. White Shirt has no such baggage.

He has no ties or responsibilities. He can be light and easygoing and spontaneous, all attractive qualities in a person. I am bound by a complicated co-parenting schedule and mortgage payments and a gigantic hole in my heart.

Lastly, there's danger. When White Shirt sleeps with other women, the worst that happens is that maybe it wasn't that great. When I sleep with other men, I am rolling the dice every single time. Even the nice, smart, educated, handsome ones can turn into monsters, remember? I remember. So there's nothing equal about non-monogamy to me. It's a totally different game for each of us, and I am so tired of playing it.

WILDWOOD

I'm in Mexico. *By myself.* In a small apartment in the old town of Puerto Vallarta, a city I love and know well. I was first here in 1998, backpacking with my boyfriend at the time, The Musician. We stayed in a little hotel for eleven American dollars per night, eating fish, freshly caught and cooked on the beach, served on sticks. It's always been one of my top vacation memories, the freedom of it, the fun.

In 2015, I was here with The Man with the White Shirt. Eight days of heady bliss, staying in an apartment on the bank of the river, buying groceries like locals, our days filled with sun, *cerveza,* and sex.

This time, in 2018, I'm in an apartment on my own, high up the hill overlooking the ocean. I'm so burnt out from work and life's demands that I don't care that no one is here with me. Okay, I *care,* but it isn't debilitating. It hasn't stopped me from coming all this way and enjoying myself. Leading up to it, I even mentally prepared that I might cry the entire time, but at least I'd be in Mexico. And this is the most progress I've made in the six years since The Bomb, to be on vacation by myself and to love it.

In truth I'm not *all* by myself. Each night I hang out with a large group of gay men that I met through a cool guy I know from Vancouver. He's in Puerto Vallarta with his husband, a thing I only discovered on Instagram after I booked the trip, delighted to see photos of his manicured toenails on the beach, painted the same blue as my own. He told me to text him when I arrived, and I thought maybe I'd have dinner with them one of the nights and that would be nice, since the idea of eating all those meals alone was daunting. But instead, he and his husband have folded me into their large group of fellas, taking me along to bar after bar, drinking and doing karaoke and dancing, not a woman in sight.

One of their friends is a young Portuguese guy I instantly click with. We become fast friends and hang out all night together, calling each other Little Brother and Little Sister, even though I'm more than a decade older. Little Brother lives in Puerto Vallarta part of the year and Toronto the other part. He's more subdued than the other guys, who are all making the most of their vacation in a manner I can only describe as hedonistic.

The night we meet, we all dance at a popular gay bar until 2:00 a.m., and when all the guys in our group disperse, Little Brother says to me, "Okay, you wanna go to a place with good music now?" and we go across the street to another bar where I don't know any of the music but it is good, really good. We dance for two more hours and in that time, I am free, more free than I've felt in all my forty-three years. I don't think about The Man with the White Shirt. Or The Ex-husband, or even Farm Boy. I don't think about work or Birdie or my family or the leaky faucet in my kitchen or the baseboards that need painting or how my car needed an oil change six months ago and I still haven't done it yet. I don't think of any of it. I just dance.

I just dance in Mexico at 4:00 a.m. in an open-air bar and don't have to worry about skeezy guys hitting on me because they're all gay here, and I am *free*. Free to move my body however I want, free to smile at people without that being an invitation to unwanted attention. Free to dance with Little Brother and not have a care in the world. In these few hot hours in this tiny bar in Puerto Vallarta, all of the last six complicated years of my life evaporate.

And this is it: unfiltered, actual happiness.

Each night I hang out with the guys and spend my days alone. I paint watercolours and read and listen to podcasts and swim in the pool that is right below my apartment window. I cook myself lunch and eat it on the tiled balcony overlooking the ocean. I nap for as long as I like. It's perfect, and I don't cry. Not once. I've finally severed The Lonely from its conjoined twin, Alone. Loneliness and being alone are no longer one and the same for me. I can be one without feeling the other. Holy fuck, *finally*. I finally feel like I'm going to find my way out of the wildwood.

I begin to shore up. I fight hard, daily, to face that dark pit of despair, that well I'm so afraid of falling down. But in order to fight it, I really have to concentrate on finding the silver lining, that thin, silvery thread that keeps me in this world. It's lucky that no matter what, I always manage to find something sparkling out of the corner of my eye, something to hold fast to. Like a flower that sprouted up in a parking lot, right there in the middle of concrete and garbage. Or the sound of a friend's big laugh — huge and deep and infectious. Or the smell of a baby's head. No, even better, the smell of a co-worker's baby's head, a baby I can hand back as soon as the crying starts.

Once I start to look, I find silver linings everywhere — in the way Birdie rolls her eyes just like I do. Or the way all the women I know elevate one another. Or the fact that we humans ever invented airplanes. And photography. And birth control. I decide to believe that there's a silver lining with me always, underneath me, inside me, because I can't lose hope to despair. If I do, despair will swallow me whole and not even taste me.

Instead, hope takes its time. Hope holds my hand.

Hope throws daggers at despair and shouts *fuck off!* and runs down the street in fits of giggles with her girlfriends.

Hope glints in the sun. It's a text that says, *I have your back.*

It's Birdie's voice calling out from her room at night, piercing the silence, "Hey, Mom? I loooove youuuu! Have a good niiiight!"

It's the glowing centre of me that's been dampened, sure, but will never be extinguished.

ACKNOWLEDGEMENTS

I have so much love and gratitude. With special thanks to:

Frank Parise for lifelong lessons in writing, optimism, and meatball making.

Tom Allen, my mentor, friend, Borg, and earliest champion of this book.

Antonette Blanchard for igniting my childhood writing and lifting me through difficult times.

Joshua Loberg, my philosopher cowboy, steady with love and intelligence, and for consistently cooking me the best eggs ever.

Kim Reeves for friendship and loyalty unparalleled — at recess and in life.

Carla Vincenzi, my anchor, no matter the distance between us.

Sergio Abegão for the fireworks and the circles, the magic and the drama.

Garvia Bailey, Nana aba Duncan, Lauren Hancock, and Reuben Maan for real talks, big laughs, tea and tears, purse tequila, all the dancing, and late night bike rides.

Marc Apollonio, the king of story structure, friendship, ear-splitting sneezes, and deep conversations.

The Ships, Vanessa Caldwell, Elizabeth Bowie, and Nora Young for being there with a shoulder to cry on, a listening ear, wisecracks, and wise words as I wrote this story.

Daemon Fairless for reading the first ten thousand words I wrote and telling me to keep going.

Scott Sellers for reminding me I was a writer, pushing me to dig deeper, and insisting that people needed to hear what I had to say.

Samantha Haywood, my cheerleader, champion, agent, and friend.

Everyone at Dundurn Press for their enthusiasm and support. And to Jess Shulman for editing with clarity, care, and humour.

Everyone at CBC Podcasts, especially Veronica Simmonds for being a magical machine, Fabiola Carletti for making the internet (and world) a better place with her generous spirit, and Leslie Merklinger and Arif Noorani, who gave me the platform to adapt this story into something people all over the world would listen to and connect with.

The fans of the podcast for your messages, tweets, and actual paper letters, proof we are never really alone. Especially to the one who designs kick-ass stickers and pins, the one who sent me hand-painted art from the crater, the one who found me while lying under a bed of desert stars, and the kindred spirit who had me in their ears as they waited for chemo … I'm grateful for the modern-day pen pals we've become. Hazak v'ematz!

Finally, to Birdie and to My Rogue for supporting this telling of our story.

Forza e coraggio,
Michelle, 2019